Metaphor and Political Discourse

By the same author

MIRROR IMAGES OF EUROPE
KOMMUNIKATIVE KREATIVITÄT
ATTITUDES TOWARD EUROPE (*co-editor*)

Metaphor and Political Discourse

Analogical Reasoning in Debates about Europe

Andreas Musolff
Reader in German, University of Durham

© Andreas Musolff 2004

All rights reserved. No reproduction, copy or transmission of this publication may be made without written permission.

No paragraph of this publication may be reproduced, copied or transmitted save with written permission or in accordance with the provisions of the Copyright, Designs and Patents Act 1988, or under the terms of any licence permitting limited copying issued by the Copyright Licensing Agency, 90 Tottenham Court Road, London W1T 4LP.

Any person who does any unauthorised act in relation to this publication may be liable to criminal prosecution and civil claims for damages.

The author has asserted his right to be identified as the author of this work in accordance with the Copyright, Designs and Patents Act 1988.

First published 2004 by
PALGRAVE MACMILLAN
Houndmills, Basingstoke, Hampshire RG21 6XS and
175 Fifth Avenue, New York, N. Y. 10010
Companies and representatives throughout the world

PALGRAVE MACMILLAN is the global academic imprint of the Palgrave Macmillan division of St. Martin's Press, LLC and of Palgrave Macmillan Ltd. Macmillan® is a registered trademark in the United States, United Kingdom and other countries. Palgrave is a registered trademark in the European Union and other countries.

ISBN 1–4039–3389–8 hardback

This book is printed on paper suitable for recycling and made from fully managed and sustained forest sources.

A catalogue record for this book is available from the British Library.

Library of Congress Cataloging-in-Publication Data

Musolff, Andreas.
   Metaphor and political discourse : analogical reasoning in debates about Europe / Andreas Musolff.
     p. cm.
   Includes bibliographical references and index.
   ISBN 1–4039–3389–8 (hardback)
    1. Discourse analysis – Political aspects. 2. Metaphor. 3. Analogy.
4. Europe – Politics and government – 1989– I. Title.

P302.77.M87 2004
401'.41 – dc22
                                                                           2004046495

10 9 8 7 6 5 4 3 2 1
13 12 11 10 09 08 07 06 05 04

Printed and bound in Great Britain by
Antony Rowe Ltd, Chippenham and Eastbourne

Contents

Acknowledgements	vii
Abbreviations and conventions	viii

1 Introduction: Metaphor and Politics	1
2 Conceptual Domains and Scenarios	8
2.1 Metaphors in a corpus of public discourse	8
2.2 FAMILY scenarios for the European Union	13
2.3 Metaphor scenarios and public attitudes	28
3 Analogical argument in political discourse	30
3.1 Metaphor and argument by analogy	30
3.2 Analogical arguments based on JOURNEY metaphors	39
3.3 Metaphorical conclusions in public debates about Europe: *paths without alternative?*	59
4 Corpora and the Semantics of Metaphor	63
4.1 Metaphors in general corpora	63
4.2 Corpus-based analysis of metaphorical meaning	69
5 Europe as a BODY POLITIC	83
5.1 Corporeal and organismic metaphors in politics	83
5.2 The LIFE CYCLE of Europe	90
5.3 HEALTH and ILLNESS of Europe	97
5.4 The ORGANS of Europe	101
5.5 Corpus data and conceptual metaphor	112
6 Discourse History in a Metaphor Corpus	115
6.1 Metaphor and discourse "evolution"	115
6.2 The development of the EUROPEAN HOUSE in British and German Euro-debates, 1989–2001	122
6.3 Do metaphors 'evolve'?	140
7 Metaphor Negotiation	146
8 Metaphor as Deception	159
8.1 Metaphors as *ignes fatui*: Hobbes's warnings of political metaphor in *Leviathan*	159
8.2 Metaphor and rhetoric	163
8.3 Metaphor as *sedition*	167

9 Open and Closed Metaphor Scenarios 173

Notes and References 178

Bibliography 193

Index 1: General 206

Index 2: Metaphor Scenarios and Their Conceptual Elements 211

Acknowledgements

I am indebted to a great number of friends and colleagues for support and encouragement during the research leading up to this book, among them the late Christopher Upward and Colin Good, as well as Saskia Daalder, Ingrid Hudabiunigg, Wolf-Andreas Liebert, Jonathan Long, Peter Rolf Lutzeier, Brigitte Nerlich, Michael Townson, Martin Wengeler and Jörg Zinken. Christina Schäffner, Josephine Tudor and Renate Henkel, who read drafts of the whole book text at various stages, made many essential suggestions for improvement and provided helpful criticism and advice. Roslyn Frank, Sheila Glasbey, René Dirven and Zoltàn Kövecses commented on versions of conference papers that became chapters in the book. Wolfgang Teubert and Pernilla Danielsson at the University of Birmingham and Eva Teubert and Heidrun Kämper at the *Institut für Deutsche Sprache* in Mannheim gave generously of their time and expertise to help me access and collect data from the *Bank of English* corpus and *COSMAS* corpora. The research for this book was supported by grants from the Art and Humanities Research Board of Great Britain, the British Academy and the University of Durham.

Abbreviations

BZ	*Berliner Zeitung*
DAS	*Deutsches Allgemeines Sonntagsblatt*
DT	*The Daily Telegraph*
E	*The Economist*
FAZ	*Frankfurter Allgemeine Zeitung*
FR	*Frankfurter Rundschau*
FT	*Financial Times*
G	*The Guardian*
I	*The Independent*
MM	*Mannheimer Morgen*
NSt	*New Statesman* (formerly: *New Statesman & Society*)
RP	*Rheinische Post*
SP	*Der Spiegel*
ST	*The Sunday Times*
SZ	*Süddeutsche Zeitung*
T	*The Times*
taz	*die tageszeitung*
TS	*Der Tagesspiegel*
W	*Die Welt*
Z	*Die Zeit*
EEC	European Economic Community
EC	European Community (organization that superseded the EEC)
ECB	European Central Bank
EMU	Economic and Monetary Union
EU	European Union (follow-up organisation of EC, since 1994)
CDU	Christlich-Demokratische Union (Christian-Democratic Union)
CSU	Christlich-Soziale Union (Christian-Social Union = Bavarian sister party of CDU)
SPD	Sozialdemokratische Partei Deutschlands (Social Democratic Party of Germany)

Conventions in the text

Metaphorical concepts, domains and scenarios: indicated by small capitals
Metaphorical expressions: indicated by italics.

1
Introduction: Metaphor and Politics

Metaphors of political discourse and political thought have had a dubious reputation for some time. More than three hundred years ago, in his treatise *Leviathan*, Thomas Hobbes described the danger of metaphors leading the human mind into intellectual and political confusion:

> (1) [. . .] The Light of humane minds is Perspicuous Words, but by exact definitions first snuffed, and purged from ambiguity; [. . .] And on the contrary, Metaphors, and senslesse and ambiguous words, are like *ignes fatui*; and reasoning upon them, is wandering amongst innumerable absurdities; and their end, contention, and sedition, or contempt. (Hobbes 1996: 36)

In recent discussions in linguistics, psychology and philosophy, the relevance of metaphor for social and political conceptualization has been acknowledged in much more positive terms. In particular, the school of cognitive metaphor analysis, which George Lakoff and Mark Johnson effectively founded with the publication of their seminal work *Metaphors We Live By* in 1980, has produced ample evidence that "metaphors play a central role in the construction of social and political reality" (Lakoff and Johnson 1980: 159). Cognitive theory views verbal metaphors and similes as reflecting mappings across domains of knowledge that underlie the language users' understanding of the world in which they live, "allowing forms of reasoning and words from one domain [. . .] to be used in the other [. . .] domain" (Lakoff 1996: 63). From the cognitive viewpoint, what matters most about a metaphor is its conceptual nature, not its 'accidental' linguistic form. In their second collaborative book, *Philosophy in the Flesh*, Lakoff and Johnson have reinforced this epistemological claim even further: "Metaphorical thought, in the form of cross-domain mappings is primary; metaphorical language is secondary" (Lakoff and Johnson 1999: 123).

It is obvious that this claim, if validated, has a massive bearing on the study of political discourse. If our social experiences and conceptualizations are organized in terms of metaphors, then politics, as part of the social domain, must also be perceived and constructed metaphorically. Cognitive theorists have indeed produced a number of analyses of political metaphor, often related to specific political issues.[1] The most systematic study has been provided by Lakoff in his 1996 book *Moral Politics: What Conservatives Know That Liberals Don't*, in which he analyses the world-views underlying political thinking in the United States of America. In his view, the conceptual metaphor of the FAMILY stands at the centre of a system of conceptualizations of society in US politics:

(2) The general metaphor looks like the following:
A Community Is a Family.
Moral Authority Is Parental Authority.
An Authority Figure is a Parent.
Moral Behaviour by Someone Subject to Authority Is Obedience.
Moral Behaviour by Someone in Authority Is Setting Standards and Enforcing Them. (Lakoff 1996: 7)

The FAMILY metaphor of Morality is by no means an isolated concept but systematically connected to other concepts such as, for instance, WELL-BEING IS WEALTH, MORAL ACTION IS GIVING SOMETHING OF POSITIVE VALUE, IMMORAL ACTION IS GIVING SOMETHING OF NEGATIVE VALUE (Lakoff 1996: 44–7). When applied to the "target" concept of the NATION STATE, this system of source concepts provides a frame of reference that "allows us to reason about the nation on the basis of what we know about a family", based on the (metaphorical) equations "The Nation Is a Family, The Government Is a Parent; The Citizens Are the Children" (1996: 154–5).

The politically significant aspect of this metaphor of the nation state is that it has two competing versions: a STRICT FATHER model and a NURTURANT PARENT model, both of which concern parents' authority over their children and their exercise of punishment and care. The two models can be roughly equated with more or less authoritarian types of family education,[2] which are "rooted in long cultural experience" in Western societies and are linked to gender role models (1996: 155). The two metaphor versions "induce" two corresponding "unconscious" patterns of moral belief systems, which, in turn, yield "conservative" and "liberal" world-views (1996: 37, 155). Lakoff also emphasizes the fact that people 'in real life' operate all kinds of combinations and sub-variants of the two basic models, which in turn may give rise to a wide range of systems of social practices and educational and moral ideologies (1996: 283–321). Nevertheless, he maintains that the two main models form the basis for all these conceptual variations (1996: 14–16, 284).

Whilst the two antagonistic basic versions of the FAMILY metaphor are, in principle, of equal status, the depth and impact of their respective application to political issues differ greatly in conservative and liberal thinking. Lakoff claims that American conservatives have developed "an elaborate language of their moral politics" from the STRICT FATHER model, which gives coherence to their views on issues such as social programmes, taxes, crime, the death penalty, the environment and abortion, whereas liberals lack a similarly powerful metaphor system, due to their uncritical commitment to an objectivist semantics that puts them "at a disadvantage in any public discourse" (1996: 386). As long as they continue to "assume that metaphors are just matters of words and rhetoric, or that they cloud the issues, or that metaphors are the stuff of Orwellian language" (1996: 387), liberals cannot even begin to redress the (im-)balance of discourse power. Lakoff's application of cognitive analysis to political discourse and theory aims at enabling them to overcome their naïve objectivism by way of exposing the STRICT FATHER model as the "unconscious conceptual framework" of political debates on moral issues (1996: 386). Cognitive metaphor analysis thus claims to look behind explicit utterances to find conceptual structures that the users themselves may not be aware of.

We shall postpone the discussion of the political and ethical implications of this "therapeutic" stance until the concluding chapters and first focus on how its epistemological claim (about unconscious conceptual metaphors underlying actual linguistic behaviour) can be empirically corroborated.[3] In *Moral Politics*, the linguistic evidence of the FAMILY metaphor consists in the first place of a short list of idiomatic phrases, such as *founding fathers, father of his country, Uncle Sam, Big Brother, fatherland*, its *sons* going to war (1996: 153–4). Such a small basis of empirical data is consistent with Lakoff's general approach to observable communication phenomena as 'surface' manifestations of underlying conceptual structures. However, it leaves underdetermined his main hypothesis about the FAMILY metaphor structuring the ideological divide in US society. The main sources that Lakoff cites to substantiate his claims about family morality in US politics are in fact popular treatises on child-rearing and research literature on socialization, political theory and public administration (1996: 143–6, 182–3, 212, 227). These overtly ideological treatises indeed appear to bear out Lakoff's analysis of the ideological divide over moral issues in US society, but they can hardly count as evidence for the existence of an unconscious conceptual framework. Far from being unconscious or hidden, they are explicit and elaborate, openly arguing in favour of specific models of family morality. Moreover, as Lakoff himself emphasizes, the STRICT FATHER metaphor is by no means the only model for morality; instead he claims that it is more elaborate, systematic and more powerful than its 'competitor', the NURTURANT PARENT model. For this hypothesis to be corroborated, we would need comparative empirical data to demonstrate that metaphors based on the STRICT FATHER model are more representative of or dominant in actual political discourse in the US than those that rely on NURTURANT PARENT concepts. If the same source domain of the FAMILY can be used to argue for both conservative and liberal world-views, who is to decide which is the dominant one in a discourse community?

It is here that corpus-based analyses can help to provide a much-needed empirical complement to cognitive linguistic theory. The studies presented here aim to investigate the possibility of such analyses by providing corpus data for the British and German discourses about a mutually relevant topic – the politics of the European Union – over the last decade of the twentieth century. The relevant data have been compiled as part of a collaborative research project on linguistic manifestations of "Attitudes towards Europe" in Britain and Germany, spanning the 12 years from 1989 to 2001.[4] This period covers a number of fundamental changes in European politics. Following the collapse of communism and faced with the impact of German unification and the re-emergence of sovereign nation states in Eastern Europe, the "European Community" (EC) – since 1994 the "European Union" (EU) – began to move towards closer economic, administrative and political integration.[5] These initiatives resulted in two new treaties, which were negotiated in (and subsequently named after) the Dutch cities of Maastricht and Amsterdam in 1991 and 1997. Among the national governments and media in the EC/EU, however, opinions were divided about the pace and direction of change. Whilst the German government, especially under the Christian Democrat chancellor Helmut Kohl until 1998, promoted fast integration, British governments took a more hesitant, if not antagonistic stance. During the first half of the 1990s, the Conservative government under John Major opposed some of the integration moves and negotiated opt-out clauses in the Maastricht Treaty, which excluded Britain from the first group of countries joining the common currency in 1999. Even after the change of government to Labour in 1997, the British media were slow to embrace integration, always fearful to lose too much sovereignty to the EU administration based in Brussels. In Germany, on the other hand, closer integration has been widely viewed as a promising economic and political prospect and as a safeguard against resurgent nationalism.

The political contrast between the two countries lends itself to comparisons of the respective national publics as discourse communities that maintain a continuous 'virtual conversation' about a particular topic. In a few cases, this conversation manifests itself in actual discussions in interviews or live debates recorded and disseminated by the public media. But such direct manifestations are not the only evidence of a continuous and coherent public debate. Rather, the whole ensemble of texts produced in public by politicians and media commentators can be assumed to form a coherent whole as long as its participants agree that they are discussing within a shared discursive context and refer to each others' statements in order to advance their arguments. The debates in Britain and Germany about EU politics can be seen as examples of such virtual conversations in the respective national public sphere. However, mutual citations, allusions and comments also often go beyond the boundaries of national discourse communities; in such cases, we are dealing with what may be regarded as the beginnings of a multinational and multilingual discourse community. It remains an open question whether, and if so when and how, the European Union will manage to establish a unified public debate across national and linguistic borders.[6]

The notion of public discourse as a virtual conversation within and between communities provides an auspicious perspective for comparing conceptual metaphors that underlie public debates in different national cultures. In the case of geographically and historically distant discourse communities, such an investigation will be more of a typological enterprise, whereas for two political cultures as closely related to each other as the German and British ones we can assume that their range of conceptual metaphors is largely similar. But this does not mean that their metaphoric discourse has to be similar – even common conceptual source domains can be used for different argumentative and ideological purposes. As Lakoff's example of the two versions of the NATION-AS-FAMILY metaphor in US political discourse shows, one and the same source domain can be employed to argue opposite political positions. The conservative and liberal sub-communities of the US public use one central element of the source domain FAMILY in particular – i.e. that of the PARENT–CHILD relationship – to advance, buttress and defend contrasting world-views, belief systems and attitudes. Thus, whilst the basic metaphor THE STATE IS A FAMILY is the same for both sides, the political and social conclusions drawn from this mapping are diametrically opposed to each other and are complemented by fitting sub-concepts – that is, the STRICT FATHER and the NURTURANT PARENT models.

However, the question remains open as to how much empirical evidence can be gathered for hypotheses about the relative weight of the two metaphor-based models of morality in US discourse. The same problem is evidently of great significance for a comparison for metaphor uses in different national communities as attempted here. We need to relate the abstractions of a 'virtual conversation' of public discourse and of its 'domination' by some conceptual metaphors to testable empirical evidence. Such evidence can be provided only by a corpus of documented data of metaphor use – even if a limited corpus never actually represents the whole ensemble of relevant texts produced in the discourse community but only comprises a sub-section. The evidence for the dominance of specific metaphors would then depend on the size and representativeness of the corpus.

In the following chapters, various aspects of a corpus-based approach to conceptual metaphors in public discourse will be discussed, using data from the aforementioned project on "Attitudes towards Europe" in Britain and Germany. In chapter 2, we shall concentrate on metaphors from the source domain of FAMILY concepts, as documented in a pilot corpus. They provide the basis for a preliminary discussion of general methodological issues of the corpus-based analysis of political metaphor. In chapter 3, the largest source domain of the pilot corpus – that is, that of PATH-MOVEMENT-JOURNEY metaphors – will be analysed with a view to clarifying the question of how metaphors are used in political *argument*. We aim to show that metaphorical argumentation constitutes a further cognitive dimension of metaphor that complements the level of categorization, which has so far been at the centre of cognitive research. The inclusion of the *argumentative* dimension requires a revision of the theoretical model linking cognitive and linguistic aspects of metaphor, which is the topic of the fourth chapter. In order to test the resulting hypotheses, we will then introduce data from a second, more representative corpus of EU-related discourse, specifically examples from the source domain of LIFE-BODY-HEALTH. The analysis of distribution patterns for metaphors from this domain in chapter

5 provides the main 'body of evidence' for the national comparison. The second corpus also provides the data for chapter 6, which investigates metaphors based on the source domain of BUILDING-HOUSING. They exemplify processes of 'metaphor evolution' as part of discourse history. Following on from these corpus-related discussions, we will return to the question of the socio-cognitive power of metaphor, drawing on individual examples of metaphor negotiation as well as on a reinterpretation of the notorious (mis-?)treatment of metaphor by Thomas Hobbes in the *Leviathan*. In the final chapter, we will use his exploration of *deceptive* metaphor to resume the discussion of the ethical dimension of metaphor in politics and its cognitive analysis.

2
Conceptual Domains and Scenarios

2.1 Metaphors in a corpus of public discourse

The notion of a "corpus" of metaphors presents two basic methodological issues: (1) how to *find* metaphors in collections of linguistic data; and (2) what to *count* as metaphors. Unlike other linguistic phenomena documented in large databases – e.g. letters, words/lexemes, morphemes or sentences – metaphors cannot be identified by external features, because they do not belong to the 'expression' side of linguistic signs but to their conceptual side. The search for a particular lexical expression in any larger database can easily yield a "concordance" of millions of instantiations of an expression and their immediate contexts, but it does not tell us whether they have metaphorical meaning. To teach a computer to find metaphors requires the researcher to define parameters by which the computer can 'recognize' relevant data, which then have to be interpreted by the researcher. In chapters 4 and 5, the methodological problems of building such a corpus will be discussed in detail.

The second problem – what data to count as metaphor – is connected to the cognitive distinction between 'underlying' metaphorical concepts (domain mappings) and linguistic 'surface' text features that are commonly regarded as metaphorical or figurative language use. As we have seen, Lakoff and Johnson (1980, 1999) regard the conceptual aspect as primary, and the linguistic level as secondary. In cognitive research literature, surveys of conceptual metaphors are usually based on inventories of idiomatic phrases containing metaphors, on the assumption that such idioms are typical of language use in general.[1] However, even extensive metaphor lists cannot be regarded as the equivalent of valid statistical evidence of their use. This is not an immediate problem for cognitive research into the lexical systems of (national) languages; after all, there is ample evidence that figurative idioms are easily identified as metaphorical by hearers and readers.[2]

In public political discourse, however, meanings of terms and phrases are typically contested and controversial, as Lakoff's own example of the two FAMILY metaphor versions in US discourse shows. Each metaphor version is as idiomatic and lexically 'correct' as the other – the difference lies in their connection to political value systems and judgements.[3] This difference is not discernible at the systemic level but can only be gleaned from the use of lexical and phraseological units in their socio-pragmatic context. Therefore, any claims about specific metaphorical concepts 'underlying', 'informing' or 'organizing' the discourse and thinking of larger social groups need to be related to empirical discourse data before any significant conclusions can be drawn.

Zoltán Kövecses (2002) introduces an important differentiation in cognitive metaphor theory that helps to deal with this problem. He distinguishes three levels of metaphor analysis: the "individual", "supraindividual" and "subindividual" level. The first level focuses on how individual speakers actually "use the metaphors [...] in actual communicative situations" and "create new metaphors" (Kövecses 2002: 242). The "supraindividual level" consists of the "conventionalized metaphors of a given language" (2002: 240), and its analysis allows linguists to arrive at generalizations about metaphor concepts that are language(-system)- or culture-specific. The "subindividual" level is concerned with the *experiential grounding* of metaphorical concepts (2002: 243–4). At this level, "primary", largely unconscious metaphors (e.g. the generic conceptualization of temporal and abstract structures in terms of spatial entities) 'embody' abstract concepts by relating them to "primary scenes" in early child development, to bodily experiences of spatial orientation, basic desires, and to neuro-physiological functioning patterns.[4]

Using Kövecses's categories, we can regard the occurrences of "individual metaphors" in a corpus as *tokens*, i.e. instantiations of conceptual mappings which represent their *types* at the "supraindividual level" (which in turn can be related to emotional and experiential aspects at the "subindividual" level). The individual tokens can be grouped, according to criteria of semantic similarity, into conceptual clusters, which in turn can be classified into larger conceptual units, i.e. *domains*.[5] These conceptual spaces display a *radial* structure in that their elements are grouped around central concepts, which provide the most characteristic and easily comprehensible examples.[6] Metaphors, as cross-domain mappings, can be analysed in a similar way by positing *central mappings* that "lead to the emergence of other mappings" and reflect "major human concerns relative to the source in question"; they are also "the mappings that are most motivated experientially" and "linguistically, they give rise to metaphorical expressions that dominate a metaphor" (Kövecses 2002: 110–12).

Cognitive research into such central mappings has provided substantial evidence for clusters of idiomatic expressions that combine to form systems of 'common-sense' knowledge in diverse cultures.[7] The conceptual metaphor ANGER IS A HOT FLUID IN A CONTAINER, for instance, has been shown to be implicit in a large number of idioms in unrelated languages such as Chinese, English, Hungarian, Japanese, Polish and Zulu (Kövecses 2002: 165–9). At the same time, the metaphor displays culture-specific features in that some of its mappings are central in one language but do not feature (or are at least not dominant) in other languages. The "entailment involving the idea of steam being produced", which is characteristic for English ANGER idioms, for instance, does not seem to be present in Chinese (2002: 169).

As regards public discourse metaphors, the issues of 'centrality' and dominance of particular conceptual mappings have to be operationalized in terms of their representation in a corpus. As Graham Low (1999) points out, inferences from metaphor data "to social behaviour and conceptual/mental organisation" should "not be assumed to be true; they need to be justified" (Low 1999: 63). In order to make plausible the claim that certain conceptual mappings are typical or characteristic of language-use in a political discourse community, it is necessary to show that they can be found in sufficient quantities in authentic linguistic data and that their distributional patterns can be related to specific sociopolitical attitudes, beliefs and value systems. Only then can we draw conclusions regarding the "supraindividual" level of conceptual metaphors, i.e. regarding their status as typical or 'dominant' concepts in subcultures, national cultures or in even larger cultural traditions (such as the 'Western cultural tradition'). Such an empirically orientated approach must not be confused with an empiricist methodology, which would demand a purely 'inductive' search procedure. Linguistic data, and *a fortiori*, their conceptual analysis, can only provide interpretative evidence. But Kövecses's distinction of different analytical levels of metaphor analysis enables us to make explicit and critically reflect upon the relationship between empirically observable uses of metaphor uttered in particular situations on the one hand, and the subindividual and supraindividual levels of metaphor on the other hand, which are arrived at by abstracting from individual circumstances of use.

The distinction between individual, supra- and subindividual levels of metaphor analysis is immediately relevant for the analysis of the corpus data from the aforementioned "Attitudes towards Europe" project. In the first instance, a pilot corpus called "EUROMETA I" was assembled, which consisted of some 2,110 texts from 28 British and German newspapers and magazines covering the years 1989–2001. The aim was to arrive at conclusions about the contextual and inter-textual effects of the individual texts and about distributional patterns for individual instantiations (tokens) of metaphorical concepts (types), which could then be put in relation to hypotheses regarding attitudinal differences towards European integration policies in both countries. In the course of this research, it became clear that beyond a 'critical' threshold of about 100 tokens per concept, the analysis needed to be refined in order to lead to meaningful conclusions at the supraindividual level. The first step was to group the conceptual elements into source domains by using lexical fields (as exemplified in standard thesaurus categories) as well as patterns of collocation and relative frequencies in the emerging corpus. Tokens from the various types of JOURNEY concepts (e.g. TRAIN, CAR, SHIP, CONVOY, AEROPLANE, BICYCLE TRANSPORT), for instance, co-occur so frequently with each other and with general PATH-MOVEMENT metaphors that their close 'ontological' links can be demonstrated in their corpus distribution. Likewise, LOVE and FAMILY source concepts co-occurred so often that it made good sense to group them together. However, at their ontological 'edges' all domains showed 'fuzzy' boundaries and less typical examples, which is in keeping with general prototypical and radial structure of concepts and categories (Lakoff 1987; Taylor 1995). Furthermore, some general source terms such as *core* or *design* seemed to collocate equally well with different sets of source domain elements, so that their allocation to a specific source domain was not always possible. This motivated the combination of some domain areas to 'super-domains' (e.g. GEOMETRY-GEOGRAPHY and TECHNOLOGY-BUILDING), which left an overall number of 12 super-domains (cf. Table 1).[8] For the heuristic purpose of the pilot corpus, the vagueness of the delimitation of domain and sub-domain boundaries was not deemed to be too problematic as long as no token was counted more than once. Each passage included contains one or more word-forms that are instantiations of lexical items that belong to the respective source domain. Once the main domains had been identified, an effort was made to find a sufficient number of passages for each domain

Table 1 Overview of the EUROMETA I pilot corpus

Source domains	Passages in British sample*	Passages in German sample*	Passages overall	Words in British sample**	Words in German sample**	Overall number of words
WAY-MOVEMENT-SPEED	214	217	431	40,900	35,300	76,200
GEOMETRY-GEOGRAPHY	95	75	170	23,100	13,800	36,900
TECHNOLOGY-BUILDING	92	132	224	18,800	24,900	43,700
GROUP-CLUB-CLASS	90	81	171	16,100	15,600	31,700
SCHOOL-DISCIPLINE	27	105	132	5,600	18,800	24,400
ECONOMY-BUSINESS	30	55	85	5,500	9,700	15,200
LOVE-MARRIAGE-FAMILY	70	62	132	13,000	14,000	27,000
LIFE-HEALTH-STRENGTH	142	165	307	23,000	29,600	52,600
GAME-SPORTS	46	60	106	8,800	8,500	17,300
WAR-FORTRESS-BATTLE	169	90	259	28,400	20,000	48,400
PERFORMANCE-SHOW	24	21	45	4,000	3,600	7,600
NATURE-WEATHER	34	19	53	4,700	2,900	7,600
Totals	1,033	1,082	2,115	191,900	196,700	388,600

in order to gain an overview over all major conceptual elements and to have roughly equal numbers of passages from both national samples. This ensured an approximate balance between the two national samples as regards absolute numbers of passages entered and thus also of words (the figures for word numbers have been rounded down to closest hundreds). Table 1 gives an overview over the source domains and the text tokens (passages).

There are just 12 text tokens altogether of source domain elements that figure in only one of the two national samples. The British sample has exclusively characterizations of politicians and economists' performance in terms of CRICKET and GOLF imagery.⁹ The German public, on the other hand, was particularly agitated by the question whether "eurozone" countries would achieve a 'landing on the precise spot' (*Punktlandung*) of a 3.0 per cent public deficit (which was one of the conditions for joining the currency union),¹⁰ with no equivalent data from the British debate. These individual, almost idiosyncratic contrasts can hardly be interpreted as indications of deep-seated cultural divisions. In general, all of the major metaphor domains and sub-domains in the EUROMETA I corpus are common to both the British and German discourse communities. It is thus only at the more specific level of individual conceptual domain elements and their configurations that we can find out whether the national discourses show characteristic patterns of metaphor use as regards the debate about EU politics.

In the following sub-chapter we shall focus on a relatively small domain of source concepts – 'small' in terms of tokens as well as of conceptual elements (types) – i.e. the conceptualization of the European Union and of relations between its member states as a FAMILY or LOVE RELATIONSHIP. As we shall see, there are similarities to Lakoff's (1996) findings at the level of central mappings in this domain. However, methodologically the present analysis takes a different approach, as only documented data of metaphor use are taken into consideration. As we shall see shortly, the domain elements tend to group into conceptual clusters representing sub-sections of the LOVE-MARRIAGE-FAMILY domain. To capture this pattern of tokens in the corpus, we shall introduce the category of "scenario" as an intermediate analytical category between the level of the conceptual domain as a whole and its individual elements.

2.2 FAMILY scenarios for the European Union

The use of the FAMILY concept as a model for the nation state has a long and distinguished history in political thinking. It can be traced back to the theories of the state developed in antiquity, and together with some of its Latin terminology it has been handed down – especially in its patriarchal version – over the centuries. We thus find the word field of *patriotism* in many European languages – for example, English *patriot, patriotism,* French *patriote, patriotisme* etc., German *Patriot, Patriotismus* and loan translations such as *fatherland, Vaterland*,¹¹ as well as the phraseological and proverbial lexicalizations that Lakoff (1996) cites (e.g. the nation *sending its sons to war, Uncle Sam* etc.). In all these cases, a sociopolitical entity is understood in terms of the conceptual complex of a FAMILY with PARENTS who are MARRIED and their CHILDREN. This is also the sense in which the concepts FAMILY, LOVE RELATIONSHIP and MARRIAGE are used in the EU-related debates with reference to 'inter-national' relationships among the member states or between single states and the whole EU and/or its institutions (e.g. the common currency).

There are altogether 132 (70 English and 62 German) text passages in the pilot corpus that contain metaphors from the LOVE-MARRIAGE-FAMILY domain. Table 2 gives an overview of the spread of texts over the period 1989–2001.

Table 2 Passages containing LOVE-MARRIAGE-FAMILY metaphors in the pilot corpus

Year	British press	German press	Overall
1989			0
1990	1		1
1991	8	1	9
1992		2	2
1993	2		2
1994	3	3	6
1995	11	3	14
1996	5	2	7
1997	11	17	28
1998	15	18	33
1999	10	6	16
2000	3	3	6
2001	1	7	8
Totals	70	62	132

The marked increase in figures in the years 1997–99 cannot be regarded as a statistically validated finding, because the pilot corpus includes a higher overall number of passages documented for the end of the decade. However, there may be a relevant historical factor: the Amsterdam Treaty, negotiated in 1997, incorporated the final decisions concerning the introduction of the *euro* currency. Many of the debates surrounding the new currency were framed in terms of LOVE-MARRIAGE-FAMILY metaphors, e.g. depictions of the *euro* as a CHILD (with the EU member states as its PARENTS) or as a MARRIAGE or ENGAGEMENT PARTNER (with the member states or former currencies as its FIANCÉS).

The following tables provide further statistical details: Table 3 lists the conceptual elements of the LOVE-MARRIAGE-FAMILY domain represented

Table 3 Conceptual elements and corresponding lexemes for the LOVE-MARRIAGE-FAMILY domain in the pilot corpus

Conceptual elements	English lexemes	German lexemes
LOVE	love (n. + v.), love-in, love-affair, love at first sight, love-rat, honeymoon, partnership, sleeping with, courting, courtship, flirting, romance, to woo	Liebe, Jawort, Liaison, Frischverliebte, Annäherung, Beziehungsdrama, Verhältnis
ENGAGEMENT	engagement	Verlobungszeit, -phase, Ehe ohne Treuebeweis
MARRIAGE	marriage (of convenience), shotgun marriage, wedding, nuptials, pre-nuptial dances	(Euro-)Ehe, Hochzeit, Flucht nach Gretna Green, heiraten, Zweckehe, Drum prüfe, wer sich ewig bindet ['Then scan thyself, if thou would'st wed!' = proverbial phrase, based on poem by F. Schiller]
COUPLE	couple, marriage	Paar, Paarbeziehung, Ehe
ADULTERY, MENAGE A TROIS	ménage a trois, triangle	Seitensprung
SEPARATION/DIVORCE	separation, divorce	Scheidung
FAMILY	(European) family	(europäische) Familie, Familienfrieden, Kleinfamilie
PARENTS	parents	
GODPARENTS	godparents	Patenrolle
FATHER(S)	(founding) father(s)	Vater, Väter, Patriarch, Paterfamilias, Gründungsväter
MOTHER	mother, mama	Mutterwährung
CHILD	child, baby, orphan, foundling, bouncer	Kind(er), Sorgenkind(er), Sohn, laufen lernen [learn how to walk], getauft werden [being baptised]
BROTHER		Bruder
COUSINS	cousins across the channel	

Table 4 Tokens for conceptual elements of the LOVE-MARRIAGE-FAMILY domain in order of overall frequency*

Conceptual elements	English tokens	German tokens	Tokens overall
LOVE	21	7	28
COUPLE	15	10	25
FAMILY	11	13	24
CHILD	9	11	20
MARRIAGE	8	11	19
FAMILY	11	13	24
FATHER(S)	7	9	16
ENGAGEMENT	2	4	6
ADULTERY, MENAGE A TROIS	6	2	8
SEPARATION, DIVORCE	4	1	5
MOTHER	2	1	3
PARENTS	2	0	2
GODPARENTS	1	1	2
COUSINS	1	0	1
BROTHER	0	1	1
Totals	100	84	184

in the corpus plus the respective English and German lexemes, and Table 4 gives figures for tokens of these concepts. Tokens are counted per lexical item denoting a conceptual element but not for word-forms; if a lexical item is repeated in a text passage, it counts as one token. Some of the passages contain combinations of individual conceptual elements: thus, the overall number of tokens is higher than that of the passages, i.e. 184.

The conceptual elements from the LOVE-MARRIAGE-FAMILY domain listed in Table 3 provide the components of a system for the conceptualization of relations between EU member states and the EU as a whole and of its main policies in the 1990s as the (re-)constitution of a *family*. The introduction of the euro is seen either as a *wedding* or as the *birth* of the EU-*parent*-nations' *baby*. Within the EU, only two nations, i.e. France and Germany, are seen as the *couple* – in that case, the euro is *their baby*. Other nations also have *love relationships* or may *wed* with the euro but they are never presented as an *established couple*. Another perspective is that of all European nations being *children of one family*, all *born with equal rights*, which informs interpretations of the collapse of the East–West divide and the plans for an EU-enlargement as a *coming home* of the *lost children* into the *fold of the family*.[12]

These conceptual elements obviously do not cover all concepts from the LOVE-MARRIAGE-FAMILY domain that are imaginable. Rather, they form conceptual clusters that focus on a few aspects of 'common-sense' knowledge and experience of LOVE-, MARRIAGE- or FAMILY- relationships. These clusters build up to "scenarios", i.e. ensembles of little scenes or story-lines, such as, for instance, THE FATE OF THE EU COUPLE, THE CHILDHOOD OF THE EURO-BABY, SOLIDARITY (OR THE LACK OF IT) WITHIN THE EC/EU FAMILY. It is at this level that evaluative arguments and judgements concerning EU politics are expressed, e.g. in terms of *family ties, marital faithfulness*, and *parental authority*. The term "scenario" seems appropriate here, because it captures the fact that there are conceptual patterns and configurations, which include assumptions about typical participants, roles, courses of action in a sense that is comparable to its source meanings known from *theatre* and *film* terminology. The *Concise Oxford Dictionary*, for instance, defines "scenario" in this sense as: "1. (Table of) scene-distribution, appearances of characters, etc., in dramatic work, outline libretto, 2. Complete plot of film play with details of scenes etc.; imagined sequence of future events" (COD 1979: 1011). We can think of a scenario as a set of standard assumptions made by competent members of a discourse community about the 'prototypical' content aspects (participants, roles, 'dramatic' story-lines) and social/ethical evaluations concerning elements of conceptual domains. This characterization seems compatible with Fillmore's (1975) general concept of "scene" as "any kind of coherent segment of human beliefs, actions, experiences or imaginings" and Lakoff's (1987) more specific definition of "scenarios" as "idealized cognitive models" (ICMs) that have a relatively rich ontology. Lakoff views scenarios as "structured by a SOURCE-PATH-GOAL schema in the time domain" and as consisting "typically of people, things, properties, relations and propositions"; among the relations are "causal relations, identity relations" and a "purpose structure" (1987: 285–6). Another term for this kind of rich conceptual structure is "script", which has been used in artificial intelligence (AI) research (Schank and Abelson 1977: 36–68; Taylor 1995: 81–92). Like *scenario*, the term *script* also has useful associations with the domains of DRAMA and FILM PLOTS, in that it conveys the idea that an action sequence constitutes a whole that can be 'scripted' and prepared and then put into action, and later described and assessed according to its 'scenic' quality. The main difference between Lakoff's and the AI concepts on the one hand and our understanding of *scenarios* on the other is the theoretical status of these constructs. Instead of being introduced a priori, "scenarios" in our study are posited as categories that reflect documented clusters of individual tokens of domain elements in the corpus.

The identification of concept scenarios aims to determine which aspects of a metaphorical mapping can be deemed to dominate public discourse for a particular topic area such as EU-politics. *Scenarios* thus complement the category of *central mappings* introduced by Kövecses, which focuses on the conceptual 'core' that informs the derivation of all metaphors within a given domain. Scenarios provide, as it were, the main story-lines or perspectives along which the central mappings are developed and extended. On the basis of the data in Table 3, we can list the central mappings and scenarios that are relevant for LOVE-, MARRIAGE- and FAMILY-metaphors in the EUROMETA I-corpus:

2.i Conceptual mappings for LOVE-, MARRIAGE- and FAMILY metaphors:

(a) A NATION STATE IS A PERSON
(b) TWO STATES CO-OPERATING OR 'BELONGING' TOGETHER POLITICALLY ARE PERSONS IN A LOVE RELATIONSHIP/MARRIAGE
(c) A LARGER GROUP OF STATES CO-OPERATING OR 'BELONGING' TOGETHER ARE A FAMILY
(d) THE RESULT OF THE STATES' CO-OPERATION IS THE FAMILY'S CHILD
(e) as an alternative to (d): THE MEMBER NATIONS OF THE GROUP ARE THE CHILDREN OF THE GROUP

2.ii Scenarios for LOVE-, MARRIAGE- and FAMILY metaphors:

(a) the PARENT(S) scenario: PARTICULAR STATES OR GROUPS OF STATES HAVE THE ROLE OF PARENTS THAT ENGENDER, BEAR AND RAISE A CHILD OR SEVERAL CHILDREN
(b) the CHILD(REN) scenario: PARTICULAR STATES OR GROUPS OF STATES OR SPECIFIC POLICIES HAVE THE ROLE OF INDIVIDUAL CHILDREN THAT ARE EDUCATED, NURTURED AND DISCIPLINED
(c) the MARRIAGE scenario: TWO STATES HAVE THE ROLE OF MARRIED PARTNERS (who have previously been LOVERS/FIANCÉS); if there is AN ESTABLISHED COUPLE, FURTHER ASSOCIATED STATES HAVE ROLES VIS-À-VIS THE COUPLE (e.g. that of EXTRA-MARITAL LOVERS/SUITORS)

The difference between the central mappings and scenarios of conceptual metaphors lies in their contrasting cognitive status. Central mappings are cognitively necessary implications of metaphors in a domain: without the central mapping A NATION STATE IS A PERSON, any talk of *states being born, being married,* or *getting divorced* etc. would be meaningless. On the other hand, there is no logical or ontological 'necessity' for the use of any particular scenario; indeed there are many examples of text passages in the corpus that focus only on one aspect of a scenario and leave others open or even include incompatible aspects. Thus, the PARENT and CHILD scenarios as manifested in actual texts of the public debate, do not have to be fully filled-in or even consistent to be comprehensible.[13] The *child(ren) of the European family,* for instance, may have just *one parent* (in the sense of a *begetter*), or have *only fathers,* or *no identifiable parents at all,* as in the following examples:

(1) [. . .] the great dream of the *founding fathers* of the original European communities – a United States of Europe. (I, 24 April 1990; italics here and in further quotations from the EUROMETA corpora indicate relevant metaphors)

(2) When the "hard ecu", Britain's alternative to the Delors plan for European Monetary Union, was first *presented to its prospective godparents* last June it was *an unappealingly premature baby. All 11 of them treated the infant with the mixture of embarrassment and derision accorded to nature's regrettable errors.* (G, 9 January 1991)

(3) [. . .] how Western Europe's *grown-up* democracies treat *the foundling-states* appearing on their eastern doorstep. (E, 7 December 1991)

(4) Europe fetes *'prodigal son'* [headline]. Britain's European Union partners yesterday feted the new government's return to Brussels *with a warmth which would not have disgraced the biblical welcome accorded the prodigal son.* (G, 6 May 1997)

(5) Genüßlich verliest Kohl die lange Liste europäischer Sozialdemokraten von Felipe González bis Lionel Jospin – *alle "Väter dieser angeblichen kränkelnden Frühgeburt".* (Z, 29 April 1998). [Kohl takes a great delight in reading out aloud the long list of European social democrats from Felipe González to Lionel Jospin – *all fathers of this allegedly sickly, premature child* (i.e. the euro, as criticized by Kohl's opponent, the then German social democrat opposition leader Gerhard Schröder)][14]

(6) Von allen *Gründervätern*, die [...] 1991 die Währungsunion aushandelten, hat er als einziger politisch überlebt. Im Kreise der EU-Mächtigen gilt der Deutsche längst als *Patriarch, als Pate, als Paterfamilias*. (Z, 29 April 1998) [Of all the *founding fathers* who negotiated EMU in 1991, he (= the then German Chancellor, H. Kohl) is the only one who has survived politically. Among EU-leaders, the German chancellor is acknowledged as *the patriarch, the godfather, the head of the family*].

As these examples show, the PARENT and CHILD scenarios cover a wide range of conceptual mappings, targeting variously all nations of the European continent, or just the states of the EC/EU, its administrative centre, or particular politicians. Among the source concepts, only one or two of these conceptual slots are usually filled, others are vaguely implied. In (3) no *parents* are identified at all. For (2) we have to assume that Britain is *the (single) parent* and all other EC members are *godparents*. In (4) the EU as a whole provides the *family*, without any *parent*-specification. In (1), (5) and (6) only *fathers* are mentioned, with no plausible *mother*-candidate. As Table 4 shows, European FATHERHOOD seems to be much more popular than MOTHERHOOD. Of the altogether three *mother* examples, the two British ones are rather pejorative, depicting as they do France as a *euro-mother in difficulties*, and the EU Commission as an over-generous *mother* figure (in the context of the nepotism scandal of 1999).[15] The only positive reference to a maternal figure in EU debates documented in the corpus is to be found in a reader's letter to the German daily newspaper *Die Welt*, in which the writer bemoans the loss of the Deutschmark as the national *mother currency* that is analogous to a nation's loss of its *mother-tongue*.[16] As an example of the PARENT-scenario in the corpus, this analogy between language-loyalty and devotion to keeping the national currency may be idiosyncratic but it shows how closely the concept of MOTHERHOOD can be connected with national symbolism.

The reasons for the apparently greater popularity of EU-/euro-FATHERHOOD seem to lie in a powerful terminological and conceptual tradition of male-centred ideologies of statehood and politics in Western culture.[17] EU-related political discourse evidently taps into this traditional imagery of politics and nationhood, associated with a male bias. However, this traditional bias of EU/euro-FATHERHOOD is a far cry from the STRICT FATHER morality that Lakoff noted as a dominant metaphor in US politics. Euro-*fathers* are not at all predominantly seen as examples of STRICT FATHER morality. On the whole, the FAMILY concept in euro-discourse appears to be much more diffuse and less ideologically 'laden' than the US example. This is probably due to two reasons. The NATION STATE-AS-FAMILY mapping (applicable to the US) is historically more established in traditions of political thinking than the CONFEDERATION-AS-FAMILY mapping (applicable to the EU). In addition, the former mapping can be seen as ontologically more coherent. When targeted at the NATION STATE concept, its FAMILY sub-mappings, GOVERNMENT-AS-PARENT and CITIZENS-AS-CHILDREN, apply easily and uniformly and lead to further mappings, such as SOLDIERS-AS-SONS.

On the other hand, it is more difficult to identify consistently PARENT(S) and CHILD(REN) for the target notion of a variable GROUP OF STATES, such as the EC/EU, and this is borne out by the evidence of considerable variation in the corpus data. However, the PARENT and CHILD scenarios still appear to be sufficiently grounded in everyday experience to allow for a wide-ranging allocation of scenario roles to referents in the target domain of EU-politics.

Relations within the EU FAMILY become more specific once we take into account the scenario of individual states forming a MARRIED COUPLE. At first sight, however, we are confronted with an apparent inconsistency in the changing application of MARRIAGE PARTNERS scenarios to either the whole group of EU states or particular states – i.e. France and Germany – as in the following examples:

(7) The reality behind *the will-they-won't-they, pre-nuptial dances* among aspirant members of Europe's monetary union club is that as long as the [. . .] economic slowdown doesn't turn into a full-blown recession the project will probably go ahead. (G, 27 January 1996)

(8) Some sceptics believe, or hope, that the strains imposed by a single currency would be too great, and that those in the first wave, *having acted in haste, would be left to regret at leisure.* (I, 21 October 1996)

(9) In the long *gestation* of Europe's Economic and Monetary Union [. . .] it suddenly seems likely this week that *the anxious parents, Germany and France, are expecting a soft baby euro.* (G, 30 May 1997)

(10) *Die französische Braut putzt sich für die Euro-Hochzeit heraus* durch Verwendung von Mitteln der France Télécom, und *der Bräutigam Deutschland* maßt sich an zu kritisieren und plant doch bereits gleiches [. . .]. (W, 30 November 1996) [*The French bride makes herself pretty for the euro-wedding* by using (the windfall profits from the pri-

vatization of) France Télécom, and now *the German bridegroom* has the presumption to criticise her for it while making similar plans.]

As examples (7)–(10) show, the MARRIED PARTNERS scenario – just like the PARENT and CHILD scenarios – accommodates several specific plots, namely that all members of the euro currency union are *married to each other* and have one *child* (the euro) together, or that two states, i.e. France and Germany, form the *couple* of *euro parents*. The first version (cf. examples 7 and 8) suggests that all Euro-zone countries are *getting married* (and presumably also become the *euro*-parents). The latter version (cf. examples 9 and 10) concentrates only the Franco-German *couple/parents* and leaves open the role of the other EU states – are they supposed to be *unofficial partners*, *distant relations*, or further *children* of the French *bride* France and her *bridegroom* Germany? These inconsistencies do not hamper the comprehension of the text passages, thus demonstrating that the source-target mapping should not be thought of as a mechanical, static relationship. Rather, a few source elements act as conceptual cues that can be combined freely to form 'story-lines', which fit a specific political interpretation of the target topic.

The distribution patterns of the TWO STATES-AS-ONE COUPLE scenario version tell a lot about national perceptions in the public debates about European politics. As Table 4 shows, the MARRIED COUPLE forms the second most frequent source concept from the FAMILY domain. In all examples, the target referents are exclusively France and Germany; no other state seems to qualify for membership of the *Euro-couple* (as it existed between 1989 and 2001). However, one further state does sometimes come into the picture as an outside suitor, i.e. Britain. This extension of the basic MARRIAGE scenario is construed and evaluated in different ways in the British and German discourse. The British press is mainly interested in their own country's chances of *replacing one of the partners in the ailing Euro-couple* or bringing about a *ménage à trois*. Changes of government in the *Euro-couple* nations regularly provide opportunities to ventilate such hopes:

(11) The tricolour flies over a new tenant in France's Elysée Palace today, but what of *the eternal triangle* at Europe's core? Will Jacques Chirac be forced by the responsibility of power to [...] declare his *true loyalty*? Is the "*Franco-German couple*" really the "heart of the European Union" [...] or are Britain's Conservatives right to imagine they have found a fellow-sceptic *to flirt with*? (G, 18 May 1995)

(12) Germany's chancellor-in-waiting seemed to herald a dramatic shift in alliances, *arguing that the Franco-German marriage was now over*. Gerhard Schröder, leader of the opposition Social Democrats, *argued in favour of a menagé [sic] à trois*, involving London, Paris and Bonn. (I, 17 June 1997, i.e. 15 months before the German general elections in 1998)

(13) [...] Germany's incoming Chancellor, Gerhard Schröder, is to meet President Chirac [...] tomorrow in Paris. Thus, Tony Blair has lost the diplomatic tussle to be the first to press a glass of champagne into Mr Schröder's victorious hand. [...] Mr Schröder himself had suggested *that the cosy Franco-German marriage might become more of a ménage à trois* [...] (DT, 29 September 1998)

(14) During his election campaign, the French were upset by Mr Schröder's suggestion that *their hitherto exclusive partnership should be opened up to form a ménage à trois with the British*. To France's relief, there has been no further mention of this distinctly touchy issue. *Was a political Viagra pill taken* this week in Potsdam *to give the ageing relationship a new fizz*? Maybe, maybe not. Talk of a possible new *Paris–Bonn–London triangle* in Europe is nothing new: every time, over the past decade, that a new president or prime minister has taken over in France, *he briefly – and in the end unsatisfactorily – flirts with the Euro-sceptical British, only to fall back in relief on the old liaison with Germany*. (E, 5 December 1998)

In these examples, the MARRIED PARTNERS scenario resembles that of a TV soap opera, which might have the title *"Europe's eternal triangle"*. Example (11) explicitly characterizes the supposition of *flirtatious advances* by the French president towards Britain as existing mainly in the wishful thinking of British Euro-sceptics. In example (12), it is claimed that the SPD's contender for the chancellorship in Germany, G. Schröder, did make similar *advances* towards Britain but close reading reveals this to be a case of metaphorical reinterpretation. Schröder is reported to have argued 'in favour' of a *ménage à trois* but, as the translation of his original statement in another article of the same newspaper issue shows, the German politician had actually used the geometrical metaphors of *triangle* and *axis*.[18] The term *triangle* seems to have acted here as a cue for the newspaper editor to switch from the geometric image to the cliché of the *eternal triangle*. The partial quotation of Schröder's statement is fitted into the extended MARRIED PARTNERS + LOVER scenario and is given a new significance, i.e. that of a political promise. This is also evident from examples (13) and (14): here Schröder is depicted as an inconstant, if not deceitful *flirter*, who, once he has become Federal Chancellor, forgets about his previous *advances* towards Britain and *flies back into the arms* of his established *partner*. True to their respective general political leanings, the strongly Euro-sceptic *Daily Telegraph* uses the MARRIED PARTNERS + LOVER scenario to denounce the German politician as a reckless *flirter*, whereas the liberal-leaning *Economist* gives a tongue-in-cheek interpretation (example 14). The magazine presents the (alleged) disappointment of Britain's hopes as the latest instalment in a popular TV saga, with the *Euro-couple* France and Germany and the *unsuccessful lover* Britain as comic characters, who almost ritually 'go through the motions' of *flirtation, marital crisis* and *reconciliation*.

This extended scenario version of the *troubled Euro-marriage* between France and Germany is used also on the German side, albeit with a different argumentative slant: a possible *break-up of the Franco-German couple* is evaluated not as a positive opportunity but as a dangerous development, and there is some sympathy for the *cheated partner's* point of view:

(15) Seit der Renaissance lebt die französische Komödie von *Dreiecksverhältnissen. Nie hat auf der Bühne der betrogene Ehemann das Mitgefühl des Publikums, sondern man lacht über ihn*. Gedankenspiele Schröders, London in das Sonderverhältnis einzuschließen, mißfallen den Franzosen zutiefst. [...] Wenn Großbritannien in Europa eingebunden werden soll, dann durch die Franzosen, nicht durch die Deutschen. *Die Rolle des cocu, des "Gehörnten", mögen andere spielen.* (SZ, 1 October 1998) [Since the Renaissance, French comedy has been based on *love triangles. The cheated husband on stage never gets any sympathy – he is the object of derision.* The French do not like at all Schröder's toying with the idea of including Britain in the special EU-relationship. If anyone ties Britain into Europe, then it should be the French, not the Germans. *The role of the cocu, the cheated husband, is not for them.*]

(16) Die Komplexe und Phobien in der *Beziehung* zwischen Paris und Berlin ernähren die Gutachter seit Jahrzehnten. [...] Seit vorigem Wochenende, seit ihrem EU-Treff in Stockholm, scheint *die vertrackte Partnerschaft* zwischen Chirac, Jospin und Schröder nun doch zu retten. [...] *Vorerst schwört der Kanzler nur Treue: Keine Seitensprünge mehr mit Tony!* (Z, 29 March 2001) [The complexes and phobias of

the *relationship* Paris–Berlin have been the bread and butter of political (psycho-)analysts for several decades. Since last weekend's EU meeting in Stockholm, however, the *troublesome partnership* Chirac–Jospin–Schröder looks as if it could still be saved. *For the moment, the Chancellor only promises marital fidelity: no more dalliance with Tony*.]

A specific feature of German discourse concerning the *Euro-couple*, which has no counterpart in the British sample, is a preoccupation with the question of who is the *stronger partner*, as evidenced in the following examples:

(17) Nach dem Prestige-Krieg um die Euro-Bank *müssen die Bonner* [. . .] *den französischen Freunden einschärfen, daß eine Ehe nicht bestehen kann, in der der Schwächere das Regiment zu führen trachtet*. (SZ, 8 May 1998) [After the prestige-war over the ECB, *Bonn must remind our French friends that a marriage cannot survive in which the weaker partner tries to dominate*.]

(18) *In dieser [deutsch-französischen] Ehe besaßen die Franzosen die Muskeln und die vergangenheitsgeschädigten Deutschen die wirtschaftlichen Energien. Schröders Versuch, Muskeln zu zeigen, und Frankreichs wirtschaftlicher Aufschwung lassen diese Vernunftehe nun erkalten*. (BZ, 29 September 1999) [*Within this Franco-German marriage*, the French had the (political) muscle, the Germans – hampered by their historical legacy – provided the economic strength. Both Schröder's attempts to show (political) muscle and France's economic recovery now contribute to *a cooling of this marriage of convenience*.]

As is the case in British public discourse, the German press employs the MARRIED COUPLE scenario to discuss developments in the Franco-German relationship. What distinguishes it from British usage is a stronger interest in the internal structure of the relationship and a more critical and warning stance regarding the possibility of a *cooling* or *break-up of the marriage*, rather than seeing it as a chance for new *flirts*. On the other hand, there is a common assumption underlying both discourses, i.e. that the EU, despite its officially egalitarian character, is based only on one really important bilateral relationship, i.e. that between France and Germany, and that the only further candidate for joining this partnership is Great Britain. The extended scenario of two or three states as MARRIED PARTNERS + LOVER thus exposes as a diplomatic sham the idea of an egalitarian status and communal solidarity, which is embodied in the more general EUROPEAN FAMILY metaphor.

In principle, of course, the MARRIED PARTNERS scenario could be applied to any bilateral international relationship; it is thus highly significant that in the EUROMETA-corpus there are no other EU-states that are said to form the *Euro-couple*. There is a single instance of a British newspaper applauding an "Anglo-German love-in" (G, 21 March 1998); however, the respective article seems to relate to one of the *flirts* that temporarily distract one of the traditional (Franco-German) *Euro-couple's partners*, not to a *lasting affair*. Any other groups of states with more than two members are covered by different metaphorical concepts and scenarios e.g. AXIS, CIRCLE, CORE VS PERIPHERY, CLUB.

Apart from the *Euro-couple*, there are numerous examples in the corpus of general LOVE or MARRIAGE metaphors covering the relationship between an individual state or one of its political/economic institutions and the EC/EU as a whole or one of its institutions. The target referents can vary, from applicant states that want to join the EU (cf. examples 19–22 below) through the currency *marriage* of individual EU states with the euro currency (examples 23–24) to Britain's problematic relationships with EU institutions (examples 25–27):

(19) Das bewährte k.u.k. Motto hat seine Auferstehung erlebt, diesmal in Verbindung mit einer Staatengemeinschaft: *Tu felix Austria nube*, und alle müßten ihren Vorteil davon haben. (Z, 17 June 1994) [The good old motto of Austrian imperial policy has been revived, this time in relation to a confederation of states. *Tu felix Austria nube.* Everyone should gain from this relationship][19]

(20) *Turkey must now be wooed* to accept EU membership. (I, 11 December 1999)

(21) Die EU will Rumänien helfen, aber die Politiker *zieren sich.* [...] *Bisher war die EU ein zögerlicher Bräutigam. Jetzt, da doch noch die Erfüllung winkt, ist es die Braut, die sich nicht traut.* (Z, 11 November 1999) [The EU wants to help Romania but its politicians *play hard to get. Up until now, the EU was the hesitant bridegroom. However, now that consummation of the marriage is close, it is the bride who is being difficult.*]

(22) Das heutige Polen will *eine reine Zweckehe* mit der EU eingehen. Es gibt an der Weichsel keine Euroföderalisten, nur Befürworter eines "Europas der Vaterländer" [...]. (Z, 14 May 1998) [Today's Poland only wants to enter into *a marriage of convenience* with the EU. There

are no Euro-federalists on the Vistula but only advocates of a 'Europe of nations'.]

(23) *Putting off the wedding* [headline] [...] Tony Blair is right to delay joining EMU [...] (G, 14 October 1997)

(24) Biedenkopf [...] plädiert für [...] *eine "Verlobung" von fünf Jahren, damit die Staaten beweisen, daß sie es ernst meinen mit der wirtschaftspolitischen Tugend* [...] *Eine Verlobung, in der man ohne Seitensprünge die Treue beweist, ist besser als eine Heirat unter Kalenderdruck. Denn eine Scheidung kann mörderisch sein, das Klima zwischen den Ex-Partnern bösartig vergiften.* (SZ, 20 September 1997) [Kurt Biedenkopf (= prominent CDU politician) argues in favour *of a five year 'engagement' period* so that member states can prove their economic *virtue. Such an engagement, in which marital fidelity can be proved by abstention from infidelities, is better than a hastily started marriage. For a divorce can be disastrous, poisoning the relationship between the ex-lovers.*]

(25) The pound's *shotgun separation* from the exchange rate mechanism is proving painful for both Britain and the rest of Europe. *The two-year marriage itself was unhappy* [...]. *As in most marriage breakdowns, there have been faults on both sides.* Sterling and the German mark – both big internationally traded currencies – were always going to be *uneasy bedfellows* [...]. (G, 2 February 1993)

(26) *Labour's honeymoon with the EU* appeared to have come to an abrupt end after a day of sharp exchanges between Mr Blair and President Chirac [...] (DT, 13 December 1997)

(27) For years, we assumed *that Britain was the great catch, with Europe the pushy suitor for our hand.* (G, 4 April 2001)

The last three quotations are representative for the strongly Euro-critical if not -sceptical attitude among British quality media as it is framed in the LOVE-MARRIAGE scenario. In example (25), Britain's 1992 withdrawal from the European Exchange Rate Mechanism (the forerunner of the currency union) is described ironically as a *shotgun separation*. In (26) the *honeymoon period* of the Labour government and the EU, once seen as equivalent in *warmth* to the *biblical welcome accorded the prodigal son* (cf. example 4, above), is said to have ended. In (27) a whole tradition of seeing the EU as the *pushy suitor for Britain's hand in marriage* is reflected upon. There are no matching examples in the

German press: the most sceptical vision is that of example (24), where a *divorce* after an ill-conceived currency *marriage* figures as the hypothetical worst-case scenario in debates about a potential postponement of the euro introduction. Even then, the envisaged political consequences amount to a *prolonged engagement period*, not a *separation*. This is far from the British condemnations of the pound–euro *relationship* or the Britain–EU *love-in*.

2.3 Metaphor scenarios and public attitudes

This survey of LOVE-MARRIAGE-FAMILY metaphors from the EUROMETA I corpus provides evidence for the relevance of source domains as conceptual structures underlying public discourse, thus corroborating basic hypotheses of cognitive theory. It also demonstrates, however, the necessity to identify central mappings and scenarios within domains to capture attitudinal and argumentative trends that are characteristic for particular discourse communities.

Specifically, the data show that the political application of the FAMILY source domain, as identified in Lakoff (1996), is also productive at the level of international politics. When combined with the mapping A NATION STATE IS A PERSON, it yields conceptualizations of bi- or multinational relationships as LOVE and/or FAMILY RELATIONSHIPS BETWEEN PERSONS. The individual metaphor data in the two national corpus samples allow us to identify central conceptual mappings that relate developments in the domain of politics to basic everyday knowledge about LOVE, MARRIAGE and FAMILY LIFE (cf. above 2.i). These mappings, which are abstracted from the data at the 'supraindividual' level, are the same for the British and German discourse communities – the list of conceptual elements contained in the corpus tokens (cf. Table 3) provides proof of this.

When we searched for attitudinal differences between the two communities, it became necessary to go beyond the general level of domains and take into account specific conceptual scenarios that relate to the central mappings but are based on frequency clusters of tokens of particular domain elements (cf. above 2.ii and Table 4). Within the LOVE-MARRIAGE scenario, British media often comment almost triumphantly on apparent *marriage problems* of the Franco-German *couple* that might lead to a *breakdown* or gradual *cooling down of the partnership* and provide Britain with a chance to establish a *ménage à trois*. The German press, on the other hand, sees such problems as a worrying threat that must be combated and averted. British media tend to emphasise the possibilities of their own national government's *divorce* or *separation* from or *end of the relationship* with the EU. By comparison, German politicians and the press talk more cautiously, e.g. in terms of a *prolonged engagement* as regards the introduction of the *euro* currency, or, with reference to new EU membership candidates, of *difficult courtships* or *marriages of convenience*. The LOVE-MARRIAGE scenario thus provides a ready-made conceptual frame of culturally shared assumptions concerning interpersonal relationships. At the same time, it allows for differences in the highlighting of particular sub-topics of inter-national relationships and their political evaluation, which are characteristic for the two national discourse communities.

Sceptical scenario versions of the FAMILY (AS PARENT and CHILD) scenario are much less frequent than for the LOVE-MARRIAGE scenario. There are no instances of texts arguing in favour of a withdrawal from the *European family* in either the British or the German sample, although debates among Euro-sceptic media and politicians about a British withdrawal from the EU are well represented in the corpus. This points to a positive 'default' bias of the FAMILY source scenario: the concepts of BEING PART OF or RETURNING INTO A FAMILY AS A CHILD, and the roles of PARENTS or GODPARENTS, are usually valued positively. It seems to be easier to conceive of a withdrawal from a *marriage that does not work* than from a *dysfunctional family*. The PARENT and CHILD scenarios appear to imply the assumption that intra-familiar relationships are, or at least should be, characterized by solidarity and mutual responsibility, which tallies with some of the basic assumptions of FAMILY-based morality in US discourse, as analysed by Lakoff (1996). However, there are also a few 'untypical' instances of pessimistic versions of the CHILD-scenario, such as those of the *premature baby* images of the "hard ecu" and the euro (cf. examples 2 and 5), which demonstrate that this scenario, too, can be used to formulate Euro-critical arguments. Clearly, scenarios can be argumentatively exploited either way in terms of the political perspectives associated with them. This leads to a further question for the analysis of metaphors in political discourse, namely that of how and why argumentative conclusions based on metaphoric scenarios come to be regarded as acceptable or even particularly persuasive. We shall study this aspect in the following chapter.

3
Analogical Argument in Political Discourse

3.1 Metaphor and argument by analogy

In autumn 1992, almost two years after her resignation as prime minister, Margaret Thatcher voiced her misgivings about EC integration policy by commenting on the then popular metaphor of the *European train leaving the station without Britain* (on account of her successor government's difficulties in ratifying the Maastricht Treaty, which was designed to *pave the way* for further economic and political integration):

> (1) Misleading analogies such as the *European train leaving the station* have been used in the debate, she says. *"If that train is going in the wrong direction it is better not to be on it at all.* The Newspeak of Orwell has returned as EMU speak." (T, 31 October 1992)

Thatcher's rejection of "misleading analogies" was closely connected with her mistrust of what she perceived as a specifically (EC-)European type of political discourse. On various other occasions, she accused the central EC administration and pro-integration politicians of using metaphors to impose political commitments on Britain, as, for example, in this passage from the autobiographical account of her time in office, *The Downing Street Years*:

> (2) [...] anyone dealing with the European Community should pay careful attention to metaphors. We in Britain were inclined to minimize their significance [...]. We had to learn the hard way that by agreement to what were apparently empty generalizations or vague aspirations we were later held to have committed ourselves to politi-

cal structures which were contrary to our interests. (Thatcher 1993: 319)[1]

As her own reinterpretation of *the train leaving the station* metaphor in (1) shows, Thatcher was by no means unable or unwilling to use analogy and metaphor. However, she sees them as dangerous rhetorical devices, whose significance she aims "to minimize" in order not to be misled like the victims of the *Newspeak* jargon in George Orwell's *1984*. It would be too easy to dismiss her criticism of analogy and metaphor as mere polemics. Leaving aside her own rhetorical flourish, one can distinguish three serious claims about political imagery: (a) that metaphors/analogies (mis-)lead and commit users to certain practical political consequences; (b) that users may not even be aware of the commitments they have entered into by subscribing to a particular metaphor; and (c) that it needs politicians like her to "minimize" the impact of metaphors by guiding the populace back to the realm of practicalities. While the last claim reflects Margaret Thatcher's special view of herself as a pre-eminent British politician, the first two claims are not miles away from the suspicions that Hobbes seems to have voiced against the use of metaphors in general (cf. quotation (1) in the preceding chapter) and that Lakoff levels against STRICT FATHER morality.

But how exactly can a metaphor, i.e. a semantic or conceptual structure, 'commit' politicians or whole nations to follow a certain course of action? Lakoff and Johnson give an answer to this question in terms of their theory of metaphorical "entailments":

(3) Metaphors have entailments through which they highlight and make coherent certain aspects of our experience. A given metaphor may be the only way to highlight and coherently organize exactly those aspects of our experience. Metaphors may create realities for us, especially social realities. A metaphor may thus be a guide for future action. Such actions will, of course, fit the metaphor. This will, in turn, reinforce the power of the metaphor to make experience coherent. In this sense metaphors can be self-fulfilling prophecies. (Lakoff and Johnson 1980: 156)[2]

The example that Lakoff and Johnson give is the WAR metaphor as used by the former US president Carter to define and further his environmental and foreign policies during the oil price crisis in the mid-1970s. The WAR metaphor can be said to 'create reality' in so far as it forms a foil against which to judge the truth of successive political statements about *battles won* or *lost*:

> (4) If you do not accept the existence of an external enemy, if you think there is no external threat, if you recognize no field of battle, no targets, no clearly defined competing forces, then the issue of objective truth or falsity cannot arise. But if you see reality as defined by metaphor, that is, if you do see the energy crisis as a war, then you can answer the question relative to whether the metaphorical entailments fit reality. (Lakoff and Johnson 1980: 158)

This account provides a general indication of how metaphors can become a 'blueprint' for political reality. However, as an explanation of the process by which a metaphor is accepted in the first place it is somewhat circular. An implication of the metaphorical mapping 'X IS WAR' can only count as an *entailment* if X has already been accepted as the source concept – otherwise, as Lakoff and Johnson themselves point out, it is meaningless. In authentic political discourse, however, there is no guarantee for an unproblematic acceptance; in fact, such an acceptance would be quite untypical, given the fundamentally competitive and controversial character of public debates. Thatcher's explicit rejection of the *leaving train* metaphor in quotation (1) provides a clear example of non-acceptance, which is typical for public disputes. She questions the suggested 'entailment' of the TRAIN JOURNEY metaphor (i.e. that it is *important to get on the train before it is too late*) and immediately introduces a new one (i.e. that it is *better not to be on the train if it is going in the wrong direction*). She thus demonstrates that it is perfectly possible to accept a metaphor mapping (i.e. A POLITICAL PROCESS IS A TRAIN JOURNEY) without subscribing to all of its entailments. Lakoff and Johnson's theory seems to work only as an explanation for those metaphors that become self-fulfilling prophecies: their source implications are confirmed in the target domain by actions that 'suit the words' and thus give them a *practical political* coherence.

But how can a metaphorical mapping suggest a certain commitment *before* it has acquired 'reality' status through political practice? In order to avoid the circularity of the self-fulfilling metaphor entailments, I propose to regard political metaphors as integral aspects of argumentative reasoning, i.e. reasoning which typically aims to prove a *contested* issue and thus also *legitimize* a certain course of action. If metaphors can be deemed to lead to conclusions that 'bind' politicians and states, they must function in some way like warrants in an argument, i.e. they must appear to give a valid justification for using particular premises in order to arrive at a certain conclusion. According to Stephen Toulmin's famous model of non-formal argumentation, warrants have the task "to register explicitly the legitimacy of the [argumentative] step involved and to refer it back to the larger class of steps whose legitimacy is being presupposed" (Toulmin 1958: 100).[3] Statements of such warrants are "hypothetical, bridge-like statements" (1958: 105) and, if questioned, have to be backed up by further data and even, if necessary, whole arguments that are specific to a particular domain of discourse and reasoning – i.e. in Toulmin's terminology, they are "field-dependent" (1958: 104). In Toulmin's own example, for instance, the conclusion that 'Harry is a British subject' is based on the premise that Harry is born in Bermuda. The warrant 'A man born in Bermuda will be a British subject' provides the link between the 'raw' data and the conclusion by adducing legal provisions for the definition of British citizenship – as these are fulfilled by the data, the conclusion is vindicated (1958: 101–2). Crucially, a warrant is not based on *entailments* in the logical sense of "necessary conditions of truth" (Kempson 1977: 39) but on *presupposed steps* of argumentation, which are assumed by the interlocutors to be uncontroversial at the time of speaking but are not logically binding truth conditions.[4] This presuppositional basis of warrants implies also a certain historicity and indexicality; for instance, the legal provisions for citizenship in Toulmin's example have changed since the days when *The Uses of Argument* was first published. The warrant conditions for the validity of a conclusion are not self-evident but "incidental and explanatory" (Toulmin 1958: 100) and may well be questioned – which then necessitates references to more general warrants that define what the respective speakers regard as fundamental "canons" of rational argument (1958: 98). Whether a metaphor functions as an argumentative warrant depends on the use of the statement it occurs in, e.g. in the political sphere, as a conclusion about a contentious issue of public concern. If so, the presupposed knowledge about the source domain that is mapped onto the target domain can lead to inferences with a particular political slant or bias. This source-induced bias seems to be the aspect of political metaphor that attracts Thatcher's and other critics' condemnation. Presuppositions that are presented as unproblematic in the metaphor, they allege, impose an "unconscious conceptual framework" (Lakoff 1996: 386) or "commit [users] to political structures" which are "contrary to [their] interests" (Thatcher).

Whether such criticism is justified still remains to be seen; however, what we need to establish first is a model of the mechanism of 'argumentation-by-metaphor'. So far, we have spoken in general terms of presuppositions that are mapped from the source onto the target domain. For such source presuppositions to become part of an argumentative warrant, however, a specific operation of analogical reasoning is required. A basic model of analogy is provided by Aristotle at the end of his famous definition of metaphor in the *Poetics* (as the last of four types of metaphor), where a relational homology between pairs of concepts is understood as the conceptual basis for exchanging the corresponding elements:

> (5) By analogy I mean cases where B stands in a similar relation to A as D does to C; one can mention D instead of B, and vice versa. Sometimes the thing to which the noun stands in relation is expressed; I mean (e.g.) a cup stands in similar relation to Dionysus as a shield does to Ares; so one may call the cup 'the shield of Dionysus', or a shield the 'cup of Ares'. [. . .] In some cases there is no existing noun for one term in the analogy, but it can nevertheless be expressed. For example scattering seed is 'sowing', but there is no noun for the scattering of fire from the sun, but this stands in similar relation to the sun as scattering does to seed; hence the expression 'sowing the god-created fire'. There is another way of using analogical metaphor: one may refer to something using the transferred noun, and negate some of its proper attributes; e.g. on might call a shield not the 'cup of Ares' but the 'wineless cup.' (Aristotle, *Poetics*, 21: 1457b, 1996a: 34–5)

Metaphorical statements, such as 'X is the father of European unity' (said about a specific politician) or 'the European train is leaving' (about a specific political decision being implemented), can be analysed as being based on this fundamental type of analogy. We can explicate them as equivalences of relationships between pairs of target and source concepts (e.g. 'POLITICIAN X + EUROPEAN UNITY' analogically = FATHER + CHILD, 'POLITICAL PROBLEM + its DECISION/IMPLEMENTATION analogically = TRAIN + LEAVING STATION). However, the analogies implicit in these metaphors do not seem to lead to contentious conclusions, probably on account of their standard, clichéd presuppositions. But if we 'spice up' the supposed utterances by using more strongly evaluative formulations, the argumentative function of the presupposed analogies becomes evident. Consider:

> (6) The *father of European Unity* must always be treated with unconditional *respect*.

(7) We *must join the European train* as quickly as possible.

Here the respective source concepts include normative assumptions about standard social roles, norms and values, e.g. about the IMPORTANCE OF (STRICT) FATHERLY AUTHORITY IN THE FAMILY, or the IMPORTANCE OF BEING PUNCTUAL FOR A TRAIN (WHICH IS ABOUT TO LEAVE). By referring to the target referents in terms of the strongly biased source concepts, the speakers also invoke the associated value judgements, thus vindicating specific political conclusions. These, too, can be explicated as analogical arguments, i.e. as inviting an inference about a conceptual pair C-D on the basis of the assumptions that the concept C is analogous to an A, and that this A is in a well-known relationship to a concept B, so that it can be inferred with some plausibility that the relation C-D is analogous to A-B:

(6″) Just as a real father (A) should (according to STRICT FATHER morality) be treated with unconditional respect (B), so the EU politician who is considered to be a *father of European Unity* (C) must be respected (D).

(7″) Just as it is (normally) preferable to catch a real train (A) in time and therefore enter it quickly when it is about to leave (B), so the political process that is considered to be the *European train leaving for the destination* of currency union (C) should be joined as soon as possible (D).

Analogical reasoning has regained theoretical recognition since the revival of rhetorical studies originating from I. A. Richards' *Philosophy of Rhetoric* (1936). In a more recent analysis, Chaim Perelman and Lucie Olbrechts-Tyteca accorded analogical reasoning a central position in their *New Rhetoric*.[5] Perelman made analogy the lynchpin of his theory of argumentation: he accorded it the status of being "one of the characteristics of communication and nonformal reasoning" (Perelman 1982: 114) and effectively subsumed metaphor under it: "for us, a metaphor is only a condensed analogy" (1982: 120). By way of interpreting Aristotle's classic examples as well as a host of metaphors from history, philosophy and poetry, Perelman elucidated the effect of analogy that lies in suggesting a similitude of proportions between aspects of the source and target concepts (in his terminology: *theme* and *phoros*), so that the relation in a pair of source aspects A-B is likened to that of the target pair C-D with special argumentative effect.

Perelman acknowledged the existence of "purely ornamental metaphor", but that is not the type of metaphor he was mainly interested in. Instead, he considered metaphor as "only successful if its value ceases to be verbal because certain aspects of the terms of the *phoros* place the corresponding terms of the *theme* in a sought after and, often affective perspective" (Perelman 1979: 93). This interest in the argumentative and conceptual dimension of metaphor is what makes Perelman's analysis compatible with more recent cognitive accounts of analogy (cf. e.g. Gentner 1988, 1989; Holyoak and Thagard 1989; Indurkhya 1988, 1992; Johnson-Laird 1989; Gentner, Holyoak and Kokinov 2001). These approaches focus on the formal properties of analogy and metaphor and their application in artificial and natural information processing as well as inferencing systems.

Analogical inferencing can take the form of highly complex and creative blendings of conceptual spaces, as shown by Mark Turner and Gilles Fauconnier (2000). They discuss, for instance, the witty counterfactual statement "If Clinton were the Titanic, the iceberg would sink", coined with respect to the former US president Clinton's ability to survive (politically) the 'collision' with attempts to instigate impeachment proceedings against him. The statement creates, rather than merely represents, an analogy: it is more than just "a cross-space mapping with the Titanic scenario as source and the Clinton scenario as target" (Turner and Fauconnier 2000: 134).[6] Its specific "blended space" has a causal and event shape structure that cannot be derived from the source, and it gives rise to inferences (along the lines of 'Clinton, contrary to the historic Titanic is [politically] unsinkable') that are not logically deducible from the knowledge about the target topic:

(8) It is uncontroversial that cases like the Clinton–Titanic example involve the basic metaphor PURPOSEFUL ACTIVITY IS TRAVELING ALONG A PATH TOWARDS A DESTINATION – the traveler projects to the agent, reaching the destination projects to achieving the goal, and so on [. . .]. But that metaphor cannot by itself yield the complex inferences outlined above. It is in the blended space that we construct and run the complex counterfactual scenario in which the Titanic sinks the iceberg, and it is that scenario which projects to the input of politics and society [. . .]. (Turner and Fauconnier 2000: 135)

We can connect this analysis of hypothetical analogical reasoning as a type of conceptual blending with the notion of scenarios as the level where argumentative, affective and evaluative inferences attach to specific source "input" spaces. The argumentative inferences in an analogical conclusion are based on – but not fully determined by – either the source or the target domain. A scenario as a blended space allows for creative exploitation of source-target mappings, as long as there are enough input spaces to enable the reader/hearer to construe the missing elements of the analogy. PARENT or LEAVING TRAIN scenarios, for instance, comprise a potentially infinite number of roles and social relations, but the conclusions concerning the target notions of a politician's 'fatherly authority' or about the 'timely participation in a political process' can be explicated as four-term analogies (cf. examples 6/6″ and 7/7″). In both cases the common-sense 'authority' of the source scenario is conferred upon a political conclusion, which otherwise might be tenuous or even implausible; however, with the backing of the analogy as a warrant it appears to be unproblematic.

Construed statements similar to those in examples (6)/(6″) and (7)/(7″), whose input presuppositions are made explicit, are rare in authentic public debates. In the majority of real-life uses, such as the examples of Euro-political discourse documented in EUROMETA I, the presuppositions (and in particular, any *problematic* presuppositions) are not spelt out but are kept implicit. This 'hiding' effect is possible because of the inferential structure of analogy. Of the four concepts involved, one can always be assumed to be tacitly understood and – as Aristotle demonstrated in the example of the 'wineless cup' – even the term for a second salient concept can be omitted in the formulation. This particular example may appear uncontroversial to modern readers, on account of its irrelevance for our world-view. But such ideological indifference is not applied to topical political metaphors whose presuppositions may lead to problematic inference that matter to us. In the cases of the FAMILY metaphor in US politics as analysed by Lakoff, or of the MARRIED COUPLE scenario in EU debates, the implications of political metaphors are by no means uncontroversial. What is hidden or played down in some instantiations of these metaphors are the normative presuppositions that 'a family should be organized according to strict father morality', or that 'a couple should stay together and its partners should refrain from extra-marital escapades'. These presuppositions are compatible with assumptions in traditional social settings, and will be accepted probably most often without much scrutiny as 'true', 'desirable' or at least as 'normal'. As warrants in an analogical argument, however, they take on a new significance because they are employed to vindicate contentious evaluative conclusions concerning the respective target concepts. In Thatcher's criticism of the TRAIN JOURNEY scenario of

EU integration (example 1 above), on the other hand, the presuppositions are made explicit, but from a critical perspective. Thatcher wants to deny the conclusiveness of the TRAIN metaphor. For this reason she engages in a kind of 'meta-metaphorical' comment by spelling out the conditions under which the presupposed analogy 'DESIRABILITY OF BEING ON THE TRAIN BEFORE IT LEAVES THE STATION equals DESIRABILITY OF JOINING THE EU INTEGRATION PROCESS IN TIME' does not hold – namely, *when the train is going in the wrong direction*.

The seemingly conclusive power of metaphors in analogical arguments is thus dependent on their scenario structure. The scenario provides more than just a cross-domain mapping: it depicts a minimal but coherent scene that is reminiscent of standard situations, which the users are familiar with as part of their shared cultural knowledge. Parts of this knowledge are assumptions and folk-theories about typical role-relations (e.g. FATHER-CHILD, COUPLE-LOVER, TRAIN-PASSENGER) and about courses of action as well as relevant social, ethical and practical norms and values that guide 'normal' behaviour (PARENTAL AUTHORITY, MARITAL FIDELITY, TRAINS LEAVING STATIONS ACCORDING TO FIXED TIMETABLES). As the various scenario elements are presupposed rather than deduced, their common-sense authority is mapped onto the target concepts automatically, unless it is explicitly challenged (as in the case of Thatcher's criticism of the TRAIN JOURNEY scenario). The source scenario can thus be employed to enhance the persuasiveness of a conclusion by supporting it with seemingly self-evident analogies, or to gloss over weak or non-existing links in an argument. Even if a hearer or reader does not consciously agree with the standard scenario assumptions and associated judgements, he or she can be expected, as a member of a discourse community, to know and anticipate these assumptions 'by default'. For this reason, Perelman called condensed analogical metaphors "the most deceiving [ones], because we are tempted to see an identification in them, although we can understand them satisfactorily only by reconstructing the analogy and supplying the missing terms" (1982: 120). He advised critics of such metaphors to "either adapt the analogy so that it corresponds better to [their] own conceptions, or to replace it by another, thought to be more adequate" (1982: 119). An example for the latter strategy could be Lakoff's plea for the NURTURANT PARENT model of state-citizen relationships in place of the STRICT FATHER model. Thatcher, on the other hand, adapts the TRAIN JOURNEY SCENARIO by highlighting the DIRECTION aspect (cf. example 1).

The identification of the presuppositions of source scenarios, which are mapped analogically onto the target topic, allows us to analyse the political bias of metaphors in public discourse. This identification is not only crucial for the interpretation of individual examples but also for elucidating distribution patterns in a corpus such as EUROMETA I. As we have seen in the case of LOVE-MARRIAGE-FAMILY-scenarios, the argumentative exploitation of conceptual metaphors in political discourse is unlimited. There is no one set of argumentative presuppositions that is associated exclusively with one source concept or domain in a discourse community. Therefore, statistics about source concepts alone, such as in Table 4, can only give a global picture of the occurrence or non-occurrence of the main source scenarios in the metaphor usage of a given discourse community. They tell us little about their argumentative function and political bias. In order to find out more about the latter aspects, we have to investigate the relative distributional frequency of argumentative conclusions associated with mappings and scenarios. Such a quantitative analysis presupposes a sufficiently large set of data. Differences in single figures, which we found for the LOVE-MARRIAGE-FAMILY domain, cannot plausibly provide a basis for meaningful calculations of percentages. One metaphor source domain that does allow for quantitative comparisons because of its high frequency in public discourse is the one from which Thatcher took her example to protest against "misleading analogies", i.e. that of JOURNEY, TRANSPORT or MOVEMENT. It is this domain that we shall study in the following sub-chapter, to test the explanatory power of what we may call the 'scenario-argument analysis' of metaphors in public discourse.

3.2 Analogical arguments based on JOURNEY metaphors

In a speech given at the Humboldt University of Berlin in May 2000, the German foreign minister, Joschka Fischer, attempted to answer a question which, in his opinion, history was putting to the European Union: "Quo vadis Europa" – *which way will you go, Europe?* (Fischer 2000). His answer was: "*onwards* to the completion of European integration" – for any "*step backwards*, even just a *standstill* or contentment with what has been achieved would demand a fatal price of all EU member states and of all those who want to become members".[7] If not all member states were prepared "to take the *leap* into full integration" immediately, he argued that an "*avant-garde* comprising a few member states" should "*push ahead* with political integration".

Fischer's plea for *fast-track* integration, and especially his argument in favour of an *avant-garde*, caught the attention of commentators in both Britain and Germany. With reference to his speech and to a similar one delivered by the French President Jacques Chirac in Berlin shortly afterwards, *The Daily Telegraph* (1 June 2000) saw an imminent danger of a "splitting of Europe into slow and fast lanes". *The Independent* (27 June 2000) spoke of "British fears" that "a sleek new Union would leave [the] UK behind". The German weekly *Die Zeit* (18 May 2000) also linked Fischer's speech to the concept of a MULTI-SPEED EUROPE. However, in stark contrast to the British papers, *Die Zeit* used the MULTI-SPEED concept as a back-up argument for an endorsement of Fischer's plans:

(9) [...] Fischer [...] hat mit der Radikalität, die ihm eigen ist, den alten Gedanken und die bewährte Praxis eines 'Europas der verschiedenen Geschwindigkeiten' zu Ende gedacht [...]. (Z, 18 May 2000) [Fischer has, in his typical thoroughgoing way, thought through the full implications of the *tried and tested concept of 'a Europe of different speeds'.*]

This barrage of TWO-/MULTI-SPEED interpretations of Fischer's and Chirac's speeches (who had not used the *two-speed* phrase themselves) is indicative of the strength of the metaphorical mapping which, even on the limited statistical evidence of the pilot corpus, can justifiably be deemed to have dominated the public debates about EC/EU integration in Britain and Germany during the 1990s. The TWO-/MULTI-SPEED metaphor is based on an analogy between the commitment of member states' governments to a policy of further political and economic integration and their RELATIVE SPEED OF MOVING TOWARDS THE COMMON GOAL.

Table 5 Passages in the pilot corpus containing WAY-MOVEMENT-SPEED metaphors

Year	British press	German press	Overall
1989	0	2	2
1990	5	1	6
1991	24	21	45
1992	14	8	22
1993	8	5	13
1994	30	7	37
1995	21	7	28
1996	21	35	56
1997	36	60	96
1998	22	46	68
1999	24	16	40
2000	8	5	13
2001	1	4	5
Totals	214	217	431

Analogical Argument in Political Discourse   41

The pilot corpus contains 431 passages (214 for the British sample and 217 for the German sample) where this mapping is present in the form of SPEED COMPARISONS or characterizations of states as TRAVELLERS or VEHICLES MOVING ALONG A PATH. The spread of documented passages per year is listed in Table 5; the main conceptual elements and their corpus frequencies are listed in Tables 6 and 7.[8] The figures for tokens are again higher than those of passages, due to frequent co-occurrences of various conceptual elements from this domain, especially in the British sample.

The two peaks in the years 1991 and 1997, with the substantial build-up in 1996 for the latter, appear to reflect the intensity of debates surrounding the Maastricht and Amsterdam Treaty negotiations.

Table 6   Conceptual elements of the WAY-MOVEMENT-SPEED domain

Conceptual elements	English lexemes	German lexemes
WAY, PATH	path, way, road, lane, track, course, middle way, third way for/in Europe*	Weg, Kurs, Route, Marschrichtung
ONE-WAY STREET		Einbahnstraße
CUL-DE-SAC	cul-de-sac	Sackgasse
CROSSROADS	crossroads	Kreuzung, Scheideweg
DISTANCE SIGN	milestone, staging post, point where you cannot go back	Meilenstein
OBSTACLE	obstacle, stumbling block	Hindernis(se)
STEP	step (forward/ backward) [not including the phrasal verb 'step up']	Schritt, Riesenschritt [not including the lexicalized lexicalized noun 'Fortschritt' (= 'progress')]
(FAST, SLOW) SPEED, TWO-/MULTI-SPEED EUROPE	fast(er/est), slow(er/est), sluggard, laggard, two-/three-/multi-/ many speed Europe	langsam(st/er), schnell(st/er), Tempo, Takt, Nachzügler, Europa der zwei/drei/mehreren/ verschiedenen Geschwindigkeiten
TIMETABLE	timetable	Fahrplan, Fahrpläne
TICKET	ticket	Fahrschein
TRAIN JOURNEY	(euro-)train, gravy train, locomotive, fat controller, (train) station, platform 24, to derail, derailment	Zug, Euro(pa)-Zug, Lokomotive, Waggon, Weichen stellen, Bahnhof, Warte-/ Hauptgleis, entgleisen, Notbremsung, abkoppeln

Table 6 Continued

Conceptual elements	English lexemes	German lexemes
MARITIME JOURNEY	ship, boat, on board, ocean liner, drag anchor, ship wreck, Titanic, fleet, flotilla, washing in the lee, convoy**	Schiff, Boot, Dampfer, Seelenverkäufer, Reling, Brücke, Supertanker, Rettungsanker, Schiffbruch, Titanic, Geleitzug**
CAR TRAVEL	car, racing car, bus, Jaguar, Mercedes, engine, motor, Formula One engine, bulldozer, juggernaut, 5000 km pit stop, change of gear, driving seat, autobahn, to drive on the European side of the road	Mercedes, Motor, Blechschaden, gegen die Wand fahren, Pannenhelfer
BICYCLE TRAVEL	bicycle, tandem	Fahrrad, Tandem
AIR/SPACE TRAVEL	plane, take-off, mission control	Punktlandung

Notes:
* Not identical with the "Third Way" politics of New Labour (cf. e.g. the Conservative Prime Minister John Major arguing for "*a third European path* besides total integration and a two-speed Europe"; G, 1 June 1994).
** In passages containing *convoy-/Geleitzug*-metaphors, references to individual *ships* have not been counted extra.

Table 7 Tokens for conceptual elements of the WAY-MOVEMENT-SPEED domain in order of overall frequency

Conceptual elements	English tokens	German tokens	Overall tokens
(FAST, SLOW) SPEED, TWO-/MULTI-SPEED EUROPE	150	72	222
TRAIN JOURNEY	41	53	94
WAY, PATH	48	41	89
MARITIME JOURNEY (SHIP/CONVOY)	32	24	56
CAR TRAVEL (MOTOR)	35	39	74
STEP	10	13	23
BICYCLE TRAVEL	5	11	16
AIR/SPACE TRAVEL	8	6	14
TIMETABLE	5	6	11
DISTANCE SIGN	6	3	9
OBSTACLE	6	2	8

Table 7 Continued

Conceptual elements	English tokens	German tokens	Overall tokens
CROSSROADS	6	2	8
CUL-DE-SAC	2	3	5
TICKET	1	1	2
ONE-WAY STREET		1	1
Totals	355	277	632

From a cognitive perspective, the high number of instantiations of WAY-MOVEMENT-SPEED metaphors in the pilot corpus comes as no surprise: Lakoff and Johnson's research has provided ample proof of their ubiquity and fundamental status as part of one of the most basic conceptual metaphor systems that we 'live by', i.e. the "event structure metaphor" (Lakoff and Johnson 1980: 41–5, 87–96; Lakoff and Johnson 1999: 137–49; Lakoff 1993; Kövecses 2002: 134–9). This metaphor structures all kinds of events in terms of spatial relationships, leading to such basic metaphorical mappings as STATES ARE LOCATIONS, CHANGES ARE MOVEMENTS, ACTION IS SELF-PROPELLED MOTION, PROGRESS IS MOTION FORWARD, PURPOSES OF ACTIONS ARE DESTINATIONS, DIFFICULTIES ARE OBSTACLES etc. In the EUROMETA I-corpus, the following central mappings and scenarios can be identified:

3.i Central conceptual mappings for WAY-MOVEMENT-SPEED metaphors:

(a) A POLITICAL PROCESS IS A JOURNEY THAT PROCEEDS FROM A DEPARTURE POINT TOWARDS A GOAL/DESTINATION ALONG A SPECIFIC PATH (or SEVERAL PATHS)
(b) POLITICAL DEVELOPMENTS HINDERING THE IMPLEMENTATION OF THE POLITICAL PROCESS ARE OBSTACLES ON THE PATH or ARE WRONG PATHS LEADING INTO CUL-DE-SACS
(c) POLITICAL DEVELOPMENTS FACILITATING THE IMPLEMENTATION OF THE POLITICAL PROCESS ARE THE REMOVAL OF OBSTACLES ON THE PATH
(d) THE PARTICIPANTS IN A POLITICAL PROCESS ARE PARTICIPANTS IN A JOURNEY, TRAVELLING TOGETHER ALONG ONE PATH or SEVERAL PATHS
(e) THE PARTICIPANTS' DEGREE OF PARTICIPATION IN THE POLITICAL PROCESS IS THE SPEED WITH WHICH THEY TRAVEL ON THE JOURNEY
(f) THE PARTICIPANTS' RELATIVE PROGRESS IN THE IMPLEMENTATION OF THE POLITICAL PROCESS CAN BE MEASURED AGAINST SPECIFIC DISTANCE SIGNS ALONG THE PATH AND A COMMUNAL TIMETABLE

3.ii Scenarios for way-movement-speed metaphors:

(a) A GROUP OF STATES CO-OPERATING IN A POLITICAL PROCESS ARE MOVING TOGETHER ALONG A PATH (e.g. STEPPING FORWARD, BACKWARD, PASSING MILESTONES, CHOOSING ROUTES AT CROSSROADS)
(b) A GROUP OF STATES CO-OPERATING IN A POLITICAL PROCESS ARE PARTICIPANTS IN A TRAIN JOURNEY (e.g. LOCOMOTIVE, WAGONS, TRAIN DRIVER, TRAIN PASSENGER)
(c) A GROUP OF STATES CO-OPERATING IN A POLITICAL PROCESS ARE PARTICIPANTS IN A MARITIME JOURNEY, either on ONE SHIP or in a CONVOY (e.g. PARTS OF A SHIP, CAPTAIN, HELMSMAN, SHIP PASSENGER, INDIVIDUAL SHIPS)
(d) A GROUP OF STATES CO-OPERATING IN A POLITICAL PROCESS ARE PARTICIPANTS IN A CAR JOURNEY (e.g. MOTOR, CAR-TYPE, BUS, COACH (1 token), DRIVER, PASSENGERS, MOTORWAY)
(e) A GROUP OF STATES CO-OPERATING IN A POLITICAL PROCESS ARE PARTICIPANTS IN A BICYCLE JOURNEY (e.g. RIDERS ON A TANDEM)
(f) A GROUP OF STATES CO-OPERATING IN A POLITICAL PROCESS ARE PARTICIPANTS IN A JOURNEY BY AIR (e.g. AEROPLANE, PILOT, PASSENGER)

These scenarios depend upon the central mappings as listed in 3.i and on one of the most fundamental mappings of political discourse which has already been introduced in the context of the LOVE-MARRIAGE-FAMILY metaphors, i.e. the mapping A NATION STATE IS A PERSON (cf. preceding chapter, 2.i.a). As Table 7 shows, the various scenarios have widely differing frequencies of tokens, ranging from the massively represented general MOVEMENT scenario to the residual one of AIR TRAVEL. However, the sheer numbers of tokens in the pilot corpus, though probably indicative of the relative popularity of particular MEANS OF TRAVEL as metaphorical sources in the respective discourse communities, do not in themselves reveal much about their argumentative value in the debate about EU politics in Britain and Germany. This value depends, as we have seen in the preceding sub-chapter, on their usefulness in providing presuppositions that are salient or intuitively plausible enough to serve as "warrants" leading to evaluative political conclusions.

In the following discussion of the six metaphor scenarios outlined above we shall therefore analyse the scenario tokens with regard to presuppositions that lead to evaluative conclusions. For instance, in the case of Fischer's 2000 speech on EU integration and its British and German interpretations quoted above, we can easily discern the scenario (3.ii.a): A GROUP OF STATES CO-OPERATING IN A POLITICAL PROCESS ARE WALKING TOGETHER ALONG A PATH. In addition, we can discern an associated argumentative structure: as the EU member states are *walking/travelling at different speeds*, Fischer pleads for an *avant-garde marching as quickly as possible towards the goal* (= the fully unified EU), while provisions are made to accommodate *slower* states that cannot or will not join the *avant-garde* now but may *catch up later*. The press comments on the speech, which were quoted above, add to this argument two phraseological labels summarizing the contentious issue – the slogans of a *two-speed Europe* and of a *Europe of fast and slow lanes*. The evaluative terms in their reports, such as 'fears', 'splitting of Europe', 'tried and tested concept', leave little doubt about the political conclusions drawn. The British newspapers cited see a *two-speed Europe* as a dangerous development, whereas *Die Zeit* endorses it as an established policy. Fischer himself, while avoiding this particular slogan (in its German version: *Europa der zwei Geschwindigkeiten*), implies its relevance in his plea for some states *moving forward more quickly* than others. All of these statements share one source presupposition, which is analogically conferred upon the target concept of EU integration: THE GROUP OF STATES THAT ARE TRAVELLING ALONG A PATH PROCEED EITHER AT THE SAME SPEED OR AT DIFFERENT SPEEDS. In the latter case, i.e. in the TWO-SPEED EUROPE version, individual member states are assumed to have the role of PROCEEDING FASTER/SLOWER THAN OTHERS.

The specific political conclusions that individual newspapers or journalists arrive at are not at the centre of this analysis, as they are motivated mainly by the respective authors' political opinions and leanings. For the cognitive analysis it is irrelevant whether they approve or disapprove of the *fast* or *slow speed progress of a nation*, or of the existence or non-existence of a *two-speed* EU. What matters most for the analysis of metaphorical warrants in public discourse are the specific configurations of scenario elements that can be observed in the corpus data. As regards the patterns of political perception of the EU in Britain and Germany, it will be particularly interesting to see if there are any presuppositions that are represented exclusively or mainly in one national sample rather than the other. It is important to bear in mind that these presuppositions have not been inferred from the source domains by way of a logical or ontological derivation but are based exclusively on the corpus material.

3.2.1 Arguments based on the general (WALKING) JOURNEY scenario

The first scenario to investigate is the basic JOURNEY schema as sketched in 3.ii.a: A GROUP OF STATES CO-OPERATING IN A POLITICAL PROCESS ARE TRAVELLING TOGETHER ALONG A PATH. This scenario covers the largest numbers of tokens, as it includes all references to EU member states MOVING TOGETHER without mentioning a specific VEHICLE as a means of transport. This general scenario is not one simple set of roles and 'story-lines' but comprises the closely connected but nevertheless ontologically different aspects of PATH and of MOVEMENT/SPEED. We therefore need to distinguish two sets of presupposed roles and story-lines. One set concerns the EU's member states PROGRESS ALONG A PATH. Their PROGRESS may be EASY/FAST or DIFFICULT/SLOW, depending on the (non)occurrence of OBSTACLES. A small but significant sub-group singles out one nation – which in all tokens happens to be Britain – as NOT FOLLOWING THE PATH or even NOT BEING ON THE PATH. These PATH-related scenario-versions are summarized in Table 8. The second main set of general JOURNEY scenario versions con-

Table 8 PATH aspects in the general (WALKING) JOURNEY scenario

Scenario aspects (roles, relations, story-lines)	EU member states or EU institutions that fill role slots in scenarios	Tokens in English sample	Tokens in German sample	Tokens in both samples
X IS THE PATH/MILESTONE/ TIMETABLE FOR THE EU'S JOURNEY; for examples cf. note[9]	X = EMU, political union, Maastricht Treaty, Amsterdam Treaty	12	9	21
THE PATH FOR THE EU'S PROGRESS LIES OPEN/IS EASY TO FOLLOW/THE EU MAKES GOOD PROGRESS; for examples cf. note[10]		7	15	22
THE PATH FOR THE EU'S PROGRESS IS DIFFICULT TO FOLLOW/IS BLOCKED BY AN OBSTACLE/THE EU MAKES SLOW PROGRESS, for examples cf. note[11]		11	16	27
THE PATH FOR THE EU'S PROGRESS LEADS INTO DISASTER/A CUL-DE-SAC/ONE-WAY-STREET, for examples cf. note[12]		5	3	8
EU MEMBER STATES HAVE REACHED A CROSSROADS, for example cf. note[13]		6	2	8
X IS OFF THE EU PATH, X = GB for examples cf. note[14]		12	1	13
Totals		53	46	99

Table 9 SPEED DIFFERENCES in general (WALKING) JOURNEY scenario

Scenario aspects (roles, relations, story-lines)	EU member states or EU institutions that fill role slots in scenarios	Tokens in English sample	Tokens in German sample	Tokens in both samples
DIFFERENT-/MULTI-/TWO-SPEED-EUROPE; for examples cf. (9) above and further quotations in text below		33	17	50
X IS MAKING (TOO) RAPID PROGRESS, for examples cf. note[15]	X = GERMANY	15	2	17
	X = FRANCE	13	2	15
	X = EU	10	1	11
	X = CORE EU[16]	2	6	8
	X = GB (all tokens referring to GB post-May 1997)	5	1	6
	X = AUSTRIA	1		1
X IS NOT MAKING FAST (ENOUGH) PROGRESS, for examples cf. note[17]	X = GB	13	11	24
	X = EU	2	8	10
	X = GERMANY		3	3
Totals		94	51	145

cerns DIFFERENCES OF SPEED among the EU member states TRAVELLING ALONG THE PATH. The tokens for this scenario version are summarized in Table 9. In both these tables, all tokens for *every* scenario aspect have been counted, to give a full picture of their relative frequency for each national sample. A passage that contains a reference to the EU's *path*, mentions the *two-speed Europe* slogan, describes Britain as a *slow traveller* and France as a *fast traveller*, is thus counted as comprising four tokens. (This is a contrast to all other tables, where tokens are only counted once per conceptual element. Tables 8 and 9 contain, for instance, tokens of conceptual elements counted separately in Table 7. The figures in Tables 8 and 9 therefore do not compare directly with those of Table 7.) Examples illustrating these two scenario versions are provided in the endnotes, as they are not referred to in the text (with the exception of uses of the *two-/multi-speed* phrase, cf. below: examples 11–17).

These overviews show patterns of political perception that are remarkably consistent. In the first place, all conceptual aspects of the basic (WALKING) JOURNEY scenario are represented across both national samples. The most significant differences between the two national samples concern the distribution of tokens regarding the EU's or the member nations' SPEED OF TRAVEL, specifically SPEED differences between Britain on the one hand and Germany, France and the EU as a whole (but without Britain) on the other. Among the British public the latter three are seen as *travelling fast* towards integration, whereas in the German press there is no discernible preference for seeing them as *fast* rather than *slow*. On the other hand, there is a significant parallel: both British and German newspapers predominantly see Britain as a member state that *makes slow progress*, if it is at all *on the European path*. It is striking that this perception appears to be especially strong in the British press, as the scenario of a STATE MAKING SLOW PROGRESS at least weakly implies a negative bias: i.e. it is typically used as a point of reference for criticism of the SLOW MOVER. There is, of course, also a possibility of turning around such a bias, e.g. in the argument 'by going *slowly* Britain is safe from *rushing* headlong into disaster' (if the EU is perceived as making *too fast progress*). This case is represented in the British sample, albeit rarely. Thus, a conservative Euro-sceptic politician, the then Environment Secretary Michael Howard, tried to present the *slow track* of European integration as preferable to the *fast lane* of EU integration:

(10) Britain might be better off *in what was falsely called 'the slow track'*. (G, 28 September 1992)

However, even such special argumentative moves as calling into question the desirability of being *fast* only underline – *ex negativo*, as it were – the argumentative bias. *Being slow/on the slow track* is not the favoured option under normal circumstances, thus Howard had to make an extra effort to explain that Britain's political position in Europe was, after all, a favourable one (and only falsely labelled as implying *slow progress*). This shows that the general (WALKING) JOURNEY scenario presupposes a distinct evaluative bias: in a *two-* or *multi-speed Europe*, movement at the *first* or *fastest speed* is normally preferred to *slower speed*.

Before we go on to investigate whether this pattern and its bias – Germany and France as *fast*, Britain as *slow movers* in Europe – is repeated in the other JOURNEY scenarios, there is one further dimension of the TWO- or MULTI-SPEED aspect to be discussed. This is the question of whether SPEED DIFFERENCES between EU states are conceptualized as an established fact or as a future danger. The German comment on Fischer's 2000 speech, for instance, saw the MULTI-SPEED EUROPE as an already practised strategy, whereas the British papers treated it as a dangerous future development. Although this contrast has no direct impact on the positive or negative slant of the scenario, it clearly makes a difference: it is one thing to speak about a specific policy as a fait accompli, another thing to see it as a future risk. Over the 1990s, a significant shift can be discerned in the development of argumentative uses of the *two-* or *multi-speed Europe* formulae, which led to the national contrast we can observe in the reactions to Fischer's speech in 2000. At the start of the decade, the *two-speed* slogan figured prominently in comments on the Maastricht Treaty negotiations, when differences of interest concerning the SPEED of EU integration between Britain's Tory government and the rest of the EU resulted in Britain's 'opt-outs' from Economic and Monetary Union (EMU) and from the planned Treaty chapter on a common social policy. These opt-outs marked an officially recognized difference between Britain and other EU countries that invited an interpretation in terms of different INTEGRATION SPEEDS being favoured by member state governments:

(11) [...] the character of the exchange rate mechanism has been irreversibly changed. It is now being transmuted into a monetary *conveyor belt* towards a single currency by 1999, but from which Britain has gained a comprehensive opt-out. [...] *This is the two speed Europe that EC leaders have continually said they are against.* (G, 11 December 1991)

(12) Die Sozialpolitik der Europäischen Union wird, soweit sie über den Status quo *hinausgeht*, zur kontinentalen Elfer-Veranstaltung [...]. Und das soll, wie Kohl und Major unisono beteuern, *kein Europa der zwei Geschwindigkeiten sein?* (FR, 12 December 1991) [The EU's Social Policy, as far as it implies any *progress* beyond the status quo, will be an exclusive affair of 11 continental member states. *And this is supposed not to be* – as Kohl and Major keep pretending – *a two-speed Europe?*]

(13) Großbritannien wird [...] den möglichen Fortschritt in der europäischen Sozialpolitik, wie schon in der Wirtschafts- und Währungsunion, wenn überhaupt, nur mit *Verspätung* fördern. (Z, 13 December 1991) [Britain's support for progress as regards the European Social policy will be *delayed*, if there is any support at all – just as in the field of Economic and Monetary Union.]

The *Guardian*'s assessment of the Treaty as a *milestone* in example (11), written by its then economic editor, Will Hutton, is ambivalent: as the *path* to EMU is deemed to be a *road to ruin*, the countries that are committed to EMU are *fast approaching disaster*, whereas a *slow* country such as Britain might be able to *avoid it*. At a first glance, this might be read as an expression of support for the incumbent Conservative government, but that is most probably not what Hutton intended. Far from commending British *slowness*, he holds the whole of the EC responsible for having created, through agreeing to EMU, a dilemma that would lead to splits among the member states. He also exposes as a sham the official rhetoric of EC heads of government, i.e. that they do not want a *two-speed* split between individual countries and the rest of the EU. In his view, the Treaty including the opt-outs increases the risk of such a split. The commentary from the German daily *Frankfurter Rundschau* (example 12) agrees with Hutton's criticism of the politicians' hypocrisy in professing to be against a *two-speed Europe* but effectively preparing the way for it. However, this time the referent is not Britain's opt-out from EMU but the one from the social policy chapter of the Treaty. Without mentioning the *two-speed* formula itself, the comment in the weekly *Die Zeit* (example 13) identifies Britain as a country that tries to *slow down European progress*, this time on account of both of the opt-outs.

These examples show that at the beginning of the 1990s the British and German media perspectives on the TWO-SPEED EUROPE concept were quite similar. They are based on a common understanding of the *two-speed* phrase as denoting a DIVISION OF INTEGRATION SPEEDS among EC member states, specifically between Britain and the rest of the EC. There are some nuances of contrast as regards the target topic: the *Guardian* commentator places the main emphasis on the EMU question, whilst the German quotations also mention the social policy opt-out. Responsibility for the perceived split is also apportioned differently: the German papers focus on Britain as the culprit, whereas Hutton, by adding the technical metaphor of a *conveyor-belt* that conjures up the idea of an automatism, apportions blame to the whole of the EC. In all texts, however, the TWO-SPEED SPLIT is seen as a future, if imminent, risk: the leftist *Guardian*, the liberal *Die Zeit* as well as the conservative *Die Welt* show no significant differences in their assessment of the topicality or urgency of the TWO-SPEED scenario. Nine months later, after the withdrawal of the British Pound Sterling and the Italian Lira from the EC Exchange Rate Mechanism (ERM) on 16 September 1992, known as *Black Wednesday*, the *different speeds* of member states' *movements* towards currency union were on the agenda again. If politicians and EU officials had been reluctant to use or endorse that slogan before, *Die Welt* (28 September 1992) now reported that 'nobody spoke of anything else' ("niemand redet über anderes als das Europa der zwei Geschwindigkeiten"). However, at the level of heads of government, open advocacy of the TWO-SPEED concept seems to have been still something of a taboo. *The Guardian* (30 September 1992) quoted the German Chancellor Kohl with a statement insisting that "rumours" of plans for a *two-speed Europe* were as credible as the "countless sightings of the Loch Ness monster", and that his government definitely did "not want a *two-speed* Europe" to come about. This laboured *dementi* illustrates how uncomfortable the TWO-SPEED scenario had by then become for EU governments. Its use by politicians of a country that was perceived as a *fast mover*, such as Germany, was seen as a threat against supposedly *slower* countries; on the other hand, any assertion of their willingness to *catch up* was interpreted as an admission that they had indeed *fallen behind*.

However, a refusal *to go faster* did not look good either, as we saw in the case of Howard's attempt to be on the *non-fast track* of the *two-speed Europe* without having to pay the political price of appearing to be *slow* (cf. above, example 10). Prime Minister Major used a different strategy to neutralize political SPEED comparisons in the EU in a speech during an election campaign for the EU parliament: he multiplied the number of SPEEDS beyond just two:

(14) The Prime Minister [. . .] held out a vision of *a multi-speed Europe in which all member states would proceed at a speed of their own choosing.* [. . .] Mr Major insisted: "I don't happen to think it threatens Europe if member states are free to do some things in their own way and at their own speed." A *multi-speed, multi-track, multi-layered Europe* was a Conservative idea in line with the mood of the people everywhere. (G, 1 June 1994)

This was a brave attempt at reversing the hierarchical bias of the *speed* comparison by suggesting a complex structure in which there were no clearly identifiable *front-runners* and *laggards*; but Major's idea, supposedly 'in line' with everyone's mood, was immediately challenged and rejected. In Britain, the Labour Party's response came in the form of FOOTBALL imagery; their campaign co-ordinator, Cunningham, portrayed Major as being "willing to offer voluntary relegation to the second division in Europe", whilst the Liberal Democrats' leader, Ashdown, warned that the Government was preparing "for Britain *being in the outer lane*" (*The Guardian*, 1 and 3 June 1994).

Nor did Major's proposition find favour with the partner governments in France and Germany. Their respective visions for the EU's future structure were explained in two near-simultaneous statements by the French Prime Minister, Edouard Balladur, and by the German Christian Democrat parties, CDU and CSU, advocating a temporary division of the Community into several *tiers* or *circles* or a firm *core* and a *periphery*, respectively. The German proposals included an explicit reference to the MULTI-SPEED metaphor. Significantly, this was now seen as a feasible and viable policy concept, no longer just a 'lesser evil':

(15) [. . .] *die Methode 'variable Geometrie' oder 'mehrere Geschwindigkeiten'* [sollte] trotz erheblicher rechtlicher und praktischer Schwierigkeiten soweit wie möglich durch den Unionsvertrag [. . .] sanktioniert und institutionalisiert werden [. . .]. (CDU/CSU-Fraktion des Deutschen Bundestages 1994) [*the method of 'variable geometry' or 'several speeds' should be sanctioned and enshrined* as fully as possible in the new EU Treaty, despite considerable legal and practical difficulties]

Ironically – in the light of later developments – the first British media reaction to the French and German statements interpreted them as "giving their open blessing to the concept of a multi-speed Community", as presented by Major a few months earlier (FT, 1 September 1994). This may have been the reading that French and German politicians had hoped for, but it was not how the supposed addressee of the "blessing" saw it. Within a week, John Major took the opportunity of a speech at Leiden in the Netherlands to object vehemently to the equation of MULTI-SPEED and CORE/CIRCLES concepts. In his view, the metaphors "of a 'hard core', inner and outer circles, a two-tier Europe" constituted "a real danger"; however, he still held on to the idea that it was "perfectly healthy for all member states to agree that some should integrate more closely and more quickly in certain areas" (DT, 8 September 1994).

If Major had hoped that his endorsement of different *speeds* while rejecting different *tiers* might prove more convincing than the French and German proposals for the further development of the EU, he was wrong. In *The Times* (8 September 1994), Michael Butler, former UK ambassador to the EC, warned that "elevating opt-outs and multi-speed, multi-track arrangements into desirable objectives" was liable "to make other member governments say to themselves that they need not bother to accommodate the British". The *Daily Telegraph*'s correspondent, Christopher Lockwood, pointed out that Major's Leiden speech failed to address the partner governments' concerns that EU integration was in danger of "falling apart" (DT, 8 September 1994). German commentators, on the other hand, criticized Major's thinly veiled rejection of the Christian Democrats' ideas as a deliberate misunderstanding and as a 'U-turn' on his own previous endorsement of a *multi-speed* EU; and they now presented the *variable geometry/two-* or *multi-speed* Europe as a well-established political practice in the EU since 1991:

> (16) *Dieses "Europa der zwei Geschwindigkeiten" ist vom Maastricht-Vertrag ausdrücklich sanktioniert*: Nicht alle EU-Staaten werden Ende des Jahrzehnts bereit und fähig sein, der Währungsunion beizutreten. [. . .] Da bietet das *Konzept der "zwei Geschwindigkeiten"* einen Ausweg: *Wer schleichen will, soll das tun, aber ohne die anderen, die voraneilen wollen, aufzuhalten*. (Z, 9 September 1994) [*This "two-speed Europe" is explicitly endorsed by the Maastricht Treaty*. Not all EU states will be ready and willing to join EMU by the end of the decade. In this situation, *the "two-speed" concept is* a way out of the impasse: *those who want to go slowly may do so but without holding back those who want to make swift progress*.]

> (17) Major hat den CDU/CSU-Fraktionstext [. . .] entweder nicht verstanden oder plump verfälscht. [. . .] *'Variable Geometrie' und 'mehrere Geschwindigkeiten' sind längst vielfältig geübte Praxis*. (Z, 16 September 1994) [Major has either misunderstood or crudely misrepresented the CDU/CSU paper: *'variable geometry' and 'multiple speed' have been widely practised for a long time*.]

In these examples, the TWO-SPEED aspect of the general JOURNEY scenario is explicitly contested by parts of the British and German public as a 'warrant', in Toulmin's terms, to suggest particular political solutions for the question of the European Union's political future. Whilst Major had tried to keep the JOURNEY scenario free from the hierarchical bias of a bipolar SLOW–FAST comparison between his own country and the rest of the EU, the majority of commentators maintained and reinforced precisely this SPEED comparison as the crucial issue for EU integration and for Britain's relationship to the other member states. Major's lack of success in avoiding and neutralizing the bias of the JOURNEY scenario marked a watershed in the international Euro-political debate: instead of reinstating Britain as a *leading* force in EU policy, Major's initiative confirmed its status as a *slow mover*.

After the 1994 climax of British–German exchanges over the TWO-SPEED concept, the political 'frontiers' of its interpretation were effectively settled. Whilst in Germany the concept was essentially seen as a descriptive, though terminologically sensitive, label for the continuing exclusion of Britain from EMU, the British EU debate was characterized by uses of the formula as a 'stigma-word', e.g. to voice misgivings that a *two-speed Europe "could leave Britain permanently in the slow lane"* (I, 20 February 1996), or *"could leave Britain sidelined in areas central to its national interest"* (DT, 18 April 1997).

This is essentially the same division of meanings that we found in the press reactions to Fischer's statement of May 2000 – British warnings of a potential split in the EU vs German acknowledgement of an existing state of affairs. These opposing evaluations were by no means predetermined: as we saw in the examples from 1991, both German and British media at first denounced a *two-speed Europe* policy as a future threat to the Community's/Union's coherence. It was in the years following the Maastricht Treaty that public attitudes and discourses in Germany and in Britain underwent changes, crystallizing in the 1992–94 disputes over the *two-/multi-speed* formula. The significant difference between British and German attitudes towards EU integration at the end of the decade lies not in the contrast of negative vs positive attitudes to the notion of a TWO-SPEED EUROPE but in its evaluation as an established political fact on the one hand and as a future, if urgent, threat on the other.

3.2.2 Arguments based on VEHICLE-specific JOURNEY scenarios

In the following section, we shall look at the scenarios listed under 3.ii.b–f above, which specify particular VEHICLES for the JOURNEY scenario of EU-politics in the 1990s. The pattern of a common British–German perception of Britain as the SLOW(EST) TRAVELLER on the EU JOURNEY and of Germany and France as FAST TRAVELLERS, plus the specifically British view of the EU AS A WHOLE TRAVELLING (TOO) FAST repeats itself to a large extent across these scenarios. In addition, the more specific scenarios allow users to highlight particular conceptual aspects that lead to further argumentative inferences, such as the contrast between a ONE-VEHICLE JOURNEY (with all EU states *travelling at the same speed* and in *the same direction*) and a MULTI-VEHICLE JOURNEY, which leaves *space* for greater national initiative. Tables 10–14 highlight the main conceptual aspects specified in these scenarios (as the examples in this section are not referred to further in the text, they are provided in the endnotes).

Analogical Argument in Political Discourse 55

Table 10 TRAIN JOURNEY scenario aspects

Scenario elements (roles, relations, story-lines)	EU member states or institutions that fill role slots in scenarios	Tokens in English sample	Tokens in German sample	Tokens in both samples
X IS OFF TRAIN/OFF TRACK/OBSTACLE IN PATH OF TRAIN, RELUCTANT PASSENGER, for examples cf. note[18]	X = GB	13	8	21
	X = TURKEY		3	3
	X = GERMANY	1	1	2
	X = ITALY		1	1
	X = DENMARK	1		1
X IS ON TRAIN /ON TRACK, LOCOMOTIVE, DRIVING THE TRAIN, SETTING THE POINTS, for examples cf. note[19]	X = GERMANY	2	3	5
	X = EU	1	4	5
	X = FRANCE	2	1	3
	X = ITALY	1	2	3
	X = FINLAND		2	2
	X = EMU		2	2
	X = SPAIN		1	1
	X = TURKEY		1	1
	X = PORTUGAL	1		1
	X = CORE EU (Germany, France, Benelux, Italy ...)	1	1	2
THE EUROPEAN TRAIN MAKES GOOD PROGRESS, for examples cf. note[20]		3	12	15
THE EUROPEAN TRAIN'S PROGRESS IS IN QUESTION, for example cf. note[21]		3	8	11
THE EUROPEAN TRAIN'S PROGRESS IS NOT SECURE/WILL END IN DISASTER, for examples cf. note[22]		12	3	15
Totals		41	53	94

Table 11 MARITIME JOURNEY scenario aspects

Scenario elements (roles, relations, story-lines)	EU member states or EU institutions that fill role slots in scenarios	Tokens in English sample	Tokens in German sample	Tokens in both samples
X IS OFF SHIP, OBSTACLE IN PATH OF SHIP, RELUCTANT PASSENGER, OFF CONVOY, SLOW(EST) SHIP IN CONVOY, examples cf. note[23]	X = GB	16	5	21
	X = GERMANY	2	2	4
	X = DENMARK	2		2

Table 11 Continued

Scenario elements (roles, relations, story-lines)	EU member states or EU institutions that fill role slots in scenarios	Tokens in English sample	Tokens in German sample	Tokens in both samples
X IS ON SHIP, FAST(EST) SHIP IN CONVOY, example cf. note[24]	X = GERMANY X = FRANCE X = CORE EU	2 2 1	2 2 1	4 4 2
THE EUROPEAN SHIP/CONVOY MAKES/WILL MAKE GOOD PROGRESS, example cf. note[25]		2	8	10
THE EUROPEAN SHIP/CONVOY'S PROGRESS IS SLOW/IN QUESTION, example cf. note[26]		3	3	6
THE EUROPEAN SHIP/CONVOY'S PROGRESS WILL END IN DISASTER, examples cf. note[27]		2	1	3
Totals		32	24	56

Table 12 CAR TRAVEL scenario aspects

Scenario elements (roles, relations, story-lines)	EU member states or institutions that fill role slots in scenarios	Tokens in English sample	Tokens in German sample	Tokens in both samples
X IS OFF CAR/BUS, RELUCTANT PASSENGER, SLOW CAR/MOTOR, examples cf. note[28]	X = GERMANY X = FRANCE X = EU X = GB X = EMU	4 2 1 2 1	7 2 4	11 4 5 2 1
X IS ON CAR/BUS, (TOO) FAST CAR/MOTOR, (TOO) GOOD OVERHAUL OF CAR/ ENGINE, examples cf. note[29]	X = GERMANY X = FRANCE X = EU X = EMU X = EU COMMISSION X = GB X = SWEDEN X = CDU	4 3 9 3 1 3 1	9 9 1 2 2 1	13 12 10 5 3 3 1 1

Table 12 Continued

Scenario elements (roles, relations, story-lines)	EU member states or institutions that fill role slots in scenarios	Tokens in English sample	Tokens in German sample	Tokens in both samples
THE EUROPEAN CAR JOURNEY'S PROGRESS WILL END IN AN ACCIDENT/DISASTER, example cf. note[30]		1	2	3
Totals		35	39	74

Table 13 AIR/SPACE JOURNEY scenario aspects

Scenario elements (roles, relations, story-lines)	EU member states or institutions that fill role slots in scenarios	Tokens in English sample	Tokens in German sample	Tokens in both samples
X IS OFF AEROPLANE, AEROPLANE/AIR TRAVELLER OFF COURSE, example cf. note[31]	X = GERMANY X = GB X = FRANCE X = EU	2	4 1 1	4 2 1 1
X IS AEROPLANE ON COURSE, example cf. note[32]	X = EXCHANGE RATE MECHANISM X = GERMANY	1 4		1 4
THE EUROPEAN PROGRESS MAY END IN AIR CRASH/ DISASTER, example cf. note[33]		1		1
Totals		8	6	14

58 *Metaphor and Political Discourse*

Table 14 BICYCLE scenario aspects

Scenario elements (roles, relations, story-lines)	EU member states or EU institutions that fill role slots in scenarios	Tokens in English sample	Tokens in German sample	Tokens in both samples
X, Y ARE PARTNERS ON TANDEM, example cf. note[34]	X = GERMANY, Y = FRANCE		8	8
	X = EU COMMISSION, Y = EU COUNCIL		1	1
X IS (SUCCESSFUL) CYCLIST, cf. note[35]	X = FRANCE		1	1
X IS (SLOW) BICYCLE, cf. note[36]	X = GB	2		2
EUROPEAN PROGRESS IS BICYCLE: MOVE (FORWARD) OR FALL, cf. note[37]		3	1	4
Totals		5	11	16

The five VEHICLE-related JOURNEY scenarios obviously differ in their overall frequency in the corpus, but with regard to the argumentative bias they exhibit clear parallels. As in the general JOURNEY scenario, their conceptual elements are typically used to express either SPEED comparisons between individual EU member states and between a state and the EU as a whole, or comparisons as regards EU member states' PARTICIPATION in and COMMITMENT to the EU's JOURNEY, or assessments of the SPEED/SUCCESS of the EU's JOURNEY. Again, Britain has the stereotypical role of the EU state that *has missed* or *is missing the eurotrain/ship/bus*, or is an *obstacle in its path*, or tries to *slow own the journey*. The seeming exceptions are the CAR TRAVEL and AEROPLANE JOURNEY scenarios, in which Germany appears more often than Britain as the *slowly moving participant* (cf. Tables 12, 13). However, on closer inspection the higher figures for Germany reveal themselves to be due to some particularly self-critical assessments of the German media during the years 1996–99 when Germany's ability to meet the "convergence criteria" for the currency union was questioned. This assessment seems to be typical of a specific internal German debate rather than a contradiction of the stereotype of Germany as a *fast mover* within the EU. The persistent expectations of strong Franco-German *driving initiative* or *power* are evident from the equally high figures for these scenarios in the German sample.

By contrast, British newspapers across the political divide see their own country almost always as the EU *laggard*. It fits this stereotype that British media and politicians often perceive the EU as a whole as *travelling (too) fast* and possibly *racing towards a disaster* (e.g. *derailment, shipwreck, aeroplane crash*), whereas warnings of a DISASTROUS OUTCOME OF THE EU JOURNEY occur only rarely in German public discourse. This shows a parallel to metaphor mappings from the LOVE-MARRIAGE-FAMILY domain analysed in the preceding chapter, where dramatic DIVORCE/ SEPARATION scenarios were more typical of British than of German debates. In line with the general stereotype, British media see Germany and France, which are assumed to be interested in maximum economic and political integration, as *fast movers/drivers*. The stereotype of the powerful joint Franco-German *locomotive-flagship-motor-tandem* is an equivalent of the EU's *couple*. In a few cases, the two scenarios are combined, as in the half-sceptical/half-optimistic prediction by *The Economist* (9 May 1998), that the Franco-German *"engine"* was *"sputtering"* but would *"for the moment, go on driving the Union"*, as the EU's *movement* still depended "on the *couple* getting along".

The JOURNEY metaphors used in British and German debates about EU politics thus show scenario patterns that correspond to contrasting attitudes towards the EU in the two discourse communities. Sceptical or hesitant attitudes towards EU integration play a much more important role among the British public than they do for German media and politicians. Britain is predominantly regarded as the SLOW(EST) MOVER, irrespective of whether newspapers or politicians approve of this or see it as a negative stigma. To appreciate the strength of this stereotype, we have to take into account that similar stigmatizations of other EU states are few and far between. On the other hand, Germany, and to a lesser degree France, are stereotyped as the EU's FAST MOVERS, and among the incidental references to other EU member states in that role, Britain is hardly ever mentioned.

3.3 Metaphorical conclusions in public debates about Europe: *paths without alternative*?

Viewed from the cognitive perspective, these findings confirm and extend the fundamental hypothesis that sociopolitical concepts and attitudes are largely metaphorical in nature. The central domain mapping A POLITICAL PROCESS IS A JOURNEY and its corollaries (3.i.a–f) inform assessments of individual nations' 'typical' performances as *travellers*. Specific political attitudes and conclusions are argued by way of analogy at the level of scenarios of MODES OF TRAVEL (3.ii.a–f). Folk-theories and common-sense assumptions regarding PUNCTUALITY IN JOINING A JOURNEY, CO-ORDINATED MOVEMENT AND SPEED, DELAYING EFFECTS of OBSTACLES ON THE PATH and DISASTER JOURNEYS serve as references to conceptualize and assess national and EU policies. The 'evidence' from common-sense expectations and everyday experience about TRAIN/SHIP/CAR/AIR/BICYCLE TRAVEL and, generally, SPEED comparisons, which is embodied in the source scenarios, is utilized to back up complex assessments of the relative economic and political positions of whole nation states and groups of states as well as the probability of future developments in the EU.

These arguments based on analogy are, logically speaking, circular. The respective metaphor scenarios suggest specific conclusions as self-evident or common-sensical in terms of the source domain (e.g. 'it is better to join the train/boat/bus/aeroplane etc. in time than to miss it'); these conclusions are (pre-)supposed to hold also for the target domain concept. Most texts in the corpus of course also cite some supposedly more 'objective' facts (e.g. statistical figures, quotes from 'authorities' on the subject etc.) to provide corroborating evidence. However, in terms of argument structure such data are not in themselves conclusive: they, too, rely on warrants that refer the argumentative step from the data to the conclusion "to the larger class of steps whose legitimacy is being presupposed" (Toulmin). In metaphorical arguments, where the warrant is analogical, the legitimacy of these data *as* evidence for the conclusion is still largely dependent upon the analogy with the source scenario and its presuppositions.

It remains intriguing that even politicians and media whose opinions can be assumed to be strongly opposed to the political bias or slant associated with specific metaphor scenarios (such as the hierarchical bias of SPEED comparisons) seem compelled to make use of these very scenarios. The British Euro-sceptical press and politicians were the first to employ the *two-/multi-speed Europe* formula and the associated scenarios of MISSING THE EU TRAIN/BOAT/SHIP/CONVOY, despite the presupposed perspective on Britain as a *laggard* in the EU. Of course, all speakers still have the option of trying to turn around the bias of a scenario, i.e. of reinterpreting it in their own favour. Nevertheless, even the overt contradiction or rebuttal of a 'biased' scenario still highlights it and promotes its use in the public debate. Even if politicians and media are aware of the hierarchical implications of the metaphor and try to avoid sensitive formulations such as the *two-* or *multi-speed* phrase, SPEED COMPARISON scenarios continue to be used as models for comments on perceived national contrasts in commitment to EU integration.

This does not mean that the public is at the mercy of its (or its media and politicians') metaphors. Metaphorical presuppositions – like any kind of presupposition in an argumentation – can be made explicit and criticized, and they can be 'turned around' and reinterpreted as regards their political bias. However, judging by the corpus data, the stereotyping power of their scenarios seems to make these biased presuppositions highly attractive for repetitive usage. At first, particular metaphorical formulations, such as the slogans of the *two-speed Europe*, of *missing the train/boat* or of the *convoy in which the slowest ship must not be allowed to dictate the speed*, are derived from the ubiquitous background imagery that depicts political processes as instances of SPATIAL MOVEMENT. If used prominently (e.g. in high-profile political speeches, election campaigns, party-political and international disputes) and repeatedly, such phrases become fixed in their references as well as in their connotative meanings, including the political bias. It is this bias that makes them sufficiently contentious to be discussed and contested by more and more political rivals and commentators, even up to the highest official level of endorsements and rejections by heads of government. Prominent scenarios finally gain a notoriety that 'forces' all the participants in the respective debate to define their attitudes towards them, perhaps even to 'suit the action to the words'.

This specific function of metaphors in political discourse, i.e. their 'power' to frame arguments into stereotypical scenarios that suggest particular conclusions, can best be analysed by way of the distributional analysis of sufficiently large amounts of corpus data, which reveal the usage patterns and relative dominance of specific scenarios. Rather than relying on anecdotal and impressionistic evidence, the corpus-based analysis relates hypotheses about the status of conceptual structures in a given discourse community to documented data that are empirically testable in terms of frequency, representativeness and consistency.

In terms of this methodological perspective, the data from the EUROMETA I pilot corpus must be regarded as limited. Even though the overall number of metaphor tokens in parts of the pilot corpus such as the WAY-MOVEMENT-SPEED domain is sufficiently large for the formulation of hypotheses about the relative weight of conceptual source elements and scenarios, the pilot corpus does not provide a reliable basis for statistical assessments. The differences in the distribution of tokens for particular scenario versions between the British and German samples can only be seen as *indicative* of 'typical' national attitudes and argumentative trends. In order to increase their validity in terms of representativeness, it is necessary to consult evidence from general corpora, which

– unlike the special corpus EUROMETA I – have been assembled independently. This demand also necessitates a further clarification of the theoretical status of our analytical categories, i.e. domains, scenarios and scenario-elements (e.g. 'role'-slots and 'plots' or 'story-lines'). So far, these categories have been derived from the data on the assumption that it makes good interpretative sense to describe the texts in question as metaphors, analogies, arguments etc. However, when looking for metaphors in a general corpus this assumption is evidently invalid. In the first place, the corpus data, i.e. linguistic items, have to be semantically identified as being metaphorical; secondly, these semantic units need to be related to conceptual categories in a systematic way. As Low (1999) and Cameron (1999) have pointed out, abstractions from metaphoric discourse data to conceptual structures need to be justified and operationalized. In the following two chapters, we shall discuss ways of characterizing the conceptual categories in terms of semantic criteria in order to gain a linguistic basis for investigating metaphor scenarios and their distribution patterns in general corpora.

4
Corpora and the Semantics of Metaphor

4.1 Metaphors in general corpora

(1) Europe's much delayed *recovery* is already faltering under the time-lagged effects of *the Asian virus* [...]. (G, 15 January 1999)

(2) After a long period of cautious equivocation, the prime minister had [...] "shifted up a gear" in his ambition to lodge Britain at its rightful place *in the heart of Europe*. And then, abruptly, *the heart of Europe got sick*. (E, 20 March 1999)

(3) Twenty-five years ago, Britain was branded *the sick man of Europe*. Germany was the model economy we should copy. Today, the influential Economist magazine says *Germany is the sick man of the euro*. (*The SUN*, 5 June 1999)

(4) [...] by the mid 1980s *Eurosclerosis* – chronically slow growth – was the *chief headache* for continental governments. (G, 24 May 1999)

The database from which the above-quoted examples are drawn is the COBUILD "Bank of English" (BoE), which was built up at the University of Birmingham and comprises over 450 million word forms, covering texts from print media, books, radio and spoken language since the beginning of the 1990s.[1] For German, an even larger corpus called COSMAS exists at the German Language Institute in Mannheim, Germany, which contains 156 specialized partial corpora with texts amounting to more than 1,500 million words drawn from print and electronic media, literature and spoken language.[2] Both the BoE and COSMAS are "general" corpora, i.e. unlike special corpora, which assemble linguistic data of a particular, predefined type, they are designed to give the best approximation to a representative overview over language systems in use (Sinclair 1991: 13–15; Hunston 2002: 14–15). Their representativity makes them an attractive basis for empirical discourse studies, in particular for contrastive analyses (Altenberg and Granger 2002b; Teubert 2002). But as regards the study of metaphor uses, the sheer volume of data available creates something of an *embarras de richesse*: how to find the needle of a metaphor in such haystacks of data? A corpus in itself does not provide any direct cues for metaphoricity. It only contains expressions; their meanings have to be interpreted by the linguist. So how can metaphors be retrieved from general corpora?

One type of approach is to look for identifiable expression units that are likely to contain metaphors, e.g. idiomatic phraseologisms. These are known from the lexicon and can thus be searched and listed in a way similar to searching for any other lexical item or collocations of these, thus yielding material for the cognitive study of the conceptual structure and usage frequency of metaphor idioms.[3] However, of the above-quoted examples only passage (3) contains a short phraseologism (*the sick man of Europe*), which might be recognizable to avid followers of Europe-related debates and to historians who know its long tradition, but without such a specialized knowledge, the phraseologism would be just comprehensible as an instantiation of the general A NATION IS A PERSON mapping rather than fitting into a whole system of ILLNESS-related metaphors (for further discussion cf. below chapter 5). In general, statements containing lexical items such as *recovery, virus, sick* or *headache* do not provide clues as to the metaphorical sense they are used in, unless they are signalled in the co-text as requiring special interpretative effort, e.g. by rhetorical "hedges" or "tuning devices" such as *so to speak, as it were, figuratively speaking* (Cameron and Deignan 2003). Using their general, non-expert background knowledge about medical topics, readers may notice that the term *Eurosclerosis* (example 4) is likely to have a special meaning, as it does not denote a well-known form of the medical condition 'sclerosis'. Even so, the term cannot be interpreted as prima facie evidence of a metaphorical meaning. *Eurosclerosis* could – conceivably – refer to some rare illness only found in Europe or to a statistical summary concerning sclerosis in European countries (as, for instance, in *Euro cancer list*, another item from the BoE corpus: "Euro cancer list shows failings", G, 17 May 1995). How can we instruct a meaning-blind database to 'find' expressions that contain metaphors pertaining to European politics and 'overlook' outwardly similar expressions without metaphorical meaning or with a thematically irrelevant metaphorical meaning?

Modern information technology helps to find a solution by providing highly sophisticated searching programmes for large amounts of data. The BoE and COSMAS can be searched with "concordancing" programmes not only for single word-forms and regular collocations, but for specific word-forms occurring at a distance from each other. The programmes also allow the retrieval of "key word-in-context" overviews of all tokens found in the search as well as of the texts or parts of the texts that they have been drawn from, plus an identification of the sources. With these technical instruments at hand, the project of building a metaphor corpus can be divided into two sets of tasks: (a) to develop programmes that enable a computer to provide plausible interpretations for metaphorical passages and (b) to identify text genres that contain material relevant for the corpus construction.

As regards the first task, impressive advances have been made in Artificial Intelligence and computational linguistics research to develop recognition and comprehension systems for figurative language, e.g. the "ATT-Meta"-project at the University of Birmingham (Barnden and Lee 2001a, b),[4] as well as the "analogy"-based knowledge and memory systems mentioned in the last chapter. In this research, the emphasis is on developing intelligent programmes that can approximate the metaphor interpreter's work.[5] It is facilitated by the creation of electronic thesauri such as "WordNet", which incorporate lexicographic and taxonomic knowledge systems. These can be taken as the basis for searching programmes like "CorMet" (Mason 2002) that detect preference patterns of domain-characteristic keywords and predicates, which are then compared to the taxonomies of the thesaurus.[6] Thus, instead of building on preconceived assumptions of a 'semantic anomaly' that predetermine what 'counts' as metaphor or not, keywords are established on a frequency basis that serves as the input for the search of Internet documents. CorMet then "examines pairs of salient concepts from the source and target domain and searches for polarized mappings between them" (Mason 2002). CorMet's results partly corroborate the "Master Metaphor List" compiled by Lakoff et al. (1989, 1991 and Lakoff 1994) and reveal the relative frequency of certain mappings (Mason 2002). However, some mappings that are predicted to be ubiquitous on the basis of the Master Metaphor List and that are generally well attested by cognitive research were not confirmed. CorMet "found the theory and architecture domain pair almost perfectly devoid of metaphoric mappings", a result which Mason interprets as "an artefact of the low quality corpora obtained for these domains", i.e. administrative documents (2002: 24).

This difficulty demonstrates that the choice and definition of the range of corpus material is decisive for the quality of search results. Random Internet searches such as Mason's do not take account of text genres and registers, which, as Deignan (1999: 196–7) points out, have an important bearing on the frequency and conceptual range of metaphor usage. From a purely 'systemic' point of view, such sociolinguistic and pragmatic variation may be a 'surface' phenomenon that is only of secondary significance, but in empirically orientated research it is one of the basic corpus parameters that must be accounted for (Sinclair 1991: 15–20; Hunston 2002: 28–30).

Furthermore, the random search for decontextualised expressions in very large databases may lead to the non-recognition and omission of important metaphor data in the search, as has been argued by Cameron and Deignan, when they warn that "if the researcher has not comprehensively pre-identified all forms "worthy of study", some "may not emerge from the data during the analysis, and an important metaphorical use may be missed" (Cameron and Deignan 2003: 151).

But how can one identify all relevant forms before a general corpus has been searched? It is here that relatively small, special corpora can play an essential heuristic role. Even though they are not fully representative, they provide a good practical basis for establishing discourse areas that are likely to yield interesting results. Cameron and Deignan (2003), for instance, compared a small classroom communication corpus with BoE data to investigate the use of hedges/tuning devices to introduce metaphors. Likewise, EUROMETA I can be viewed as a pilot corpus for investigating metaphors in public discourse in Britain and Germany, if one accepts the assumption that the 12 super-domains presented in chapter 1 (Table 1) provide a heuristic overview of the conceptual source areas employed in Euro-political debates.

When, in 2002, the opportunity arose to search the BoE and COSMAS to build a second metaphor corpus that was comparable in theme and period range to EUROMETA I but was based on a more representative set of data, several selection steps were taken so as to avoid the collection of data irrelevant for the purpose of the analysis. In a first step, all US-American, Australian, Austrian and Swiss press texts, which are also contained in BoE and COSMAS, were completely discarded, together with data from non-print-media sources. This left texts from the following newspapers and magazines: *The Times*, *The Guardian*, *The Independent*, *The Economist* and *The SUN* in the British sample, and *Mannheimer*

Morgen, Frankfurter Allgemeine Zeitung, tageszeitung, Frankfurter Rundschau, Berliner Zeitung in the German sample. Even after this 'assimilation' of the types of texts in both samples, exact comparability could not be achieved, because apart from the 1:3 difference in the overall volume of the corpora, the range of media sources and the selection of documented texts differ across the years. The BoE records one tabloid (*The SUN*) but no regional newspapers, whereas COSMAS has a high number of texts from one regional paper (*Mannheimer Morgen*), but no tabloids. Some sources have been documented with different intensity for specific years, e.g. the *Frankfurter Allgemeine Zeitung* in COSMAS only for 1993 and 1995 (there are also gaps for some newspapers in the BoE for 1996–97). Apparently the selection procedures underlying the corpora have been different in the two research institutions, on account of their particular objectives, histories, technological standards, manpower etc. Nevertheless, due to their extended range of sources, which cover most of the mainstream political spectrum, and to the high number of texts documented, the BoE and COSMAS must be regarded as the best publicly available approximations to representative collections of English and German language data in this register.

Thanks to the existence of the pilot corpus, the relevant linguistic forms to be searched could also be identified more comprehensively than would have been possible on the basis of a thesaurus or random Internet searches. So an inventory of all lexical source items known from EUROMETA I was compiled and then augmented by as many further members of their respective semantic fields as possible. In the actual searches the items from this augmented list were combined with the word-forms *Euro/euro, Europe* (plus their inflected forms) for the BoE, and *Euro* and *Europa* (also plus their inflected forms, which are automatically available in COSMAS) for the German corpus. It soon became evident that these word-form combinations when searched by way of standard concordancing generated large numbers of relevant examples. No use was therefore made of automatic metaphor detection programmes such as the ones mentioned above. This limits the statistical significance of the findings. However, given the above-mentioned discrepancies between the two source corpora, the creation of a 'balanced' new corpus,[7] which could justify full statistical validation, would have led to a massive reduction of the database, because only small parts of BoE and COSMAS are directly comparable. The reliance on concordances meant that only 80–90 per cent of the examples generated were relevant in the sense that they contained metaphors with Euro-political target reference. The remaining irrelevant examples had to be sifted out 'by hand'.

The search was specified to find text passages that contained source and target (*euro-*)elements as single lexical items or as parts of compounds at distances of between zero and five 'intervening' word-forms. The reason for this 'five-words-maximum-distance' rule was a practical one: after several trial-runs, it seemed to yield the best results as a search procedure. Beyond a distance of five words, the probability of finding relevant uses decreased rapidly in proportion to the distance between the combination elements, especially when the sentence limit was transcended. As regards the "co-text" of the source articles, it would have been ideal to incorporate the complete texts in order to ensure a similarly comprehensive documentation as in the pilot corpus. However, given the high number of texts to be compiled and exported into the new special corpus this seemed neither feasible nor necessary, considering that the analysis did not aim at an exhaustive interpretation of the individual texts but was focused on distributional comparisons of metaphor scenarios and their elements. On the other hand, reliance on mere concordance lines would have been insufficient, because strings of 10–20 words often do not give enough information to determine whether an expression is used metaphorically and what the precise topic of the passage is. The general corpora were therefore searched twice:

(a) The overview of the 'key-word-in-context' concordances, which was a result of the initial search, provided the basis for the selection of potentially relevant examples, i.e. concordance lines that seemed to contain metaphorical expressions, which pertained to the topic of EU politics/economy.

(b) The retrieval of 100–500 word passages of the source texts for the selected lines was the basis for eliminating non-metaphor cases and metaphors and figurative idioms that co-occurred with *Europe*-terms but did not concern EU-politics (e.g. phrases such as "those sick-soul-of-Europe art movies", I, 13 May 1999).

The result of these searches was a new special corpus, called EUROMETA II, which consists of English and German text passages in BoE and COSMAS that contain all Euro-politically relevant tokens of metaphors covering the various domains known from the pilot corpus. All in all, EUROMETA II comprises more than 19,000 entries, amounting to about one million words.[8] In this and the following chapter we shall use only the data for two domains to investigate further the argumentative exploitation of metaphors in British and German public discourse, i.e.

the domains of LIFE-BODY-HEALTH and ARCHITECTURE-BUILDING-HOUSE. The main advantage of the EUROMETA II corpus over the pilot corpus and other collections of press texts is that, thanks to its enhanced representativity and the much higher numbers of examples, it permits reliable distributional analyses of not just source domain elements but also of whole metaphor scenarios. This in turn allows comparisons of *relative* frequencies of scenarios within each national sample, which helps to overcome to a degree the shortcomings resulting from the lack of full statistical harmonization and validation of the samples. Even though it is impossible to compare absolute frequencies between data from corpora as distinct as BoE and COSMAS, it should at least be possible to assess the status of specific scenarios in each sample, and to formulate testable hypotheses concerning how representative they are of national discourses.

4.2 Corpus-based analysis of metaphorical meaning

Before we can analyse the results of our corpus searches in detail, it is necessary to go back to the principal methodological question posed at the end of the last chapter: what are the criteria for interpreting *linguistic* metaphor data as evidence of underlying *conceptual* metaphors? Without a 'working hypothesis' to answer this question, the theoretical and methodological status of the text passages in EUROMETA II remains unclear. The process of selecting and grouping the BoE and COSMAS data into domains and scenarios requires a linguistic reformulation of the cognitive hypotheses and criteria implicit in the searches. Otherwise, any inference from the data to their cognitive significance would be circular.

As a first approach, one might attempt to simply rephrase the conceptual distinction of source and target domains in terms of lexical meaning. For instance, we could assign a feature "+ medical" to the meaning of terms such as *recovery*, *virus*, *sick* and *sclerosis* in examples (1) to (4), which contrasts with the meanings of their respective referents, i.e. political or economic entities of the EU. This semantic contrast or opposition could be assumed to indicate the existence of a metaphor. Such a simplistic account would, however, be open to the criticism that Max Black levelled as early as 1954 at what he dubbed the "substitution" and "comparison" theories of metaphor (Black 1954, 1962, 1993). These views of metaphor as a mere lexical replacement or shortened simile are, Black argued, psychologically implausible and semantically invalid. They presuppose an equation of meaning and reference which is particularly absurd in the case of metaphor, as the whole point of using a metaphor is to provide a sense that differs from that of a literal paraphrase whilst keeping the referents identical. Examples (1) to (4) can, for instance, be paraphrased without using any medical expressions, but this would not at all capture the specific meaning of the metaphors in question – it would only refer to the same referents.

In order to capture the specific aspect of metaphorical meaning, Black, building on I.A. Richards' *Philosophy of Rhetoric* (1936), proposed an "interaction" view of metaphor that highlighted the predicative structure of metaphoric statements, as consisting of a literal "frame" (as the "primary subject") and a non-literal "focus" (as the "secondary subject") (Black 1962: 38–44 and Black 1993: 25–8). The traditional view of metaphor as an extravagant, semantically anomalous phenomenon was thus replaced by a syntagmatically orientated concept of metaphor as a dynamic relation of semantic elements in a predication. This approach acknowledged the creative aspect of metaphor use and also tackled the old paradox of 'literally true' negated metaphors. A statement *Nation X is not the sick man of Europe* is literally true (in the trivial sense that nations are not physically sick, as they have no physical bodies) and at the same time it is as valid a metaphor as the assertion *Nation X is the sick man of Europe*. In Black's perspective, the interaction between the concepts of NATION and SICKNESS is present in both the asserted and the negated statements – hence they can also both be interpreted as metaphors. The result of the semantic interaction is a filter-effect that arises from the application of the "system of associated commonplaces" evoked by the metaphorical focus to the primary subject of the statement (Black 1962: 39–43).

By discarding the 'substitution' and 'comparison' views of metaphor and interpreting Richards' interaction concept in *gestalt*-theoretical terms of conceptual *focus-frame* and *filter*-effects, Black foreshadows to some extent the cognitive approach – indeed, he explicitly introduces and discusses the notion of "metaphorical thought" as "a neglected topic of major importance" (Black 1993: 31). However, when it comes to the question of the linguistic "recognition" of metaphors, he is curiously diffident:

(5) Our recognition of a metaphorical statement depends essentially upon two things: Our general knowledge of what it is *to be* a metaphorical statement, and our specific judgment that a metaphorical reading of a given statement is here preferable to a literal one. The decisive reason for the choice of interpretation may be, as it often is, the patent falsity or incoherence of the literal reading – but it

might equally be the banality of that reading's truth, its pointlessness, or its lack of congruence with the surrounding text and nonverbal setting. The situation in cases of doubt as to how a statement is best taken is basically the same as in other cases of ambiguity. And just as there is no infallible test for resolving ambiguity, so there is none to be expected in discriminating the metaphorical from the literal. (Black 1993: 34).

From a critical perspective, Black might be accused of reintroducing here the vague criteria for metaphor interpretation known from substitution and comparison theories, e.g. *patent falsity, banality, lack of congruence* etc. Moreover, his assumption of a "general knowledge of what it is *to be* a metaphorical statement" seems to clash with his subsequent assertion that "there is no infallible test discriminating the metaphorical from the literal". Such caution should, however, be taken seriously. We may well know what a metaphor is in principle without always being able to decide precisely whether a particular linguistic structure constitutes a metaphor 'proper', or a metonymy, a semi-literal allusion etc. Some statements (e.g. the well-worn example *Anchorage is a cold city*) can be true literally and metaphorically at the same time (Kittay 1987: 178–213; Leezenberg 2001: 69–97, 173–86). Sensory-motor perception, metonymic and metaphoric conceptualization have been shown to be so interwoven and mutually interdependent (cf. Lakoff and Johnson 1999 and the contributions in Barcelona 2000 and in Dirven and Pörings 2002) that it is implausible to draw a sharp dividing line between literal meaning in the sense of 'normal' or 'basic' meaning and figurative meaning as 'deviant' or 'secondary'. Even basic or primary perceptions and concepts appear to be integrated into focus-frame-, mapping- and blending-structures, which would traditionally have been considered relevant only for 'figurative' meaning.

Still, the traditional literal/non-literal distinction seemed to gain a further lease of life in the context of pragmatic analyses of metaphor as an intended violation of normally obligatory rules for communication. The most influential models among these have been H. Paul Grice's view of metaphor as a "conversational implicature" inferred from the apparent violation of the "maxim of quality" (Grice 1975, 1989) and John Searle's interpretation of metaphor as an "indirect speech act" (Searle 1993). These theories are based on the assumption that a special inferencing process is triggered by the hearer/reader's discovery of an apparent falsity or absurdity of a statement in a situation when it is implausible to suspect deliberate falsehood or irrational behaviour on the part of the speaker. Assuming that the speaker is being rational and communicatively co-operative, the hearer is thought to seek a further reading by searching for hitherto unnoticed 'resemblances' or 'similarities' between the non-fitting part of a statement and contextually accessible experience or knowledge. According to Searle, the successful use of metaphors presupposes "shared linguistic and factual knowledge" on the parts of speaker and hearer (to work out the literal meaning) as well as "shared strategies on the basis of which the hearer can recognize that the utterance is not intended literally", because it would be "obviously defective" (1993: 108).[9] Although Searle does not demand that the hearer always "goes consciously" through a "set of steps" starting with a literal interpretation, he insists that his assumption of the primacy of literal meaning in the understanding of metaphors is necessary for the "rational construction of the inference patterns that underlie our ability to understand metaphor" (1993: 102). These and similar accounts of metaphor have come under sustained criticism for several reasons:[10]

(a) like traditional semantic accounts, the pragmatic approaches rely on a notion of categorial/semantic anomaly as the basis for metaphor recognition without being able to name a generally applicable, clear-cut test for it;
(b) they do not provide unambiguous criteria for distinguishing different types of conventional violations of conversational maxims or of indirect speech acts (e.g. *irony* vs *metaphor* vs *metonymy* etc.);
(c) there is no psycholinguistic evidence for the assumption that actual metaphor recognition involves an initial anomaly reading;
(d) by basing metaphor interpretation solely on pragmatic aspects, they arbitrarily separate it from the semantic analysis of other statements.[11]

The last-mentioned argument is of special importance for corpus-based metaphor analysis. If an exclusively pragmatic account of metaphor were true, we would have to give up any hope of finding metaphors in a corpus on the basis of linguistic criteria, because the identification of metaphors would then essentially depend on extra-linguistic knowledge (e.g. about speakers' intentions, the situation of use and the wider political context). However, in determining source domains, scenarios and presuppositions in the corpus data we are *not* relying in the first place on (assumed) speakers' intentions and extra-linguistic features but on our semantic competence to recognize linguistic structures as metaphors. We have thus got to look for a semantic account of metaphor that avoids both an overreliance on extra-linguistic information and the pitfalls of the traditional 'semantic anomaly' view, but which instead provides interpretations that are compatible with the cognitive analysis of conceptual metaphor.

In the remainder of this sub-chapter, I shall outline three relatively recent attempts to develop such a semantic account, without claiming to provide a full critique of their theoretical and epistemological implications. Rather, they will be considered with regard to their potential to mediate between the empirical level of linguistic phenomena we find in general language corpora and the level of *conceptual* domains and scenarios, which are amenable to cognitive and sociocultural analysis. The three approaches to be discussed are: (1) Eva Feder Kittay's (1987) application of *semantic field* theory to the study of metaphor; (2) the psycholinguistic studies of a group around Sam Glucksberg, Boaz Keysar and Matthew McGlone (Glucksberg and Keysar 1990, 1993; Glucksberg and McGlone 1999; McGlone 1996, 2001; Glucksberg 2001); and (3) the work on a non-truth-conditional semantics of metaphor by Josef Stern (1985, 2000) and Michiel Leezenberg (2001).

Based on a detailed critique of 'atomistic', word-based semantic theories of metaphor as well as of Davidson's opposition to them, Kittay (1987) has presented a "perspectival theory" of metaphor as an interrelation between *vehicle* and *topic* meanings. It builds on the insights of *structural semantics* into the organization of the lexicon and its underlying 'semantic space' into *fields*, whose elements stand in systematic relations to each other. Such relations can be paradigmatic (for example, synonymy, antonymy, hypo- and hyperonymy, prototype vs marginal category and so on) as well as syntagmatic (collocations of nouns and verbs, nouns and adjectives etc.).[12] The analytical framework to capture these relationships distinguishes three levels: "content domains", "lexical fields" (that is, sets of lexical items as labels) and "semantic fields" which are "content domains that have been articulated by lexical fields" (Kittay 1987: 229). Kittay acknowledges that the concept of *field* has its shortcomings – e.g. the fact that it oversimplifies semantics by focusing on relational structures within a two-dimensional model at the expense of the signification aspect (1987: 249, 256), but she still finds it useful to capture the "conceptual import" of metaphors. In her view, a metaphorical utterance is the "process in which the structure of one semantic field", represented by the *vehicle* term(s), "induces a structure on another content domain", namely that of the *topic* (1987: 258).[13] Field theory thus allows us to analyse metaphors in terms of "relational shifts, which can be specified as changes in the semantic relations governing the semantic fields" (1987: 288).

Compared with traditional semantic or pragmatic accounts, Kittay's theory has the advantage of making the relationship between the linguistic and conceptual levels explicit by positing the *semantic field* as the crucial 'mediating' category between lexicon and conceptual content domain. This way the conceptual structure of metaphor can be analysed in terms of the systematic semantic relationships of the topic field as being 'induced' by those of the *vehicle* field. Such an approach is particularly useful for the study of creative cognitive effects of metaphorical statements, e.g. where a highly specified semantic field is imposed on a hitherto less structured or completely new domain.

Stern (2000) acknowledges Kittay's diligence in providing "detailed analyses of a number of complex metaphors" but criticizes her approach for not drawing a clear enough "distinction between speakers' knowledge of language or semantic competence, on the one hand, and their empirical, extra-linguistic beliefs and the kinds of skills that enter into their use of language, on the other" (2000: 242–3). Without such a distinction, the semantic analysis 'proper' is overburdened with extra-linguistic content aspects (2000: 246). As a consequence, Stern chooses a radically different semantic approach that avoids assimilating too much extra-linguistic knowledge into semantic competence (cf. below). Stern's criticism is of interest to us as it highlights a similar problem to that of the relationship between *linguistic* and *conceptual* metaphors. The latter are abstractions of the former and can be illustrated by them, but such an illustration does not *prove* their cognitive relevance and even less their structuring/organizing power at the semantic level. In the pilot corpus searches, we encountered, for instance, the problem of precisely delimiting *domains*: it is relatively easy to construe *in abstracto* well-defined and logically ordered conceptual domains, but on the empirical level of discourse data, we had to leave the boundaries between source domains as ill-defined areas, and resorted to the ad hoc assumption of "super-domains". Kittay sees a similar problem: she concedes that the precise boundaries of semantic fields are hard to define and introduces a distinction of *superfields* and *proper fields* – only the latter provide distinct structures for metaphorical transference, whereas the *superfields* encompass several proper fields and may also intersect and merge with each other (1987: 251, 292). However, this move only relocates the problem of how to delimit the knowledge "articulated" in a lexical field from extra-linguistic world knowledge and belief systems to the level of *superfields*. Unlike "super-domains", *superfields* are supposed to be again linguistic/semantic structures, i.e. empirically testable and manifest – which would entail their precise, operationalized definition. They therefore cannot help to solve the problems of delimitation of semantic fields. As long as semantic and conceptual structures are assumed to be somehow parallel or homologous *fields*, the circular nature of metaphor interpretation cannot be resolved. For this reason, the term "field", with its suggestion of conceptual and lexical parallelism, will not be employed further. Nonetheless, Kittay deserves credit for having highlighted the need to explicate this relationship by explicitly distinguishing *lexical*, *semantic* and *conceptual* structures. The systematic relations of these three analytical levels have to be accounted for if the cognitive account of metaphor is to be linguistically operationalized, so as to be amenable to the analysis of corpus data.

Glucksberg et al. refer to Kittay (as well as to Black and I. A. Richards) as theoretical pioneers of a renewed semantic approach,[14] which they aim to develop further. Glucksberg and Keysar (1990) revive the old distinction of metaphor and simile as distinct types of mapping. However, unlike in the classical tradition of rhetoric, the two mappings are *not* conceived of as the respectively 'abbreviated' or 'extended' versions of one and the same underlying comparison, but as involving two distinct meanings:

(6) When someone says "My job is a jail", the intention is for the hearer to understand that the job in question has all the properties of the attributive category that is called "jail". If instead one said, "my job is like a jail", then one is likening that job to an actual "jail", not to the superordinate "jail". When the metaphorical form is chosen over the simile form, the very choice is communicative. If one chooses the simile, then the hearer presumably recognizes that choice and would therefore infer that the speaker was not attributing all the properties of the class "jail" to "my job", but only some of them. (Glucksberg and Keysar 1993: 413)

Whilst a simile is effectively a comparison between categories at the same categorial level, metaphors are "class inclusion statements" (Glucksberg and Keysar 1993: 415) that subsume the *topic* category (e.g. MY JOB) under the "superordinate" class of properties that is exemplified by the *vehicle* (JAIL). This "class inclusion" view of metaphor accounts for language users' intuitions about clines of metaphoricity, specifically the intuition that a simile is a weakened form of metaphor, with the comparison term "like" acting as a hedge (Ortony 1979; Glucksberg 2001: 26–47). It is also based on psycholinguistic evidence that priming subjects with lexical items from a given source domain does not significantly shorten their reading time for stories containing domain-consistent vehicles, compared with inconsistent vehicles (Glucksberg and McGlone 1999: 1547–8; McGlone 2001: 101–2). Furthermore, it accounts for a new perspective on results from experiments that were originally seen as a corroboration of claims about the automaticity of access to conceptual source domains, i.e. subjects' preference for domain-consistent over domain-inconsistent use of metaphor vehicles in the completion of stories. Glucksberg and McGlone reinterpret these results as evidence for general cognitive processing strategies that depend on the particular context. They conclude that only if "a metaphor vehicle exemplifies a category to which the metaphor can be assigned in an interesting way, people will take that category as the ground of the metaphor", otherwise they will not; and on occasions "that warrant contemplation and analysis, such as the study of poetry or creative writing", analogical retrieval of categories exemplified by the vehicle will typically be "conscious and deliberate, *not* unconscious and automatic" (Glucksberg and McGlone 1999: 1555–6).

Glucksberg views the comprehension of metaphorical statements as a function of semantic constraints on both the topic and the vehicle, which leads him to propose a modified version of Black's "interaction" theory (Glucksberg 2001: 55–9). Thus, Richards/Black's theory of an 'interactive' semantic relation is reinstated as the basis for metaphor identification and interpretation, with the important further specification, however, that the metaphorical vehicle expresses a property attribution that leads to the construction of a superordinate categorial class. This is a more precise characterization compared with Black's hints at "systems of associated commonplaces" evoked by the vehicle. It has the advantage of covering non-commonplace metaphors, and also of being supported by a substantial body of psycholinguistic comprehension experiments. However, it is still an open question on what *semantic* grounds this class inclusion process works, and in particular, how a linguistic account of this process deals with the extra-linguistic factors that are part of the context.

Building on David Kaplan's *Logic of Demonstratives* (Kaplan 1978, 1979), Josef Stern and Michiel Leezenberg propose answers to this question by treating metaphor as a matter of the *semantic form* of a statement, i.e. its *character*, rather than of its propositional *content*. Like the semantic description of indexical expressions (which has to take account of their dependency on variable situational contexts without predicting any specific contents of these context 'slots'), a semantic account of metaphors need not be burdened with having to determine "for each utterance of a metaphor which feature or resemblance it expresses on that occasion" (Stern 2000: 68). Instead, a theory of metaphor understanding should address "only the interpreter's *knowledge of meaning specific to metaphorical interpretation*" (Stern 2000: 68, italics in the original). Following the model of Kaplan's proposal of an indexical operator "Dthat", Stern introduces an operator "Mthat" (2000: 107, 115), which represents the language users' knowledge that statements have a metaphorical meaning *whenever* certain conditions apply, namely when the accessible context-knowledge contains sets of presuppositions that call for a non-default interpretation (2000: 113–14).

When applied to Romeo's utterance, *Juliet is the sun*, for instance, it stipulates that certain properties are "m[etaphor]-associated" with the expression *is the sun*, e.g. being 'something around which his life revolves', 'something that nourishes him' and 'something that he worships'. These properties are, as presuppositions, preserved under negation as well as under modal modification, e.g. in statements such as *Juliet is not the sun, Juliet might be the sun* (2000: 114). The semantic *content*-aspect of any statement about *Juliet's being the sun* depends on the truth-value of the contextual presuppositions, which involves extra-linguistic information; but this individual content can be excluded from the account of metaphor as a *character*-aspect. Stern's account is concerned with the 'conditions of the possibility' to assign a truth-value to metaphorical utterances, not the actual fulfilment of these conditions.

In his account, Stern relies on Stalnaker's (1974) pragmatic characterization of presuppositions as fulfilling the "primary function" to "constrain and enable what the utterance can appropriately assert" (2000: 126). On this basis, he introduces two distinctions: The first one differentiates between *A- (Assertion)* and *I- (Interpretation)* sets of presuppositions, which are needed to avoid redundancy and inconsistency in the evaluation and generation of metaphorical utterances (2000: 127–9). The second distinction connects with the interaction theory of metaphor by assigning sets of presuppositions to the context/frame and to the focus/vehicle respectively: a *productive (p-) presupposition set* is associated with the metaphorical expression, and a *filter (f-) presupposition set* is associated with its linguistic and non-linguistic environment (2000: 139). This complex model of presupposition sets activated in metaphors enables Stern to differentiate the applications of presuppositions at the various stages of metaphor construction and comprehension. At the "presemantic" stage, the *p-presuppositions* generate a first knowledge that a statement in question is metaphorical; at the semantic stage, the context-based *f-presuppositions* 'filter out' those aspects of the *p-set* that would be inconsistent with the topic. At the "postsemantic" stage, the truth-value and appropriateness of the utterance that contains a metaphor is asserted and evaluated. This complex analysis may appear cumbersome but it provides an explicit account of where extra-linguistic factors come into the process of constructing/understanding a metaphor, i.e. at the initial stage and in the last stages of completed interpretation. It thus leaves a space for a genuinely *semantic* interaction between "p-" and "f-presupposition" sets at the central stage.

Leezenberg, whilst critical of Stern's understanding of presupposition and of the logical status of the "Mthat" operator (Leezenberg 2001: 191–5, 202–8), pursues a similar aim of basing metaphor recognition and interpretation not on the propositional *content* but on a *character*-rule. In addition to Kaplan's *Logic of Demonstratives* he relies on Bartsch's (1987) concept of *thematic dimension*, i.e. the contextual set of properties that specifies the theme of a discourse (Leezenberg 2001: 165–71). In a maximally context-free, 'literal' statement, the thematic dimension is "internally" determined, i.e. "associated with dimensionally strongly determined expressions by default"; but ordinarily, i.e. in indexically co-determined language use, the thematic dimension is also determined by "external" dimensions (in the form of predicate-limiting adverbials) and "contextual dimensions" (based on extra-linguistic and intertextual information). In metaphors, "the internal dimension of the predicate [. . .] is suspended or neutralized by the contextual or external one" so that a new thematic dimension is established, which is directly accessed: "the hearer can just bypass the question of whether the sentence is literally true, and determine a metaphorical content directly, on the basis of the contextually available information" (2001: 173–4).

In this "direct contextual interpretation" theory, the problem of metaphor recognition, which still features in Kittay and Stern's accounts, "simply drops out" (2001: 230). Leezenberg does not view the set of contextual presuppositions as necessary to construct/understand the metaphor: for him, "it is not the relevant property itself that is presupposed but rather the thematic dimension determining that property" (Leezenberg 2001: 221). However, Stern's theory also includes such a dimension when he describes the cognitive effects of metaphor as the introduction of a new *perspective*, a *way of seeing-as* that is grounded not in one isolated "m-associated" property but in a whole *network* of presuppositions (Stern 2000: 277–85). Stern's "Mthat" theory and Leezenberg's thematic dimension approach thus need not be considered as incompatible with one another – nor, for that matter, as irreconcilable with cognitive metaphor theory.[15] In fact, Leezenberg places great emphasis on the 'interface' of semantic-linguistic and cognitive aspects of metaphor. He devotes a whole chapter to the discussion of epistemological, anthropological, psycho- and sociolinguistic theories to elucidate the close relationship between the *thematic dimension* view of metaphor and the cognitive interest in analysing the structure of *ad hoc concepts, folk theories, quasi-theories*, their social function and their evolutionary background (2001: 251–304). In the course of this discussion, he arrives at a further reinterpretation of Max Black's interaction theory as a model for recategorization processes. If, for instance, a metaphorical ad hoc concept of SUN [as in *Juliet is the sun*] is "integrated into existing theories, the new application becomes established as 'subconcept' of *sun*, which is thus turned into a polysemic complex" (Leezenberg 2001: 293). The relevance of this genetic view of metaphor meaning for corpus analysis will become clearer when we look at changes in metaphor use (cf. chapter 6).

For the immediate purpose of relating conceptual and linguistic levels of metaphor analysis, we can summarize the preceding discussion of Kittay, Glucksberg et al., Leezenberg and Stern's accounts as pointing in a common direction. They all demonstrate the possibility of providing a semantic analysis of metaphor that takes into account its dependency on extra-linguistic factors without relinquishing its linguistic definability. This is achieved through reconstructing the notion of *context* in terms of semantic character, i.e. as a set of presuppositions that provide semantic constraints on the respective metaphors whilst allowing for variable contents.

Glucksberg (2001) discusses, for instance, the metaphors *some roads are snakes* and *some lawyers are snakes*. The source domain of the vehicle is in both cases in some sense identical. However, the attribution of properties in these two metaphors is clearly variable, as it is "a joint function of the categories that the vehicle can exemplify (e.g. 'things with twisting shape' and/or 'things that are devious and malevolent') and the relevance constraints imposed by the respective topics (e.g. shape for roads, character for lawyers)" (Glucksberg 2001: 55).

This context-dependency of metaphors also showed in our corpus examples from the BODY-HEALTH domain. Thus, the identification of the expressions *Europe's much delayed recovery, (sick) heart of Europe, sick man of Europe* and *Eurosclerosis* in examples (1) to (4) as metaphorical depends on contexts where the "thematic dimension" of HEALTH/ILLNESS is applied to topics such as national economies or the EU. We can describe the corpus data as representing categorizations that rely on two sets of presuppositions, which make up a context that requires a metaphorical interpretation. One set of presuppositions consists of the topic-related background assumptions (e.g. about economic/political entities and their relations). The second set introduces the source perspective based on the knowledge of ILLNESS as a medical condition that can afflict PERSONS. This perspective includes, for instance, the presupposed scenarios of PERSONS BEING DIAGNOSED AS SICK, as SUFFERING FROM SPECIFIC ILLNESSES, as BEING INFECTED (e.g. by a VIRUS), of SPECIFIC ORGANS BEING SICK, and of RECOVERY. These notions are part of the standard folk-knowledge about the general theme of ILLNESS. In the contexts of utterances about Euro-politics, these aspects of knowledge about ILLNESS knowledge gain a semantic role as properties that are attributed to the topic. We can thus locate the category of *scenario* in the sets of presuppositions that are activated at the central semantic stage of metaphor interpretation.

The neo-semantic account of metaphor confirms the intuition that examples such as (1)–(4) are not interpreted by going through the construction of a literal meaning and its subsequent rejection. In this model, the question of whether the properties introduced through the set of source presuppositions are attributed 'literally' or not does not even arise in the comprehension of examples such as (1) to (4), as there is no ambiguity about the topical referents: after all, they are the only ones available. Thus, no 'semantic anomaly' assessment is required to recognize these meanings as metaphorical. All that is needed is the application of a basic version of the communicative "co-operation principle" to justify that the hearer/reader looks for a non-default interpretation as the most plausible meaning hypothesis at the "pre-semantic" stage. The semantic interpretation of an utterance *as* a metaphor makes use of the folk-theoretical scenarios as well as of their normally associated evaluative presuppositions that fit the most plausible thematic perspective (e.g. that it is highly desirable to avoid illness or to recover from illness etc.). The argumentative exploitation of these assumptions for inferences about the target topic is then a matter for the full explication of the utterance, which may go well beyond purely semantic criteria and take into account pragmatic and rhetorical factors.

Irrespective of their differences in semantic modelling and psycholinguistic corroboration, Glucksberg et al., Stern and Leezenberg's accounts show that metaphorical source/vehicle concepts can be analysed in *semantic* terms as thematically constraining presuppositions of utterances-in-context. It thus complements the cognitive insight into the systematicity of source concepts as parts of interrelated domains of experience and knowledge that organize our perception and conceptualization processes. The reformulation of the semantic account of metaphor in terms of *meaning character* avoids the problems of traditional, *content*-fixated approaches, and it has the further advantage of helping to explicate the relation between linguistic data and conceptual categories, and of highlighting the status of metaphorical source concepts as presuppositions. This ties in with the general account we gave of the *argumentative* function of metaphors in the preceding chapter. More semantic modelling is needed to clarify the exact relationship between those argumentation-orientated presuppositions with the types of presuppositions that Stern identifies.

As regards the implications for corpus-based approaches in metaphor analysis, the semantic accounts sketched above provide more than just a general link between cognitive and linguistic levels of description. They also give a theoretical underpinning to the category of "scenarios". In chapters 2 and 3, we saw that the data from the pilot corpus did not cover all conceptual 'areas' of the respective source domain in a regular, evenly weighted manner but were concentrated instead on a few conceptual elements manifested as lexical items. We characterized these conceptual clusters as "scenarios" that incorporated typical roles for participants and scenes or story-lines for their actions, as well as associated attitudes and values, which served as sources for analogical arguments concerning the target topic. We can now define these "scenarios" as prominent sub-sets of presuppositions within a specific *thematic dimension* or *perspective*. Their 'prominence' is not a matter of conjecture but a result of their distributional rank in a given corpus. We thus have a justification for drawing conclusions from the occurrence and distribution of specific scenarios in the corpus to the cognitive function of source concepts when applied to the target topic of EU politics. In the following chapter, we shall investigate such cognitive implications for the domain of corporeal and medical concepts, using both the data from the EUROMETA I pilot corpus as well as those from the "Bank of English" and COSMAS that are contained in the EUROMETA II corpus.

5
Europe as a BODY POLITIC

5.1 Corporeal and organismic metaphors in politics

The mapping of source concepts of the (HUMAN) BODY onto sociopolitical INSTITUTIONS has had a long tradition in political discourse and thought, dating back to antiquity and permutating over the centuries:

> (1) Originating as an expression of the unity of the Greek *polis*, it became in turn an important concept in the arsenal of the Stoic philosophers, Christian theologians, and spokesmen for the rising monarchies of the late medieval Europe. [. . .] The English Renaissance witnessed the final flourishing of the idea of the body politic, while at the same time it produced [. . .] challenges to the anthropomorphic view of the universe [. . .]. (Hale 1971: 47)

One strand of the BODY POLITIC tradition was focused on the person of the ruler, as epitomized in the theory of the *King's two bodies*, analysed in the seminal study, first published in 1957 by Ernst Kantorowicz (Kantorowicz 1997). In this tradition the ruler was seen, in the words of the Renaissance lawyer Edmund Plowden, as having "in him" both a "Body natural [. . .], subject to all Infirmities that come by Nature or Accident" and a "Body politic" that "cannot be seen or handled, consisting of Policy and Government, and constituted for the Direction of the People, and the Management of the public weal" (Kantorowicz 1997: 7). Here we find a basic analogy between the concrete, natural body of an individual person and the abstract political and legal powers he holds. The analogy serves to highlight the differences between the two categorial levels involved so as to enable legal and political theorists to distinguish the mortal and potentially deficient body of a person (who 'happened to be' the ruler) from the immortal, supposedly divinely legitimized system of authority, justice and dynasty (1997: 7–23 and passim).

By contrast, in the mapping 'THE WHOLE OF STATE IS A BODY' the emphasis lies on explaining the functions of parts of the political entity by reference to the parts and organs of the body and their state of health (Hale 1971; Struve 1978, 1984; Bass 1997). The traditional contention, as expressed in the above-quoted statement from Hale's book, was that the BODY POLITIC concept ceased to function as the basis of a political world-view by the time of the change from the Renaissance to the early Enlightenment. This received view has been based mainly on the evidence of the most prominent works of political theory and philosophy.[1] In political discourse as well as in literature, however, the use of BODY, LIFE and HEALTH source concepts for the conceptualization of society has in fact remained very active up to the present time. Not only do we still speak of *heads of state* or *government*,[2] but in modern extremist and totalitarian ideologies, for instance in Nazi ideology and discourse, the conceptualization of the nation as A BODY THAT MUST BE SHIELDED FROM DISEASE AND PARASITES AT ANY COST has gained new potency, with horrific consequences.[3] In her famous essay *Illness as Metaphor*, first published in 1978, Susan Sontag analyses in detail how dramatic ("master"-)ILLNESS source concepts, such as those of CANCER and TUBERCULOSIS, have been used to envisage and justify 'severe measures' against the supposed CARRIERS OF DISEASE (in the form of specific social groups) (Sontag 1991: 84). Cognitive research has revealed that the superordinate metaphor system of mappings between inanimate, animate, social and spiritual domains, known as the "GREAT CHAIN OF BEING" (Lovejoy 1936; Tillyard 1982), of which the BODY POLITIC concept is but one part, is indeed far from being obsolete but, on the contrary, fully 'alive' and productive in popular folk-theories of, *inter alia*, social systems (Lakoff and Turner 1989: 167; Kövecses 2002: 124–7).

Traditionally, the target referent of BODY POLITIC mappings has been a nation state and its socioeconomic system. In the case of the EC/EU, however, it is a multi-state confederation, whose legal and political status is still undecided and highly contentious. Its *corporeal* conceptualization is probably helped by the ubiquity of *organismic* metaphors in economic thought and discourse (White 2003: 134–43). The EUROMETA I pilot corpus has 188 passages comprising lexical elements that depict the EU, its institutions or member states as an *organism* or *body* (or part of it) that *is born, lives, dies, falls ill* and *recovers*, and which can thus be assigned to a domain LIFE-BODY-HEALTH. Of these, the English sample has 102 tokens, and the German sample has 86. In EUROMETA I, the tokens from this domain were initially subsumed together with those from the domain of STRENGTH-FIRMNESS under a 'super-domain' LIFE-HEALTH-STRENGTH (cf. Table 1) because of their close conceptual links and some evidence of collocation. However, many STRENGTH-FIRMNESS tokens appear as quasi-lexicalized verbalizations of statistical economic information about the *strengthening/weakening* of the euro or EU economy etc., in conjunction with news reports about the *rising/falling movements* of currency or interest rates.[4] As the latter have little to do with LIFE-BODY-HEALTH scenarios, general STRENGTH-FIRMNESS concepts are excluded from the following discussion. Tables 15 and 16 show the recorded conceptual elements sorted by basic mappings and frequencies respectively. For subordinate conceptual categories, sub-totals have been indicated (in italics) in Table 16, which are part of the figures for the whole conceptual element category (in regular font). Overall figures are calculated only for the latter.

Table 15 Conceptual elements of the LIFE-BODY-HEALTH domain in the EUROMETA I pilot corpus

Source concepts of LIFE-BODY-HEALTH domain	English lexemes	German lexemes
LIFE	to live, life-cycle	
BIRTH/BABY	(premature) birth, birth pangs, midwife, baby, babe in arms, clone, infant, infancy	Geburt, Frühgeburt, Baby
ADULTHOOD	coming of age	erwachsen werden
DEATH	death, dead, lethal	Tod, tot, sterben
ILLNESS/DISEASE (I/D, in general)	ill, illness, sick, sick man of Europe, disease, diseased, ailment	krank, kranker Mann Europas, kränkelnd
I/D: HEART DISEASE	rotten, sick, diseased heart, blood clot, blocked arteries	Herzklappenfehler
I/D: EUROSCLEROSIS	Euro(-)sclerosis, sclerotic	Eurosklerose
I/D: FURTHER 'EU-SPECIFIC' ILLNESSES	anorexia europa, eurosis	Subventionitis
I/D: PARALYSIS	paralysis	gelähmt
I/D: WASTING/TBC		Schwindsucht, schwindsüchtig
I/D: FAINTING		Schwächeanfall
I/D: ALIEN BODY		Fremdkörper
I/D: PSYCHIATRIC/PSYCHOLOGICAL	neurosis, madness	

Table 15 Continued

Source concepts of LIFE-BODY-HEALTH domain	English lexemes	German lexemes
I/D: PATIENT	patient	Patient
I/D: PAIN	pain	
FEVER[5]	fever	Fieber
POISON	poison, cyanide, opiate	
CURE/THERAPY/CARE	cure	Medizin, Frischzellenkur, Therapie, Pflege, pflegen
CURE: PILL/TRANQUILIZER	euro pill; morphine	Beruhigungspille, Euro-Baldrian
CURE: FITNESS PROGRAMME		Fitnessprogramm
CURE: VITAMIN		Vitaminstoß
CURE: SURGERY	ops, surgery	
CURE: KISS OF LIFE	kiss of life	
CURE: HOMEOPATHY	homeopathic remedies	
RECOVERY	to recover	erholen, Erholung
FIT/HEALTHY	health(y), fit(ness), vitality	gesund, fit, Fitness
BODY PART: HEART	heart	Herz
BODY PART: MUSCLE	muscle(s)	Muskeln
BODY PART: ARTERIES	arteries	Arterien
BODY PART: LIVER	liver	
BODY PART: GALL BLADDER	gall bladder	
BODY PART: HEAD	head	

Table 16 Tokens for conceptual elements of LIFE-BODY-HEALTH source concepts in EUROMETA I in order of frequency

Source concepts in LIFE-BODY-HEALTH domain	Tokens in British sample	Sub-totals	Tokens in German sample	Sub-totals	Tokens overall
ILLNESS/DISEASE	36		49		85
I/D: general		13		28	
I/D: HEART DISEASE		9		1	
I/D: EUROSCLEROSIS		5		7	
I/D: FURTHER 'EU-SPECIFIC' ILLNESSES		2		1	
I/D: PARALYSIS		2		1	
I/D: WASTING/TBC				3	
I/D: FAINTING				2	

Table 16   Continued

Source concepts in LIFE-BODY-HEALTH domain	Tokens in British sample	Sub-totals	Tokens in German sample	Sub-totals	Tokens overall
I/D: ALIEN BODY				1	
I/D: PSYCHIATRIC/ PSYCHOLOGICAL		2			
I/D: PATIENT		2		5	
I/D: PAIN		1			
BODY PARTS	45		11		56
BP: HEART		37		7	
BP: MUSCLE		2		2	
BP: ARTERIES		3		2	
BP: LIVER		1			
BP: GALL BLADDER		1			
BP: HEAD		1			
BIRTH/BABY	30		24		54
FIT/HEALTHY	6		8		14
CURE/THERAPY/CARE	6		10		16
C/T/C: general		2		7	
C/T/C: PILL, TRANQUILISER				1	
C/T/C: FITNESS PROGRAMME				1	
C/T/C: VITAMIN				1	
C/T/C: SURGERY		2			
C/T/C: KISS OF LIFE		1			
C/T/C: HOMEOPATHY		1			
DEATH	3		5		8
RECOVERY	2		3		5
POISON	3				3
FEVER	1		2		3
ADULTHOOD	1		1		2
LIFE	2				2
Total	135		113`		248
Number of passages	102		86		188

On the basis of these data, both the "Bank of English" and COSMAS corpora were searched for all combinations of the word-forms: English: *Euro/euro, Europe*, and German: *Euro/euro, Europa* plus all word-forms for lexical items denoting corporeal and medical entities and terms of *living/alive* etc. known from the pilot corpus, within a distance of 0 to ±5 word-forms. The results are given in Tables 17 and 18.

Table 17 Conceptual elements of the LIFE-BODY-HEALTH domain in EUROMETA II

Source concepts	English lexemes	German lexemes
LIFE, SURVIVAL	to live, life, alive, survival	Leben, leben, lebendig, überleben, Weiterleben, ins Leben rufen
BIRTH/BABY	birth, rebirth, born, stillborn, premature birth, abortion, baptism, baby, (bouncing) child	Geburt, geboren, Wiedergeburt, Frühgeburt, Mißgeburt, Kind, Baby
DEATH	death sentence/warrant/knell	Tod, tot
ILLNESS/DISEASE (general)	ill, illness, sick (sick man of Europe)	krank, kranker Mann Europas, kränkelnd
I/D: EUROSCLEROSIS	Euro(-)sclerosis	Eurosklerose
I/D: MADNESS	(Euro-)madness	
I/D: INFLUENZA	Asian (economic) flu	Grippe
I/D: VIRUS	virus	
I/D: COLIC	colic	
I/D: WOUND		Wunde, Narbe
I/D: WASTING/TBC		Schwindsucht
I/D: HURT		Wehtun
CURE/THERAPY/CARE	therapy, diagnose	Pflege, pflegen, Nachsorge
HEALTH/FITNESS/ RECOVERY	to recover, recovery, revive, health, healthy	Gesundheit, gesund, gesünder, gesunden, sich erholen, Fit, Fitness[6]
BODY PART: HEART	heart	Herz
BODY PARTS: EYES		Augen
BODY PART: HEAD		Kopf
BODY PARTS: LEGS		Beine
BODY PARTS: FEET		Füße
BODY PARTS: MUSCLES		Muskeln
BODY PART: BOTTOM	backside	

Table 18 Tokens for conceptual elements of LIFE-BODY-HEALTH source concepts in EUROMETA II in the order of frequency

Source concepts	Tokens in English sample	Sub-totals	Tokens in German sample	Sub-totals	Tokens overall
BODY PARTS	210		377		587
BP: HEART		209		336	
BP: EYES				19	
BP: HEAD				9	
BP: LEGS				6	

Table 18   Continued

Source concepts	Tokens in English sample	Sub-totals	Tokens in German sample	Sub-totals	Tokens overall
BP: FEET				5	
BP: MUSCLES				2	
BP: BOTTOM		1			
ILLNESS/DISEASE	60		137		197
I/D: SICK/ILL		40		92	
I/D: EUROSCLEROSIS		12		32	
I/D: MADNESS		4			
I/D: INFLUENZA		2		3	
I/D: VIRUS		1			
I/D: COLIC		1			
I/D: WOUND				5	
I/D: WASTING/TBC				3	
H/I: HURT				2	
BIRTH/BABY	58		100		158
HEALTH/FITNESS/ RECOVERY	37		111		148
LIFE, SURVIVAL	23		55		78
DEATH	4		8		12
CURE/THERAPY/ CARE	2		7		9
TOTALS	394		795		1189
Number of passages	184		485		669

The 2.5:1 ratio of COSMAS to BoE passages (plus the resulting 2:1 ratio of tokens) should not be interpreted as evidence of a greater popularity of LIFE-BODY-HEALTH metaphors in German press language. It is most probably due to the fact that the German sample contains many more texts for the same period than the BoE (apart from being thrice as large overall). It would be sheer speculation to derive comparative conclusions about the use of individual lexical items in the two national discourse communities.

Except for the sub-domain CURE/THERAPY/CARE,[7] the EUROMETA II data confirm the prominence of those LIFE-BODY-HEALTH concepts that were identified in the pilot corpus in the public debate on Europe in Britain and Germany. These are the concepts of the LIFE CYCLE (particularly BIRTH), the notion of the HEART and the complex of HEALTH-ILLNESS concepts (with the emphasis on certain types of ILLNESS, the condition of being the SICK MAN OF EUROPE, phases of RECOVERY and FITNESS).

We can now turn to the characteristic scenarios in which these source elements occur and their instrumentalization for political arguments about the EU. On the evidence of the EUROMETA II data, the basic mapping from the source domain of LIFE-BODY-HEALTH concepts to the target domain of Euro-political INSTITUTIONS, i.e. INSTITUTIONS ARE (HUMAN) ORGANISMS, can be divided into three sub-mappings and concomitant scenarios:

5.i Conceptual mappings for life-body-health metaphors

(a) AN INSTITUTION HAS A LIFE CYCLE THAT LASTS FROM BIRTH TO DEATH
(b) AN INSTITUTION HAS A BODY THAT COMPRISES VARIOUS PARTS AND ORGANS
(c) AN INSTITUTION (and any of its parts, cf. 5.i.b) CAN BE IN A MORE OR LESS HEALTHY/ILL STATE.

5.ii Scenarios for LIFE-BODY-HEALTH metaphors

(a) *LIFE CYCLE:* AN INSTITUTION IS CONCEIVED, CARRIED AND BORN; IF IT CONTINUES TO FUNCTION IT SURVIVES AND GROWS UP; WHEN IT CEASES FUNCTIONING, IT DIES
(b) *HEALTH/ILLNESS:* AN INSTITUTION CAN SUFFER INJURIES TO ITS BODY OR FALL ILL, RECOVER, AND UNDERGO MEDICAL TREATMENT
(c) *BODY:* THE PARTS OR ASPECTS OF AN INSTITUTION ARE LIMBS AND ORGANS OF ITS BODY (which can also BECOME ILL and then may AFFECT THE WHOLE BODY).

In the following sub-chapters we shall investigate each of these scenarios on the basis of data from both EUROMETA I and EUROMETA II with regard to their conceptual and distributional characteristics and their significance for argumentative trends in the British and German debates.

5.2 The LIFE CYCLE of Europe

The main focus of the LIFE-CYCLE scenario in the EUROMETA corpora is on the concepts BIRTH and BABY. These are employed to categorize momentous and innovative political developments, such as the restructuring of Europe after the collapse of the Warsaw Pact in 1989/90, the institutional reforms of the EC/EU, which were agreed in the Treaties of Maastricht (1992) and Amsterdam (1997), as well as new economic institutions, in particular the common currency, the "euro". More than 75 per cent of all BIRTH/BABY tokens in EUROMETA I and EUROMETA II have the euro as their target concept. They comprise a variety of mini-scenarios such as those of pre-, peri- and post-natal problems (STILL BIRTH, PREMATURE BIRTH, TEETHING PROBLEMS) as well as emphatically positive descriptions of a HEALTHY BABY. At first sight, the distribution of these scenarios, all of which connect to arguments and conclusions about the success of the currency introduction, seems to give the lie to some of the assumptions about the relative strength of Euro-scepticism in Britain and Germany, as indicated in chapters 2 and 3.

Whereas tokens for the characterization of the euro introduction as a PROBLEM BIRTH in the British sample account for less than 35 per cent, they make up the great majority, i.e., 63 per cent, in the German sample (9 out of 26 BIRTH tokens in the English sample of EUROMETA II, 50 out of 79 BIRTH tokens in the German sample). A closer study of the reasons for this apparent lack of confidence in the EURO-BIRTH amongst the German public reveals that 90 per cent of all of the German tokens consist of citations of and/or comments on a particular statement by the then opposition contender for the German Chancellorship, the Social-Democratic minister-president of Lower Saxony, Gerhard Schröder. In March 1998, Schröder augured that the euro start might be a PREMATURE BIRTH. He was not the first politician to do so,[8] but he was by far the most prominent; and he made his statement at a crucial time in the run-up to the federal elections in Germany, which were to take place in autumn that year. For the last two years of the conservative government under Kohl, opinion polls showed that a majority of German voters were sceptical about the replacement of the Deutschmark by the new currency.[9]

For a politician who wanted to win over indecisive voters, a metaphorical warning phrased so as to sound like a helpful suggestion while at the same time expressing some reservations about the precipitate introduction of the new currency promised maximum electoral profit. Immediately after the EU Commission had declared all candidate states to be *fit for the euro*, and with enough time in hand to make an impact on the election campaign, Schröder warned that a hastened arrival of the euro was going to *deliver a sickly, premature baby*:

> (2) Einen Tag, nachdem die Europäische Kommission in Brüssel den Startschuß für den Euro [...] gegeben hat, meldet sich der Kanzlerkandidat Gerhard Schröder: Die Währungsunion komme überhastet und führe zu einer *kränkelnden Frühgeburt*, moniert er. (W, 27 March 1998) [One day after the European Commission in Brussels has given the green light for the euro [...], the opposi-

tion's candidate for the Chancellorship, Gerhard Schröder, decries EMU as coming too soon and producing a *sick, prematurely born child*.]

The incumbent Chancellor, Helmut Kohl, and his foreign minister, Klaus Kinkel, attempted to launch a counter-attack by condemning Schröder for having denounced the euro-birth as a *miscarriage* ("Fehlgeburt") or even as a *monstrosity* ("Mißgeburt").[10] Schröder in turn accused his opponents of mis-quoting him and demonstrated how carefully he had chosen the specific scenario he favoured for the *euro-birth*: of course, he stated, 'a *miscarriage* and a *premature birth* were completely different things'.[11] Calling the *birth* of the euro a *miscarriage* would have implied an utterly pessimistic attitude, namely, that the *child was doomed to die*, whereas the diagnosis of a *premature birth* could be interpreted as a plea for *extra care* and *support* so that *the child could still survive*. Needless to say, Schröder considered his own party to be *best qualified to give that support* and he reiterated this assessment on the election campaign trail:

(3) [. . .] Schröder kennzeichnet "die überhastete Währungsunion" als "*eine kränkelnde Frühgeburt*". *Damit das Kind durchkommt*, müsse man in der Steuer-, Sozial- und Umweltpolitik noch ganz schnell einiges tun. (SP, 14/1998). [Schröder characterizes the 'rushed currency union' as '*a sickly, premature child*'. *In order for it to survive*, urgent measures are needed in the fields of tax policies as well as social and environment policies.]

(4) [. . .] in Leipzig wiederholte Schröder seine *Diagnose einer Frühgeburt, die gepflegt werden müsse*. "Das können wir am besten", sagte er [. . .]. SZ, 3 April 1998). [in Leipzig, Schröder reiterated his *diagnosis of a premature child that needed care*. 'It's us (= SPD) who are best equipped to provide that *care*', he said.]

Sensing the attractiveness of his opponent's metaphor for the electorate, Chancellor Kohl tried once more to weaken its appeal. He now denounced Schröder's *premature birth*-perspective on the currency introduction as isolating Germany among the other *euro-fathers*, especially his opponent's own political allies, i.e. the Social-Democratic governments of EU member states (cf. example 5 in chapter 2, p. 19). These tactics might have worked if it had not been for the fact that the *euro-fathers'* commitment to the *health* of the *baby* euro was put into question by inter-governmental disagreements, such as the quarrel over who should be the first president of the European Central Bank, which led to critical commentaries on the *euro baby's difficult birth*.[12] As an assessment of the *euro baby's chances of survival*, Schröder's metaphor thus appeared to be more plausible than the picture of *euro fatherhood* (by 12 fathers altogether!) painted by Kohl.

Soon after his victory in the general election, Schröder was charged, as acting president of the EU Council of ministers from January to June 1999, with *caring* for the *child* whose allegedly *premature birth* he had criticized only a few months before. He quickly assumed the role of the responsible, caring *father* even when confronted with his *premature baby* statement, e.g. in this passage from an interview by the magazine *Der Spiegel*:

(5) *Spiegel*: Sie übernehmen den Vorsitz im Rat der EU in einem Augenblick, in dem das historisch einzigartige Experiment des Euro anläuft – *eine "Frühgeburt", wie Sie meinten*. Immer noch skeptisch? – *Schröder*: Wir müssen den Euro zu einem Erfolg machen. (SP, 1/1999) [*Spiegel*: You are taking over the EU presidency just at the start of the historically unique experiment of the euro – *a 'premature child'*, *as you called it*. Are you still sceptical? – *Schröder*: We must make the euro a success.]

Some commentators ridiculed the new Federal Chancellor for his erstwhile pessimism. The weekly newspaper *Die Zeit* declared that, contrary to Schröder's and others' gloomy prognoses, the euro-*baby* had 'turned out to be a *bouncing bundle of joy*' ("putzmunterer Wonneproppen"; Z, 7 January 1999). Six months later, they condemned his 'ill-chosen' *premature birth* warning as typical of the lack of depth and urgency, which in their view characterized the German EU debate ("Schröder, samt seinem Unwort von der *'kränkelnden Frühgeburt'* [ist] ein sehr typisches Kind der Republik"; Z, 8 July 1999). As late as spring 2000, parts of the German press harked back to Schröder's 1998 statement. The regional newspaper *Mannheimer Morgen*, for instance, used his *premature birth diagnosis* ("Schröder, der den Euro einst als *'kränkelnde Frühgeburt'* abgetan hatte") to highlight its contrast with Schröder's more upbeat comments on the then topical decline of the euro's exchange rate as being 'nothing to shed tears over' ("Wir müssen nicht weinen, wenn etwas der deutschen Exportwirtschaft nutzt"; MM, 12 May 2000).

The debates about Schröder's and others' comments on the euro BIRTH PROBLEMS had a massive impact on the distribution patterns of *birth* tokens in the EUROMETA II corpus. From the early 1990s until spring 1998, tokens are quite rare: they are in evidence once a year on average. PROBLEM BIRTH scenarios then begin to pick up in both national samples, which can be explained with reference to the approaching date for the introduction of the euro currency (1 January 1999). But this increase is insignificant compared with the sudden inflation of tokens for the more specific PREMATURE BIRTH scenario, which exclusively dominate the German sample for the following four weeks and which make up the bulk of all BIRTH tokens up to October 1998 (i.e. the time of the general election). After this peak their frequency decreases but still remains at a higher level than before March 1998. Some of these later occurrences do not refer back to Schröder's phrase; they apply the general PROBLEM BIRTH scenario to the new currency's difficulties in the financial markets:

(6) Nie war er *so schwach wie heute* [headline] Der Euro hat *seit seiner Geburt* acht Prozent an Wert verloren. (taz, 6 March 1999) [It was never *so weak as today*. Since its birth, the euro has lost 8 per cent of its worth.]¹³

(7) Two months after its *birth the euro is suffering an attack of colic*. (G, 6 March 1999)

(8) Am Ende des ersten Jahres nach der vertragsrechtlichen *Geburt des Euro* summieren sich jedoch Zweifel am Erfolg des gigantischen Währungsprojekts. (FR, 29 December 1999) [At the end of the first year after the contractually agreed *birth of the euro*, doubts about the gigantic currency project are mounting.]

(9) The *struggling euro has been dubbed a "stillborn baby"* in a withering audit of its first two years. (*The SUN*, 11 September 2001)

We can observe how one sub-group of scenarios, i.e. here the PROBLEM BIRTH scenarios – with a focus on one special target topic (the euro currency introduction) – provide the bulk of tokens in the corpus, due to particular historical developments. Once the scenario has been used by a prominent politician in a salient context (e.g. in an election campaign), it becomes widely known through further comments and reinterpretations. In the short term, the metaphor remains the 'property', as it were, of its author and serves his argumentative needs – thus, the PREMATURE BIRTH metaphor helped Schröder to sound sufficiently euro-sceptical to ingratiate himself with the German electorate of 1998. Within a few months, in a changed political context, the metaphor started to be quoted against him in the context of comments suggesting that Schröder's *premature birth* warnings had sounded too sceptical to be offset easily by his new posturing as a *caring euro father*.

The lesson for the interpretation of corpus data is that the sheer frequency of occurrences of tokens for specific scenarios cannot in itself be regarded as evidence of a particular argumentative or ideological bias of the source. It would make little sense to conclude from the number of tokens of the PREMATURE BIRTH scenario that the German public was more sceptical towards the euro than the British. The scenario provided Schröder for the time of the election campaign with an opportunity to suggest that under Kohl the euro's *birth* was likely to be *premature* and to pose as the better *euro father*. This argumentative opportunity was in principle open to any politician, but it happened to be Schröder who made use of it. Not only did he launch it successfully but he managed to defend it and, when challenged, to recontextualize it in a convincing manner. Such further argumentative exploitation is not part of the set of presuppositions that make up the scenario itself; it rather depends on the tactics of participants in the 'virtual conversation' of the public debate. An initially prominent scenario can 'spawn' a number of variations, each of them designed to counter or ridicule rival scenario versions put forward by the political contestants. In these cases, the 'virtual' public conversation becomes more similar to real arguments or disputations, where each comment represents a "turn" in the discussion. We shall deal with the discourse-historic aspect of such 'conceptual contests' in the following chapter; for the moment, we shall turn to the other elements of the LIFE-CYCLE scenario.

The opposite pole to the concept of BIRTH within the LIFE CYCLE, i.e. DEATH, is mentioned only eight times in EUROMETA I and twelve times in EUROMETA II. Most of the few references in the German sample are parts of statements about the *life-threatening* consequences of certain events or actions for Europe. The daily *Frankfurter Rundschau*, which usually holds pro-EU integration views, for instance, warned in 1997 that the then German government was 'committing *economic suicide*' by trying to achieve the Maastricht criteria for EMU 'for fear of *endangering the life of Europe*' (FR, 28 February 1997: "[. . .] was Bonn unter dem Diktat von Maastricht [. . .] verordnet, läuft auf *wirtschaftspolitischen Selbstmord* hinaus *aus Angst vor dem Tode Europas*"). The same newspaper later quoted the EU finance commissioner, De Silguy, alerting the public to the effects of a delayed currency introduction as 'the *death* of the euro' (FR, 21 July 1997: "De Silguy [antwortete]: '*Dann ist der Euro tot.*'"). In other cases, the DEATH concept was explicitly refuted. In 1993, the *tageszeitung*, for instance, rejected as premature the *death* pronouncements on EMU as a consequence of difficulties of the European Exchange Rate Mechanism:

(10) Die *Totengräber* stehen bereit: Wenn das Europäische Währungssystem (EWS) nun *zu Grabe getragen* wird, wollen sie die europäische Wirtschaftsunion gleich *mit beerdigen*. [. . .] Es ist jedoch nicht anzunehmen, daß die europäischen Regierungen jetzt einfach die Flinte ins Korn werfen.' (*taz*, 6 August 1993). [The *gravediggers* are ready: they want to *bury* the economic union together with the Exchange rate mechanism. But it is hardly likely that the European governments will simply throw in the towel now.]

In the British sample, the few recorded examples come from the extreme Euro-sceptical end of the political spectrum. Margaret Thatcher was quoted likening "the [impending Maastricht] treaty to a national *suicide note*" (FT, 28 July 1991), and in January 2000, *The SUN* triumphantly announced that the ECB president's "sensational admission" that Britain would "not join the single currency for years" sounded "the *death knell* for the euro" (*The SUN*, 31 January 2000).

Such *death* pronouncements are of dubious value as argumentative moves in public debates, because they run the risk of being factually falsified by future compromise solutions that give a new *lease of life* to the economic or political projects in question. Mainstream media and politicians usually try to sound more cautious in their warnings of dangers for the *survival* or the *life expectancy* of political projects. In 1999, *The Independent*, for instance, pointed out that the euro's "design faults" could lead to a recession, which "might *put at risk even the euro's very survival*" (I, 3 March 1999). In 1998, the incoming Bundesbank president, Ernst Welteke, was quoted stating that 'the euro's *life depended* on the ECB's independence from political intervention' (FR, 6 November 1998: "[. . .] der Euro *lebe davon*, daß die Zentralbank frei von politischer Einflußnahme sei"). Other LIFE CYCLE-related statements in the German sample put emphasis on the distinction between abstract political concepts on the one hand and the *vitality* of the EU, as in one example praising youth exchanges as activities in which Europe 'really comes alive' (FR, 11 June 1999: "[. . .] ein Austausch, der Europa für viele Jugendliche erst *lebendig* mache").

In these examples, as well as in most instantiations of the BIRTH concept, one basic attitudinal 'bias' is discernible, which has the deepest possible experiential grounding – namely, that being alive and maintaining and supporting a life is preferable to death or dying. In terms of real-life experience, this may appear to be a commonplace truth. However, in a cognitive perspective, it is significant that complex and highly abstract issues such as the introduction of a new currency or problems with political acceptance of the EU are 'brought home' to the general public's perception by way of tapping into this experiential basis via the LIFE CYCLE scenario.

5.3 HEALTH and ILLNESS of Europe

A similarly strong experiential grounding can be assumed for the second group of scenarios under the INSTITUTION-ORGANISM mapping, i.e. the conceptualization of the EU as a whole, or of member states or the euro as *organisms afflicted by illness* or *disease*. Under normal circumstances, a good state of health is preferred to a condition of being ill, sick, injured or crippled. Consequently, metaphors describing an institution as *ill* are used for critical judgements, and the promise of *recovery*, *care* or, if need be, *medical treatment* is valued positively. So we find a variety of ILLNESS-TREATMENT-RECOVERY scenarios in the corpus, comprising physical as well as psychological and psychosomatic conditions, intoxication and concomitant effects such as PAIN and AGONY, and also forms of THERAPY and PREVENTION, such as FITNESS PROGRAMMES, HEALTH TESTS, PILLS OR MEDICINES (cf. Tables 15 and 17). The concept of FEVER would also seem to belong in this category. However, in the uses documented in the corpus, the lexical items *fever* and its German equivalent *Fieber* do not appear to be associated with notions of PAIN or SUFFERING, which are typical for other ILLNESS conditions, but are used in a wider and almost neutral sense of 'frantic activity' or 'agitation'.[14] For this reason they have been excluded from the ILLNESS/DISEASE scenarios (but are still considered part of the whole LIFE-BODY-HEALTH domain).

The most general terms for concepts in the ILLNESS domain, *disease* and *illness*, *ill* and *sick* in English, and German *Krankheit*, *krank* as well as *kränkeln* ('poorly', 'to begin to be ill'), collocate in some cases with more specific ILLNESS terms (e.g. *kränkeln* with *Frühgeburt* in Schröder's *sick, premature birth* warning), but most tokens appear in the fixed phrase *the sick man of Europe* (in German: *der kranke Mann Europas*). This phrase is by no means new to European discourse – the *sick man of Europe* formula can be traced back to the late seventeenth century and enjoyed special prominence in the nineteenth century as a reference to the declining military and economic power of the Ottoman Empire – this usage is still remembered in the British press.[15] More recently, in the 1970s, Britain, which was just entering the "EEC" as it was then called, and whose economy was suffering from recessions, strikes and the effects of de-industrialization, was also dubbed the *sick man of Europe* – a stigmatization that is even more poignantly remembered. It was thus with considerable relief, and in a few cases with considerable *schadenfreude*, that British media passed the stigma label onto Germany, when the erstwhile model of a *healthy economy* in Europe experienced the threat of recession and of not meeting the EMU stability criteria:

(11) *Germany has become the sick man of Europe*: growth is slowing, exports [. . .] have dipped. (E, 20 March 1999)

(12) Market-friendly politicians [. . .] now complain of Germany being a *blockierte Gesellschaft* (blocked society). Unblocking it will take determination. Without that, *Germany is unlikely soon to shed its title as the sick man of Europe*. (E, 5 June 1999)

(13) Twenty-five years ago, Britain was branded *the sick man of Europe*. Germany was the model economy we should copy. Today, the influential Economist magazine says *Germany is the sick man of the euro*. (*The SUN*, 5 June 1999)

(14) How times have changed. Thanks to radical union reform, widespread economic liberalisation and sensible monetary and fiscal policies, *the UK has transformed itself from the "Sick Man of Europe" to the best-performing G 7 economy* this year [. . .]. And it is *Germany, once the economic powerhouse of the Continent, that is looking decidedly ill*. (T, 26 October 2001)

The *sick man of Europe* formula accounts for 29 of the 40 British SICK/ILL(NESS) tokens in EUROMETA II, i.e. 72 per cent, with most of them harking back to Britain's past status as the *sick man* (15 tokens). This appears to corroborate the *Guardian*'s verdict that "Britain still seems to be living with the psychological consequences of [. . .] the lingering inferiority complex from when we were seen as the 'sick man of Europe'" (G, 16 February 1999). Germany comes second (10 tokens); apart from it only Albania and the euro carry this stigma (each once), plus two historical references to Turkey. The British view of Germany as the current *sick man of Europe* is repeated on the German side, though on a smaller scale. Of the 13 tokens of *kranker Mann Europas* (= 14 per cent of the 92 tokens of the general ILLNESS lexemes: *krank/Krankheit/kränkelnd*), five name Germany as the target (with single tokens for Russia, Greece and Spain each, plus two historical references to Turkey and three acknowledgements that Britain has left the negative image behind). The public image of Europe as it is manifested in the British and German press language thus seems to include the notion of a *sick list* of nations (cf. e.g. G, 9 June 1999; "[. . .] Germany comes off *sick list*"), which is continually updated, with one nation being singled out as the worst *afflicted* one.

Whilst the *sick man of Europe* phrase presupposes a mapping from the concept of SEVERAL PERSONS to DIVERSE EUROPEAN STATES, so that one of them can be identified as *the* SICK MAN, an alternative perspective is that of the EU as ONE INTEGRAL ORGANISM THAT SUFFERS FROM AN ILLNESS OR DISEASE. This concept underlies the two remaining ILLNESS scenarios that occur in substantial numbers in the EUROMETA corpora, i.e. the scenario of the special ILLNESS called *Eurosclerosis* and that of an affliction of THE HEART OF EUROPE. As the latter of these falls into the BODY PART category, it will be treated separately in the next sub-chapter.

Eurosclerosis is the only 'medical' metaphor in Euro-discourse that has achieved the status of a well-known key term that can be identified in its own right in a general corpus. The pilot corpus does include two similar coinings, namely "eurosis" and "anorexia europa", but these seem not to have spread beyond the individual articles in which they appeared (in G, 18 December 1995; G, 12 December 1998 respectively). By contrast, *Eurosclerosis* is the single most frequently used 'disease' term referring to EU politics in the BoE and COSMAS, and thus in EUROMETA II. It seems to have gained prominence first in the early 1980s as a term to warn against a decrease in economic and institutional *flexibility*,[16] in keeping with its source meaning of "morbid tissue hardening", e.g. in the form of "arteriosclerosis" as a hardening of the tissue of blood vessels (*Concise Oxford Dictionary* 1979: 1014–15). In a speech from the early 1990s, Helmut Kohl contrasted the situation of ten years before with the now (supposedly) much happier situation:

(15) Vor knapp zehn Jahren [. . .] war das meistgebrauchte Wort in der EG *"Eurosklerose"*. Heute spricht man [. . .] nicht mehr von *"Eurosklerose"* – wir haben vielmehr Grund, von einem neuen Abschnitt europäischer Geschichte zu sprechen. (Presse- und Informationsamt der Bundesregierung, 1992). [Ten years ago, *'Eurosclerosis'* was the most frequently used buzzword in the EC. These days, nobody speaks of *'Eurosclerosis'* any more – instead we have every reason to speak of a new chapter in European history.]

Kohl's *diagnosis* of a Union *healed of Eurosclerosis* for the 1990s turned out to be wishful thinking. At the end of the same year, when negotiations about budget plans at the EC summit conference in Edinburgh proved to be particularly difficult, the magazine *Der Spiegel* stated that the politicians 'had not managed to heal *the prolonged, almost chronic Eurosclerosis that the EC was suffering from*' (SP 51/1992: "[...] *die verschleppte, inzwischen fast chronische Eurosklerose,* von der die EG *befallen ist,* [konnte] nicht *geheilt* werden"). On the British side, *Eurosclerosis* was also far from forgotten. In 1993, *The Economist* stated a *relapse* into the 1980s *illness* (cf. example 16 below), and during the second half of the 1990s, the verdict of *Eurosclerosis* was again used in the British press to condemn slow growth and rising unemployment in continental member states. On the Euro-sceptical side of the political spectrum, these *diagnoses* were used to promote abstention from Monetary Union (cf. examples 17 and 18):

(16) The Delors who arrived in Brussels in 1985 was obsessed by economic decline. The commission's single-market programme promised to vanquish *Eurosclerosis*. The EC gained a net 7m jobs in the three years from 1988 to 1990, and Mr Delors moved on to other things. But deepening recession has shifted his attention back to employment. (E, 19 June 1993)

(17) These social market policies [in Germany and France] have produced Europe's unemployment rate of over 11 per cent. The single currency would cement this high unemployment in place and extend it to Britain. *It would make Euro-sclerosis incurable.* [...]. *This was the British disease of our socialist period* [...], *it is now the German disease, the French disease, the Spanish disease, the European disease in general.* (T, 4 April 1996)

(18) In the real world, it is far better for the UK to avoid *eurosclerosis* and rules such as the withholding tax on savings than to join the euro at a rate we would rue. (T, 25 January 2000)

In the latter examples, *Eurosclerosis* has become a *contagious disease that spreads across the EU* as an epidemic spreads through a population. Strictly speaking, this is not compatible with the source concept of SCLEROSIS, as its medical definition does not include any CONTAGION aspect. But if one EU nation can be *cured* of it or avoid it whilst the others still *suffer* from it – as is argued in (17) and (18) – there must be several PATIENTS. As in previous scenarios, we find here a counterfactual blend of different sets of input presuppositions, i.e. one set concerning SCLEROSIS and a second, more general notion of DISEASE that includes the possibility of CONTAGIOUS SPREADING. Following Turner and Fauconnier (2000), we can analyse this conceptual blend as being based on two "mental input spaces", SCLEROSIS and CONTAGIOUS DISEASE, both of which are parts of the ILLNESS/HEALTH domain, as well as several "target spaces" (EU ECONOMY, NATIONAL ECONOMIES). The resulting blended space can be described as denoting 'a paralysing condition affecting the EU countries that participate in the single currency'. It is neither 'entailed' by any one of its source inputs, nor is it a self-evident qualification of the target concepts, but rather a "selective projection" (Turner and Fauconnier 2000: 136) from both types of inputs, which creates an ad hoc concept designed to denounce the single currency as a dangerous political project.

It is also significant that in the rhetorically most powerful passage, i.e. (17), the emphasis is on *national diseases spreading*: "[...] the German disease, the French disease, the Spanish disease, the European disease in general". This formulation is reminiscent of traditions of ascribing strongly feared or embarrassing contagious diseases to individual nations, as in 'euphemisms' such as *French disease, German measles, English sickness, Spanish gout*, etc.[17] In these cases, the concept of DISEASE is the target notion and its 'national' specification is motivated by historical factors, such as alleged first manifestations of a disease in one nation according to popular and often highly prejudicial folk-theories. In (17) and (18), the combination of input notions of a debilitating medical condition (SCLEROSIS) and of contagious diffusion achieves a maximum scare effect, which serves the authors' specific purposes of boosting Euro-sceptical attitudes. It would be mistaken to attribute this bias to the term *Eurosclerosis* itself. However, the possibility to invest it with associations of deep-seated fears concerning sweeping epidemics makes it especially attractive for intimidating use. Here we have evidence of a linkage of discourse data not just to the "supra-" but also to the "subindividual" level of metaphor, in so far as it is grounded in the anthropologically fundamental notion of an EPIDEMIC. Its argumentative appeal reaches not just into rational consciousness but also into the affective system and, possibly, into the evolutionary memory of human beings.

5.4 The ORGANS of Europe

If the European Union can be *alive* or *dead* and *fall ill*, it must – in the logic of the metaphor – have a BODY that consists of various ORGANIC PARTS. The two EUROMETA corpora contain tokens of altogether nine BODY PARTS, of which only one, however, constitutes a significant source concept for Euro-metaphors: i.e. the HEART. As Tables 16 and 18 show, the remaining BODY PART concepts (ARTERIES, BOTTOM, EYES, FEET, GALL-

BLADDER, LEGS, LIVER, MUSCLES) have so few tokens that they are statistically insignificant. Furthermore, many of them appear, as we shall see, in special one-off formulations that have the HEART source concept as their principal semantic clue.[18]

The heart has traditionally been regarded as the *seat* of courage, personality and character not only in individual human beings, but also in the BODY POLITIC and has given rise to a vast number of metonymic and metaphorical concepts represented in idioms and proverbs.[19] Niemeier (2000) has shown that this integration of metaphorical and metonymic meaning aspects is grounded in salient bodily experiences and in the apparent immediacy of the conceptual link between HEART and PERSON:

> (19) Thus, starting with their most basic bodily experiences, people have a heart and they can feel it acting differently according to the emotions they experience: the heartbeat quickens, slows down, stops altogether, etc. Already in ancient times emotions were assured to reside in the most conspicuous body organ (the only one everybody is able to paint – though physiologically incorrectly) – at least in Western cultures – and the heart was taken as a metonymy for the whole body and thus it stands for the whole person experiencing a specific emotion. It is on the basis of this archetypal metonymy that the other understandings could arise and flourish. This thought was further developed and commonplace experiences strengthened the idea that the heart must be a very valuable and important organ. (Niemeier 2000: 209–10)

Niemeier divides English idioms involving figurative conceptualizations of HEART into four main types along an axis from maximally metonymic to maximally metaphorical "meaning clusters": HEART as a metonymy for a PERSON, as in *she set all hearts on fire*; HEART as a LIVING ORGANISM, as in *two hearts that beat as one*; HEART as an OBJECT OF VALUE, as in *to win somebody's heart*; and HEART as a CONTAINER, as in *to pour out one's heart to somebody* (Niemeier 2000: 199–209). Such idiomatic phrases also turn up in the EUROMETA corpora but are of little relevance for the target notion of the EU AS A POLITICAL INSTITUTION.[20] The two conceptualizations in the corpus data that are relevant for our analysis are: (a) an understanding of the HEART as the CENTRAL PART of the BODY, and (b) the notion that the HEART as an ORGAN can suffer damage from INJURY or DISEASE, and that (given the HEART's central function) such damage is LIFE-THREATENING to the whole ORGANISM.

The CENTRALITY aspect of the HEART concept is, first of all, manifest in references to the localization of countries, regions or cities *in the heart of Europe*. These are statistically by far the most prominent uses of the phrase *heart of Europe* in the EUROMETA II German sample (with 257 out of 336 tokens), and still make up a substantial portion in the English sample (34 out of 209). Nearly half of the German tokens – 116 out of the 252 tokens – refer to Germany as a whole or to German cities (Berlin, Frankfurt and, at least for the *Mannheimer Morgen*, Mannheim) as being *(in) the heart of Europe*. There are no similar references to places in Britain or to Britain as a whole in either the British or the German sample of the corpus. As regards continental Europe, the HEART = CENTRE equation extends not just over the countries of central Europe – that is, Poland, the Czech Republic (in particular, Prague), Austria and Slovenia besides Germany – but also includes Belgium, the Franco-German border regions (Alsace-Lorraine, Burgundy and the Palatinate), Switzerland, and the Balkans. In 2000, the *heart of Europe* was even considered to be *moving northwards*, on account of the planned completion of the bridge linking Jutland with the rest of Denmark:

(20) Am 1. Juli 2000, sagt Dänemarks Ministerin für Industrie und Handel, "*rückt das Herz Europas nach Norden*". (BZ, 18 October 1999) [On 1 July 2000, *Europe's heart will move to the North*, says Denmark's minister for trade and industry.]

The references to the Balkans form a special topical sub-group: all of them deal with the war in the former Yugoslavia. As the following examples show, the emphasis is on the fact that the war takes place *in the heart of Europe*, with the implication that what happens *in the heart* is or should be of special importance to ('fellow') Europeans:

(21) As the war has dragged on, the possibility of Bosnia's Muslims being completely dispossessed of land has increased, intensifying the prospect of a new Palestinian problem *in the heart of Europe*. (E, 12 December 1992)

(22) [Letter to editor:] *Mortal danger in the heart of Europe*. Sir: Having just returned from an aid effort in Bosnia, I can safely say that our reputation among the citizens and humanitarian workers has reached new depths of contempt. (I, 20 July 1995)

(23) Von 1991 bis 1995 wurde *im Herzen Europas* ein Krieg geführt, dessen Brutalität und Menschenverachtung wir der Vergangenheit

angehörig glaubten. (Z, 18 February 1999) [Between 1991 and 1995, a war was fought *in the heart of Europe* with a brutality and inhumanity which we had thought belonged in the past.]

(24) [Letter to editor:] *Headlines about this war being in the "heart of Europe"* [. . .] *and other similar comments* [. . .] *have the implication that if this was happening thousands of miles away it would be more explicable and almost normal.* (G, 5 April 1999)

The last passage shows that there is a close connection between the HEART-AS-CENTRE and the HEART-AS-SEAT OF EMOTIONS concepts. What is *in the heart* is – or should be, according to standard cultural assumptions in the West – *close to, and thus of particular importance for, one's emotional centre.* The critical comment on press headlines in (24) is based on this association; otherwise the implication and the attached accusation of double standards would not make sense. This emotional and deontic dimension of positioning a nation *in the heart of Europe* is also discernible in some cases of references to candidate states for the EU enlargement process, such as the Czech Republic, Poland and Hungary.

(25) "Prag, Warschau und Budapest gehören *zum Herzen Europas*", sagte er [= Eberhard Diepgen, then Lord Mayor of Berlin]. (taz, 2 January 1995) ['Prague, Warsaw and Budapest belong *in the heart of Europe'*, he said.]

(26) Trotzdem ist die Einbindung Osteuropas in ein gemeinsames Europa notwendig und sinnvoll, um [. . .] die historischen *Wunden*, die Faschismus und Stalinismus *im Herzen Europas schlugen, zu heilen.* (FR, 9 August 1999) [Nevertheless, the integration of Eastern Europe into a Common Europe is necessary and useful in order to *heal the wounds which fascism and communism have inflicted on the heart of Europe* in the past.]

(27) Some may see the accession of the Czech Republic, Hungary and Poland mainly as a righting of historical wrongs, as the final step in overcoming the division of Europe which followed the Yalta agreement in 1945 and Stalin's imposition of *an iron curtain in the heart of Europe*. Yet such a view would miss the real significance of enlargement – which lies not only in correcting past injustices but in preparing for a common future. (*The Economist*, 13 March 1999)

The implication here is that the countries in question have so far not been acknowledged sufficiently in their central relevance for Europe, with the historical culprits for this discrimination being named in (26) and (27). The allocation of HEART OF EUROPE-status is meant as an acknowledgement or promise that certain nations have a historic 'right' to belong not just to Europe, but to its HEART. The localization of a nation (or metonymically, of its capital, as in example 25) *in the heart of Europe* is seen as more than mere geographic CENTRALITY: it is presented as a privilege resulting from the success of the post-Second World War reconstruction of Western Europe, which is hoped to spread further eastward.

This emotive dimension of the HEART OF EUROPE concept is also prominent in the British public debate about Britain's relations to the EU in the 1990s: whilst there was no question of Britain being *in the heart of Europe*, the question of whether the nation could be *at its heart* attracted a fair amount of attention. As in the German *premature birth* debate, a prominent political utterance stood at the beginning of the public discussions. Just four months into his premiership, the successor of Margaret Thatcher as British Prime Minister and Tory Party leader, John Major, visited Germany and gave a speech in Bonn, in which he promised:

(28) [. . .] Britain would work "at the very heart of Europe" with its partners in forging an integrated European community. (G, 12 March 1991)

Over the following months, Major's *heart of Europe* slogan triggered a host of interpretations and variations, which were even more wide-ranging than those of Schröder's *premature birth* statement. But after only three months the *Economist* magazine was already asking: "how would Britain fare outside a single-currency area – and how does staying out square with *his oft-repeated wish to be 'at the heart of Europe'?*"; and it added presciently: "Those questions will not go away" (E, 22 June 1991). For a while, most comments followed the prime minister's lead and treated the scenario of Britain WORKING AT THE HEART OF AN INSTITUTION as equivalent to the notion of its BEING CLOSELY INVOLVED WITH IT. The political evaluations attached to this perspective of course differed strongly, according to the Euro-political preferences of commentators in Britain and Germany:

(29) Most galling of all, the British prime minister has decided that Britain is at the '*very heart of Europe*'. Here is a dangerous new twist to British pragmatism. (E, 23 March 1991)

(30) Statt außen vor zu bleiben, versucht Großbritannien unter ihm, *'im Herzen Europas' Politik zu machen*. (Z, 22 May 1992) [Rather than staying on the sidelines, Britain under him attempts to influence (literally: 'make') politics *'at the heart of Europe'*.]

(31) [Iain Vallance, chairman of British Telecom] urged the Government *to put Britain at the heart of Europe* and play a full part in debates over monetary union, employment, social costs [. . .]. (G, 16 November 1993)

(32) [. . .] if we cannot remind our politicians of their responsibilities, we can at least make plain to others how little they speak for us. With regard to foreign policy alone, *Great Britain has been at the heart of Europe far too long*. (I, letter to the editor; 16 August 1995)

In 1994, the joint parliamentary groups of the Christian Democratic Union (CDU) and Christian Social Union (CSU) parties, which formed part of the incumbent German government coalition, even used the reference to Major's statement in an EU-political manifesto to express their 'hope . . . that Britain should *play its role at the heart – i.e., at the core – of Europe*'.[21] The *Guardian* commented that this CDU/CSU paper was "by far the most important recognition by *a political body indisputably – as opposed to rhetorically – at the heart of Europe* that the Maastricht project will now be rethought" (G, 3 September 1994). The thinly disguised condemnation of the Conservative government as being 'only rhetorically at the heart of Europe' signalled that the dominant political interpretation of the BRITAIN-AT-THE-HEART-OF-EUROPE notion had changed. Major's promise from 1991 was by now seen as hollow.

In the following years, German media repeatedly quoted it as evidence of his apparent about-turn to a Euro-sceptical position, in a way not unlike their strategy of confronting Schröder with his former *premature birth* misgivings. *Die Zeit* even concluded 'that the British *never really put their heart into Europe*' and that Major 'who once declared he wanted to lodge Britain *at the heart of Europe,* had no firm conviction'.[22] In the British debate, similar attempts were made to remind Major of his erstwhile euro-enthusiasm,[23] but there were also more rhetorically sophisticated challenges to his BRITAIN-AT-THE-HEART-OF-EUROPE. Major's phrase was adapted to more pessimistic scenarios of a HEART FAILURE after the Pound Sterling's withdrawal from the European Exchange Rate Mechanism and delays in the ratification of the Maastricht Treaty had begun to slow down the integration process:

(33) *Coronary in Europe's new heart* [headline]. [...] after a currency debacle set up partly by the march towards Maastricht, it is almost comical for John Major to say to gleeful Euro-sceptics within the Conservative Party that the treaty is good for Britain. (E, 26 September 1992)

(34) [....] if Mr Major wanted to be *at the heart of Europe*, it was, presumably, *as a blood clot*. (I, 11 September 1994)

(35) [In the debate on Britain's obstruction policy in 1996 in the wake of the EU's boycott against British beef] Sir Edward Heath, the former prime minister, said that the non-co-operation policy had achieved nothing. *"The Prime Minister was right when he said Britain must be at the heart of Europe. But you can't be at the heart of Europe if you spend your time blocking its arteries,"* he said. (DT, 21 June 1996)

In these examples, the HEART concept is integrated into the ILLNESS scenario, and is thus treated specifically as a BODY ORGAN concept. By highlighting life-threatening physiological phenomena, such as coronary, blood clot or artery blockage, a particularly powerful double-effect of conceptual blending and analogical reasoning is achieved. The mental spaces of CENTRALITY and ILLNESS are combined to build an apparently conclusive argument: 'If you want to be central to the heart of a (political) body, then pursuing an obstruction policy will endanger the health of the heart and thus, of the whole body.'

As if such HEART FAILURE scenarios had not been enough to give the *heart of Europe* a bad name, a further damning version emerged with the publication of a strongly Euro-critical book written by the former EU official Bernard Connolly in 1995, entitled *The Rotten Heart of Europe*. It quickly captured the headlines of the British press,[24] and it led to his sacking by the EU Commission. The ROTTEN HEART scenario also constitutes a special blend, insofar as the long-standing and idiomatically well-established mapping: SOCIAL ENTITIES THAT HAVE DETERIORATED ARE ROTTEN/ROTTING ORGANISMS[25] is applied to the concept of HEART in its metaphorical meaning of the CENTRE and CHIEF ORGAN of the EU. It conveys a sense of a particularly dangerous and advanced type of DETERIORATION, which is hard to *heal*, if at all. It was in this sense that the ROTTEN HEART scenario was applied to the nepotism scandal which led to the mass resignation of the EU Commission under Jacques Santer in 1999:

(36) [...] changes in personnel will not be enough to stop the *rot at the heart of the EU*. There must also be reform of its institutions. (*Daily Mail*, 17 March 1999)

(37) The European Commission is undemocratic. *The truth is the rotten heart of Europe will never be cleaned out*. (*The SUN*, 17 March 1999)

Another variant of the HEART concept that suited the March 1999 scandal was that of a HOLE IN/AT THE HEART:

(38) [...] last week as *a hole suddenly opened up at the heart* of the European Union (I, 21 March 1999)

The *diagnosis* of a HOLE IN/AT THE HEART OF EUROPE on the occasion of the commission's resignation suggests that the EU Commission itself is seen here as the HEART of the EU. This reading is also supported by example (36) above, as well as by a number of other references to *the heart of the EU* without further elaboration.[26] This particular scenario leads to a neat analogical conclusion: CORRUPTION IN EU COMMISSION = HOLE or ROT IN/AT THE HEART OF ORGANISM, with the strong insinuation (made explicit in example 37) that the damage is irreparable.

By contrast with the British debate, DISEASED HEART metaphors are very rare in the German sample. In the pilot corpus we find one HEART token that refers to a row between the French and German governments over financial policy as 'the *real illness*, i.e. the *faulty cardiac valve behind the fainting fit*' (SZ, 16 June 1997: "der Kampf um Pakt und Kapitel hat erneut *die eigentliche Krankheit* dramatisiert – den *Herzklappenfehler* hinter dem *Schwächeanfall*"). In the EUROMETA II sample there is one single further characterization of the *heart of Europe* as *ill*. It is part of a quotation from an allegation by an extremist right-wing party that '*Germany, as the heart of Europe, is ill* due to its humiliation by the Western powers after World War II' (taz, 12 January 1990: "[...] die 'Verbiegung des Charakters des deutschen Volkes' durch die Siegermächte – *Wenn das Herz Europas krank ist, kann Europa nicht gesunden*"). There are a few references to the *cold* or *empty heart of Europe*[27] that fit folk-theories about the HARDENED or CLOSED HEART, which are based on the HEART-AS-PERSON metonymy and on the HEART-CONTAINER metaphor (Kövecses 1986, 1995; Niemeier 2000) but do not concern the HEART's SURVIVAL. The remainder are neutral or positive about the *heart of Europe's* STATE OF HEALTH, and a sub-section of 25 tokens is made up of references to British debates. Six of these mention the title of the above-mentioned book by Bernard Connolly (1995), translated variously as "Das kaputte" (*broken*) or "verrottete" (*rotten*) or "verkommene" (*depraved*) "Herz Europas", without, however, endorsing this strongly negative characterization.[28]

Even on the occasion of the 1999 nepotism scandal, which elicited as much critical coverage in Germany as it did in Britain, we find no equivalent of the British *rot at the heart of Europe* tokens. There is just one mildly ironical reference by the *Frankfurter Rundschau* to Tony Blair as a would-be *dragon slayer* [of the 'monster of EU-corruption'] *at the heart of Europe* (FR, 24 March 1999: "Drachentöter im Herzen Europas"). The article went on to praise Blair for 'really trying, unlike the Tories, to put Britain *at the heart of Europe*' ("Blair will, im Kontrast zu den britischen Konservativen, sein Land wirklich 'im Herzen Europas' ansiedeln"). This use of the phrase *putting Britain at the heart of Europe* with regard to Blair betrayed a good knowledge of the British debate on the EU at the time. Blair had 'inherited', as it were, the role of promoter of the *Britain at the heart of Europe* slogan from his predecessor Major. Since he was elected prime minister for the first time in May 1997, he has been quoted time and again restating Britain's claim to a place *at the heart of Europe*.[29] Together with that claim, he has inherited the challenges to it in the form of DISEASE/ILLNESS scenarios. Within less than two months of Blair's election, *The Guardian* published a comment on non-committal Labour's Euro-policies that echoed Heath's above-quoted reference to *blocked arteries* (cf. example 35):

(39) If Britain carries on laying down the law [on EMU] [. . .] while maintaining its opt-out, other EU regulars may get cheesed off. Britain may be advised *that it can't be at the heart of Europe if it is detached from its arteries*. (G, 10 June 1997)

At the end of Blair's first term of office, another *Guardian* article depicted Britain as it allegedly looked from the outside, i.e. from continental Europe:

(40) Having heard our press and politicians pour scorn and disdain on them for generations, the Europeans are exacting their revenge. They are seeing *Britain as Europe's sick man*, a charity case which needs their help. When the time finally comes for Tony Blair *to make good his promise to be "at the heart of Europe,"* he may find the dynamic has changed. Far from welcoming him as a young, energetic saviour, *the neighbours might offer him a look of pity and a cup of sweetened tea* – but

only after he has wiped his feet in a trough of disinfectant. (G, 4 April 2001)

Example (40) follows the pattern of integrating the phrase *heart of Europe* into ILLNESS/DISEASE scenarios, which had been set by the reinterpretations of Major's phrase (cf. examples 33–35). However, it goes further than they do in that it links the slogan of *being at the heart of Europe* and the *sick man of Europe* formula with an allusion to the 2001 "foot and mouth" epidemic in Britain, which necessitated public hygiene measures such as wiping one's feet in disinfectant when entering or leaving areas where livestock were present.[30] The connection between the HEART concept and the FOOT AND MOUTH EPIDEMIC scenario is rather tenuous. Still, the latter, by way of conceptual blending, provides a context of HEALTH/HYGIENE PROBLEMS that affects the understanding of the *heart of Europe* phrase, suggesting inferences that the EU might after all not want Britain to be *close to its heart* because of its perceived INFECTION.

The integration of the HEART concept into an ILLNESS/DISEASE scenario, which we have found in the preceding examples, not only introduces a particular thematic perspective but also special ironical viewpoint, due to the contrast of the optimistic *being/working at the heart*-appeal and the alleged probability of a GRAVE HEALTH RISK. This striking juxtaposition produces a sarcastic effect by exposing an apparent lack of realism on the part of the *heart of Europe* promoters/supporters. Some combinations of the HEART concept with other BODY PARTS, which are documented in EUROMETA II, also achieve striking contrasts, which leads to grotesque effects:

(41) These are just a handful of the issues which echo around Brussels' conference and dinner tables. There are many more in a similar vein – and one thing binds them together. *They bear no relationship to the British "debate", hearts, livers, gall bladders and all.* (G, 1 December 1997)

(42) The contempt with which the French government treats Britain [in the dispute over the "Sangatte" refugee camp near Calais] is beyond belief. *Tony Blair says he wants Britain to be at the heart of Europe. Well it looks this morning as if Europe is showing us its backside.* (*The SUN*, 3 September 2001)

The concepts GALL-BLADDER, LIVER and BOTTOM can hardly be said to be habitually associated with the BODY POLITIC of Europe (cf. their minimal token figures in Tables 16 and 18 above). But as parts of the general notion of BODY, they serve the purpose of ridiculing the *heart of Europe* phrase by way of foregrounding contrasting physiological allusions.

Apart from these idiosyncratic uses that are designed to achieve special rhetorical effects, there are formulations in the corpus in which an idiom comprising references to BODY PARTS other than HEART is applied to the EU as its target, namely the concepts EYES, HEAD, FEET and LEGS, and MUSCLES.[31] In terms of frequency they do not compare with the HEART metaphors; however, unlike examples (41) and (42) they provide genuine conceptualizations of the EU as a BODY. The most significant one is the scenario of *Europe* (metonymically standing for the EU's citizens and/or governments) SEEING, and thus BEING A WITNESS OF, problematic political developments, often with the suggestion that it has a moral obligation to contribute (more) to solving a problem, but has failed to fulfil that obligation:

(43) Fast vier Jahre nach dem Fall der Mauer hat Brüssel noch keine auch nur halbwegs konkreten Vorstellungen entwickelt, wie das ganze Europa aussehen soll. Maastricht ist der Versuch, das westliche Europa abzuschotten *und die Augen zuzumachen*. (taz, 3 August 1998). [Nearly four years have passed since the fall of the Berlin Wall and still Brussels has not developed any proper plan of what the whole of Europe should look like. [The Treaty of] Maastricht is nothing but an attempt to secure Western Europe and *close its eyes to the rest*.]

(44) In den letzten Jahren sind alle wesentlichen Probleme im ehemaligen Jugoslawien entweder mit Gewalt oder aber überhaupt nicht gelöst worden. Und dies alles geschah und geschieht *vor den Augen Europas*. (taz, 16 August 1997) [Over the last years, all really important political problems in the former Yugoslavia have been 'solved' either by brute force or not at all. And all this happened *before Europe's very eyes*.]

References to Europe's HEAD are more varied than those to the EYES. Two tokens are folk-geographical conceptualizations of Spain as *Europe's head*, as seen in historical paintings (FR, 16 July 1998 and 17 October 1998). Another two are idioms based on the metonymy: TYPICAL GESTURE for EMOTION, in this case: *to scratch one's head* (or the more drastic German version: *sich den Kopf zerbrechen*, 'to break one's head') for a STATE OF PERPLEXITY (E, 20 March 1995; BZ, 5 May 1998). The remaining tokens are contained in creative adaptations of a saying coined by Karl Marx about 'putting philosophy from the head onto the feet'. They highlight a perceived chance or necessity 'to put the EU back *from its head onto its feet'* ("Europa wieder *vom Kopf auf die Füße zu stellen"*) – in the sense of 'making Europe matter to the citizens on the ground rather than just to bureaucrats and politicians (taz, 19 December 1995; FAZ, 4 May 1995; FR, 13 February 1997; FR, 2 January 1998; MM, 11 May 2000).

This last usage type also accounts for all tokens of FEET, so that only LEGS and MUSCLES remain. The LEG metaphors, all of which come from the German sample, are idiomatic applications of the conceptual metaphor: STANDING UP IS BEING IN CONTROL/READY TO ACT, as in "Europa ist *auf den Beinen"* [Europe is *on its feet* (literally: *on its legs*)]; "[der] Euro *kommt nicht auf die Beine"* [the (weak) euro *is not back on its feet* (again, literally: *on its legs*)] (taz, 4 September 1992; MM, 8 June 1999). MUSCLES metaphors, which can be found in both national samples, play on idioms of *showing* or *growing muscles* as an indication of BODY STRENGTH, one example even supplying a rhyming headline that refers to a planned increase in the EU Commission and Parliament's competencies: "Muscles for Brussels" (E, 20 March 1999).[32]

5.5 Corpus data and conceptual metaphor

The analysis of the LIFE-HEALTH-BODY metaphor data shows that elements of conceptual source domains and their configurations in scenarios can be identified in general corpora by using keyword searches for pairs of lexical items that belong to the hypothesized source and target domains. This marks an advance from illustrative metaphor corpora that exemplify preconceived mappings. The EUROMETA II corpus allows us to formulate hypotheses about the elements and structures of particular conceptual domains in public discourse on the basis of data from two corpora (BoE and COSMAS) that were assembled independently and that are the best available approximation to representative corpora for press language in the respective languages.

On the other hand, the findings show that conceptual domains as such do not provide a sufficiently well-defined basis to explain the distribution patterns of source concepts that are characteristic for the respective discourse communities. The evidence from the LIFE-HEALTH-BODY domain data in EUROMETA II confirms the hypothesis from the pilot corpus data that within a domain central mappings and their corresponding scenarios have a privileged, prominent status. They account for most of the tokens of metaphorical concepts and for the cognitively and textually most elaborate variations. In the course of the public debate within a discourse community, micro-traditions of metaphor use emerge, in which specific scenarios and special formulations (e.g. *premature birth, being at the heart of Europe, Eurosclerosis, the sick man of Europe*) become the foci of further extensions, variations and reinterpretations. These emerging traditions culminate in 'conceptual contests', in which no major participant in the public debate can afford to remain silent; hence a sudden inflation of tokens for the respective scenarios in the corpus at particular points in the discourse history of that community. Some of these contests become so prominent that they are reported in a neighbouring discourse community (such as the British claims of being *at the heart of Europe* that were commented on in the German media). In the course of these debates, the ideological and argumentative bias of source concepts may change drastically. Thus, the initially positive *heart of Europe* phrase was turned against its authors in comments that highlighted *diseases* of or *injuries* to that *heart*; and Schröder's verdict on the euro's *birth problems* was quoted against him, as well as twisted around by himself to suit his rhetorical needs once he was installed as chancellor. By focusing on such traditions of use and their turning points, corpus-based metaphor analysis can highlight the argumentative tendencies and assumptions that are associated with specific scenarios, rather than remaining at the abstract level of source domains, which due to their generality are largely politically indifferent.

These results confirm criticisms of an exclusive reliance on the notion of inter-domain mapping as the defining characteristic of metaphor (Jackendoff and Aaron 1991; Stern 2000; Leezenberg 2001; Bartsch 2002). Whilst the domain-mapping model is plausible enough at the conceptual level, it needs to be translated into linguistic, semantic criteria in order to be applied to empirical discourse data. Modern semantic accounts (Kittay 1987; Stern 2000; Leezenberg 2001) can provide such criteria by defining metaphorical meaning constitution as context- or, in Kittay's terminology, "field"-dependent. Within this new model, lexical items documented in a corpus and their distribution patterns can be understood as indicators of specific, non-default thematic dimensions/perspectives that have been introduced into the discourse by speakers to achieve specific argumentative objectives. Whilst the argumentative orientation may change in the course of the debate due to extra-linguistic reasons, the semantic perspective that provides the basis for the metaphor constitution and its main foci, i.e. the dominant scenarios, remain structurally the same. It is thus at the level of documented *linguistic* data that major tendencies of metaphor usage within a discourse community can be identified and then interpreted as evidence of *conceptual* and *ideological* strategies that may be typical or significant for the respective discourse community.

The analysis of LIFE-HEALTH-BODY metaphors also showed that the most frequently used and argumentatively dominant source scenarios were based on metonymic and metaphoric blends and that their contextualization in texts often adds further dimensions of conceptual blending. The resulting conceptual structures are not directly deducible from either the source or the target input(s) but they suffice to constitute coherent discourse patterns that are characteristic for a given discourse community.

This model of corpus-based metaphor analysis does not imply an empiricist claim of sole reliance on primary observational data. Obviously, a high degree of interpretative hypothesis-building has gone into the selection of data. Nonetheless, the analytical distinction between the *semantic/linguistic* level of identifying the relevant discourse data and the *conceptual/cognitive* level, i.e. their interpretation as evidence of socially significant scenarios, allows us to make the various steps in the data analysis transparent and in principle empirically testable.

The corpus-based approach also opens a research perspective on *diachronic* processes of metaphorical concept-formation. Emergent discursive traditions, which eventually may lead to the lexicalization or quasi-lexicalization of metaphorical concepts (e.g. *Eurosclerosis, the sick man of Europe*), must first be manifested at the level of discourse phenomena. On this basis, conclusions can be drawn as regards the significance of conceptual traditions for a discourse community (at the "supraindividual" level, in Kövecses's terminology) and as regards their 'grounding' in experiential or cultural patterns (at the "subindividual" level). In the following chapter, an attempt will be made to analyse in more detail the dynamics of metaphor emergence and tradition-building with regard to the conceptualization of the EU as a HOUSE or a related type of CONSTRUCTION.

6
Discourse History in a Metaphor Corpus

6.1 Metaphor and discourse "evolution"

In the last chapter, we noted that some metaphorical formulations have a history of their own; e.g. the *sick man of Europe* phrase, which dates back to the seventeenth century, *Eurosclerosis*, which has been around for some 25 years, or the more short-lived depictions of the euro introduction as a *premature birth* and of British EU policies as attempts to lodge Britain *at the heart of Europe*. When we relate these specific formulations to the conceptual mapping INSTITUTIONS ARE ORGANISMS and its sub-mappings, their micro-histories in the 1990s turn out to be parts of long-standing traditions of thinking and speaking about politics and society within Western culture. Some of these can be traced back to antiquity, such as the notion of the GREAT CHAIN OF BEING, which, in the words of Alexander Pope, "from God began" and encompasses "Natures aethereal, human, angel, man, beast, bird, fish, insect, what no eye can see, no glass can reach; from Infinite to thee, from thee to nothing" (Pope 1994: 51). In this universal chain, 'higher-order' entities or structures (e.g. HUMAN SOCIAL INSTITUTIONS) can be metaphorically 'replaced' by 'lower-order' ones (e.g. ORGANISMS), because all are part of an overarching whole, in which not the tiniest link must be broken. The BODY POLITIC theories mentioned in the last chapter form part of this GREAT CHAIN concept.

The GREAT CHAIN OF BEING notion – or rather, complex of notions – has been shown by Arthur O. Lovejoy (1936) to connect ancient systems of ideas – via their neo-platonic, medieval and Renaissance reinterpretations – with modern thinking, reaching as far as nineteenth-century Romanticism and evolutionist theory (1936: 246–313). Lakoff and Turner (1989) have argued that its folk-theoretical version "still exists as a contemporary unconscious cultural model" (1989: 167).[1] For a corpus-based study, these conceptual traditions present at first similar problems to those discussed in chapter 4, i.e. how to operationalize the notion of conceptual and semantic structures (here: in the diachronic dimension) so as to identify and analyse them on the basis of corpus data. Except for a few special terms and phrases, such as the *sick man of Europe* formula, which may receive explanatory comments or glosses in the respective texts,[2] there are usually no explicit indicators for the relevance of specific conceptual traditions for the understanding of the respective metaphors.

This problem points to an even more fundamental question: on what basis can we posit the existence of conceptual and discursive traditions as regards metaphors? In chapter 2, the construct of a virtual conversation was introduced to capture the pragmatic coherence of public debates: they are viewed as a special type of discourse among debating parties that exchange their statements more often via the mass media than in face-to-face situations. Strictly speaking, this virtual conversation model only covers contributions to the public debate that refer explicitly to other contributions, such as, for instance, one participant's approval or rejection of a metaphor formulation used by other participants (for example, Mrs Thatcher's criticism of "misleading analogies") or ironical allusions to previous prominent uses (such as Major and Blair's *heart-of-Europe* promises or Schröder's *premature birth* warnings). For other uses that do not contain such explicit references, however, there is no immediate evidence of their being part of a tradition, even if they can be grouped together in a particular source domain or scenario. Thus, unless they happen to study the history of political thought, present-day users of the INSTITUTIONS ARE ORGANISMS metaphor cannot plausibly be expected to be aware of the BODY POLITIC or GREAT CHAIN OF BEING traditions that go back hundreds or thousands of years.

Even if a corpus such as EUROMETA II contains recurring manifestations of a metaphorical mapping in texts that cover a relatively brief period of time and often explicitly refer to each other, the data cannot be assumed a priori to provide evidence of conceptual traditions in the discourse community. Alternatively, they may for instance be regarded as 'generic' metaphors that are shared universally or almost universally, on account of being grounded in basic physiological or psycho-physical experience acquired in early childhood (cf. the 'primary' metaphors analysed by Grady, Taub and Morgan 1996; Grady and Johnson 2002). This kind of analysis, however, mainly concerns mappings of high generality (e.g. TIME PASSING IS MOTION), and in order to derive conclusions from it, corroborating evidence from the fields of biology, neurophysiology, and anthropology is required.

But this type of evidence does not answer the question of how cultural traditions, i.e. "supraindividual" conceptual traditions in the use of highly complex "individual" metaphors, such as our corpus data, can be accounted for. Long-term tendencies in discourse communities are observable not so much at the level of primary metaphors as at the level of characteristic configurations of complex metaphors – i.e. at the level of scenarios. We thus have to look for theoretical models that allow us to interpret metaphor scenario data in terms of their development as conceptual traditions. Traditionally, the diachronic development of concepts has been the object of the "history of ideas", be it in the form of phenomenologically and hermeneutically orientated versions of *Begriffsgeschichte* or *histoire des mentalités*, or in the vein of more pragmatically orientated Anglo-American "conceptual history".[3] Over the past decades, several new approaches have attempted to liken the concept of conceptual history to that of "evolution" in the biological sense established since Darwin, i.e. as a 'chain' of minimal changes in the genetic make-up of organisms, which are 'motivated' by ecological pressures. The application of the biological model of genetic adaptation in linguistics (and in the humanities in general) is by no means a recent phenomenon. Nineteenth-century linguistics, for instance, seized upon Darwin's theory and construed national languages as *organisms* that had 'familial' *lines of descent, life cycles, mutations* etc. (Hoenigswald and Wiener 1987; Nerlich 1989). Whilst these attempts relied on the classical version of Darwinist theory, the focus of more recent applications has shifted towards the application of insights from the modern genetic sciences. They interpret evolutionary changes in terms of the statistical distributions of genotypes in populations of life forms in an environment. In his 1976 book *The Selfish Gene*, Richard Dawkins proposed the concept of "memes" as cultural counterparts of genes. Like the latter, memes – e.g. "tunes, ideas, catch-phrases, clothes fashions, ways of building pots or of building arches" – are thought of as "replicators" of strings of information: "Just as genes propagate themselves in the gene pool by leaping from body to body via sperms or eggs, so memes propagate themselves in the meme pool by leaping from brain to brain via a process which, in the broad sense, can be called imitation" (Dawkins 1989: 192). In *The Extended Phenotype*, first published in 1982, Dawkins concedes that there are fundamental differences between genetic and cultural reproduction, but he maintains the validity of the basic analogy: like genes, memes are supposed to compete for optimal conditions of reproduction and diffusion. The more "vehicles" – i.e. human brains – a meme can replicate itself into, the better are its chances of survival; memes that do not replicate sufficiently are in danger of 'dying out' (Dawkins 1999a: 109–12). Likewise, Susan Blackmore in her 1999 book *The Meme Machine*, which provides a general outline of possible applications of Dawkins's hypothesis, concedes that genes and memes are "very different" in many respects; their comparability rests only on the functional aspect that "both are replicators, but they need not work in the same way" (Blackmore 1999: 17–18).

If the gene–meme analogy were to be validated, its potential for application to cultural phenomena would indeed revolutionize cultural and conceptual history: all kinds of symbol structures, including linguistic forms, are in principle conceivable as 'competitors' for dissemination by the greatest possible number of "vehicles" (i.e. human brains) and their phenotypical extensions (e.g. texts, mass media, Internet etc.). Blackmore (1999: 82–107) and Worden (2000) have used the notion of the meme to propose new theoretical approaches to the origin and general evolution of language and have sketched research programmes for analysing language structures, such as semantic role selection, typological patterns and morphological rules, in terms of their functional fitness for spreading memes as widely and quickly as possible. Gabora (1997) and Conte (2000) have designed mathematical models to account for the social dissemination and evolution of memes by individuals' minds as meme-evolving agents. So far, however, meme theory cannot claim to be based on independently corroborated scientific evidence; it rests essentially on an argument by (multiple) analogy. As Dawkins in his foreword to *The Meme Machine* explains, the meme concept was meant to persuade readers of *The Selfish Gene* of the notion "that the gene was only a special case" of the fundamental unit of selection, i.e. the "replicator", which could be "any unit of which copies are made, with occasional errors, and with some influence or power over their own probability of replication" (Dawkins 1999b: xvi). This supposition in turn rests on a further analogy between genetic distribution probabilities and purposeful action. Dawkins views genes as "perform[ing] a task analogous to prediction", but he himself insists that of course they "do not think of it as a prophecy, they do not think at all: they just build in a thick coat of hair [in the case of polar bears], because that is what they have always done before in previous bodies, and that is why they still exist in the gene pool" (Dawkins 1989: 55).

Talk of genes *predicting* and *performing* is thus in itself a metaphorical shorthand expression for statistical probability calculations of opportunities for gene reproduction. The gene–meme analogy is superimposed on this basic analogy, making it a kind of 'double-blend' metaphor. Its status as a secondary analogy does not invalidate the concept a priori but should be taken into account when talking of concepts as 'replicators' that are 'interested in' or 'intent on' propagation, just like the 'selfish' genes themselves. Even one of the staunchest defenders of an "intentional stance" in evolution theory and epistemology, Daniel C. Dennett,[4] concedes that "the prospects of elaborating a rigorous science of memetics are doubtful", but he maintains that "the prospect provides a valuable perspective from which to investigate the complex relationship between cultural and genetic heritage" (Dennett 1995: 369). The new perspective is characterized by a switch of attention from the vehicle's supposed interest (i.e. the survival and/or well-being of a single whole organism or a single Cartesian 'Self') to that of the replicator (i.e. genes or memes). The 'selfish gene' perspective is meant to help explain cases where evolutionary adaptation seems to work against the organism and to contradict evolution theory. From the "gene's eye point of view" seemingly extraordinary adaptations are still plausible as mechanisms to ensure the propagation of the gene in further generations. The same justification should hold, if we follow Dennett, for memetic approaches: "Only if meme theory permits us better to understand the deviations from the normal scheme will it have any warrant for being accepted" (Dennett 1995: 364).

However, as Dan Sperber (1996, 2000) and other critics have argued,[5] the crucial difference between the "replication" of genes and memes is still unaccounted for. Whereas genes are normally replicated with high fidelity, exact copying occurs rarely in the cultural sphere, e.g. in the exceptional cases of facsimiles, computer viruses and chain letters (Sperber 1996: 102–4). Consequently, conceptual structures have a vastly higher rate of change than genetic mutation.[6] The reason for the rapid change of concepts lies in their dependency on a continuous transformation from "mental" to "public representations" and vice versa as the only mode of reproduction available to their vehicles, i.e. human brains. In Sperber's view, this likens them to viruses rather than to genes:[7]

(1) Just as one can say that a human population is inhabited by a much larger population of viruses, so one can say that it is inhabited by a much larger population of mental representations. Most of these representations are found in only one individual. Some, however, get communicated: that is, first transformed by the communicator into

public representations, and then re-transformed by the audience into mental representations. A very small proportion of these communicated representations get communicated repeatedly. The question is: Why do some representations propagate, either generally or in specific contexts? To answer such a question is to develop a kind of 'epidemiology of representations'. The epidemiological metaphor can help us, provided we recognize its limits. (Sperber 1996: 25)

Sperber's proviso at the end of this passage is intended as a warning against reifications such as those invited by the meme–gene analogy. The change from mental to public representation and 'back' is modelled on *linguistic* communication, not on genetic reproduction in general or even on the mode of replication observed in epidemiology (Sperber 1996: 25). The conditions for the much more rapidly occurring transformations of representations are determined not just by the need to survive and propagate, as in the case of genes and viruses, but by the general tendency to produce "contents that require lesser mental effort and provide greater cognitive effects" (1996: 53), according to the principle of relevance (Sperber and Wilson 1995). This tendency of conceptual representations requires an explanation not in terms "of some global macro-mechanism" but in terms of "the combined effect of countless micro-mechanisms" (Sperber 1996: 54) that are amenable to empirical research.

Corpus-based cognitive analysis can provide an ideal testing ground for an epidemiological approach to cultural studies. The phenomena in question, that is, conceptual structures such as metaphors, can be observed and studied in the form of public representations, i.e. linguistic data distributed over a population (for example, in our case, the public discourse of a national discourse community as it is represented in a general corpus). These distribution patterns can be interpreted as the indicators of communicative transformations resulting from the interplay of the language users' representations, building up to traditions of use that can be related to political attitudes and argumentative trends in the respective discourse community. In this evolutionist perspective, the conceptual elements and scenarios that we have identified in the EUROMETA corpora can be understood as representations that compete for 'evolutionary' success in terms of the widest possible distribution among texts produced by the members of a discourse community.

As regards public discourse, this view is also pragmatically plausible, because it reflects to a large extent the intentions of its main participants. Both the politicians and the media are interested in the fastest and widest possible dissemination and acceptance of their representations (or, in 'epidemiological' terms: in the transformation of the public representations they produce into the mental representations of members of the general public). This interest on the part of the speakers probably accounts for the density of micro-changes in usage patterns that we observed in variations and reinterpretations of certain prominent metaphor formulations (e.g. the PREMATURE BIRTH and HEART DISEASE scenarios discussed in chapter 5). The 'competitive' pressure of the public debate may also be a key factor in the 'surfeit' of TWO-/MULTI-SPEED tokens we noted in chapter 3. The predominance of such tokens especially in British Euro-discourse, which regularly depicted Britain as the SLOW(EST) MOVER in the EU JOURNEY, seemed at first sight to contradict conclusions that by and large the British public (as it is represented in the print media) is more Euro-sceptic than, for instance, the German public. Here the 'meme's eye view' could perhaps provide an explanation: despite the fact that the TWO-/MULTI-SPEED scenario does not easily serve their communicative purposes, British politicians and media are 'compelled' to use its public representations because of its optimal flexibility in highlighting contrasts in the EU member states' commitment to political integration. Attempts to bend the logic of the SPEED COMPARISON, such as the one made by Michael Howard when appealing for support of his view that "Britain might be better off in what was falsely called 'the slow track'" (example 10 in chapter 3, p. 48), can be interpreted as adaptations to suit a specific communicative environment (i.e. Euro-sceptic discourse). The TWO/MULTI-SPEED scenario could be regarded as an example of a particularly successful 'competitor' in the 'pool' of EU-related metaphors.

The corpus-based analysis of conceptual metaphors from an evolutionist viewpoint provides, at least in principle, a chance to put to the test some of the hypotheses about cultural evolution formulated by Blackmore, Dennett and Sperber. These hypotheses concern: (a) explanations for the occurrence of seemingly 'exceptional' cases of conceptual development (e.g. the case of the TWO-SPEED metaphor discussed above); and (b) the spread of particular versions of a concept at the expense of others, understood as the "combined effect of countless micro-mechanisms" (Sperber 1996: 54). In order to formulate and substantiate these hypotheses about the evolution of public discourse, we need to rely on a corpus that comprises sufficient amounts of data to reconstruct the transformational steps between successive, dominant public representations of the concepts and scenarios in question. The

EUROMETA II corpus is an attempt to advance in this direction as regards the study of public discourse metaphors. Its advantage over a manually collected corpus such as EUROMETA I lies in its greater representativity, which results from the fact that it has been assembled from general corpora. This almost guarantees a much higher number of tokens for lexical items per conceptual scenario and domain, which in turn allows for more detailed analyses of frequency distribution patterns in sub-sets of the corpus (for example, in the English and German samples and in different time periods). However, EUROMETA II cannot yet give evenly matched accounts of the transformational steps from one set of dominant scenarios to the following one for both national samples, due to the imbalances between its 'mother corpora', BoE and COSMAS. Therefore, the conclusions about argumentative directions in the British and German discourse communities presented so far have had to remain tentative. In one case, however, EUROMETA II does provide sets of data that allow us to outline the contours of a corpus-based metaphor analysis of conceptual developments. This case is provided by data from the domain of ARCHITECTURE-HOUSE-BUILDING, in particular the concept of a (COMMON) EUROPEAN HOUSE. The analysis of the data for this domain will be at the centre of the following discussion.

6.2 The development of the EUROPEAN HOUSE metaphor in British and German Euro-debates, 1989–2001

The source concept of a BUILDING – or, more specifically, of a HOUSE – has been in use for some time to denote the entity 'Europe' in its geopolitical sense. Hugo Young (1998) quotes a speech by Winston Churchill from 1950 in which he advocated the establishment of a European army as a message "from the house of Europe to the whole world" (Young 1998: 74). It builds on traditions of metonymic identification between a political entity and the dynastic HOUSEHOLD (e.g. *the House of Windsor*) or other ruling institutions (e.g. the British Parliament as the *House of Commons*). The further conceptual background is provided by the ancient symbolization of a national-cum-religious community being a HOUSE for its God (as in the biblical concept of the HOUSE OF ISRAEL).[8]

The application of the BUILDING concept to a supranational political entity such as the EU includes a number of sub-mappings that cover its functional and structural aspects. Kövecses (2002) counts the domain of BUILDING among the most important source domains used for the conceptualization of abstract complex systems of any kind in terms of substances or things that we are familiar with from everyday experience, i.e. the "Complex systems metaphor" (2002: 127), which in turn fits into the GREAT CHAIN OF BEING metaphor system. Kövecses characterizes the central mapping of BUILDING-based conceptualizations of "abstract complex systems" as follows:

(2) CREATING A WELL-STRUCTURED AND LASTING ABSTRACT COMPLEX SYSTEM IS MAKING A WELL-STRUCTURED, STRONG BUILDING, which consists of several simple metaphors, such as CREATING AN ABSTRACT COMPLEX SYSTEM IS BUILDING, THE STRUCTURE OF AN ABSTRACT SYSTEM IS THE PHYSICAL STRUCTURE OF THE BUILDING, AND A LASTING ABSTRACT SYSTEM IS A STRONG BUILDING. (Kövecses 2002: 131)

The three "simple" mappings themselves represent a summary of a list of more detailed mappings that Kövecses has distilled from BUILDING-based metaphor idioms found in the Bank of English:

(3) (a) foundation ⇒ basis that supports the entire system
 (b) framework ⇒ overall structure of elements that make up the system
 (c) additional elements to support the framework ⇒ additional elements to support the structure of the system
 (d) design ⇒ logical structure of the system
 (e) architect ⇒ maker/builder of the system
 (f) process of building ⇒ process of constructing the system
 (g) strength ⇒ lastingness/stability of the system
 (h) collapse ⇒ failure of the system (Kövecses 2002: 111)

Kövecses' list is largely corroborated but also added to by the EUROMETA II data. Tables 19 and 20 below give the conceptual elements used in British and German Euro-debates and their frequencies as recorded in EUROMETA II. Again, as for Tables 16 and 17 in the preceding chapter, sub-totals are given in italics for subordinate conceptual categories, which contribute to the figures for the whole conceptual element category; overall figures are calculated only for the latter.

The enormous discrepancy between the British and German samples (see Table 20) can only partly be explained by differences in the overall size of the 'mother' corpora, BoE and COSMAS. Whilst the ratio between the two general corpora is roughly 1:3, the ratio here is between 1:6 and 1:7, depending on whether we count passages or tokens. The range of lexical items searched for each conceptual element was the same for both corpora. Even if some degree of distortion is allowed for, which

124 Metaphor and Political Discourse

Table 19 ARCHITECTURE-HOUSE-BUILDING source concepts in EUROMETA II[9]

Source concepts	English lexemes	German lexemes
ARCHITECTURE, ARCHITECT BLUEPRINT	architecture, architectural, architect plan, blueprint, drawing board	Architektur, Architekt, Konstrukteur Konzept, Baupläne, Reißbrett
(ABANDONED) BUILDING SITE	building site	Baustelle, Bauruine
FOUNDATION(S)	cornerstone, foundation	Fundament, Grundfesten, Grundstein
BUILDING MATERIAL	building blocks	Stein, Baustein, Sandstein, Mauerstein, Zement
PILLAR	pillar	Pfeiler, Eckpfeiler, Säule
WALLS	walls	Mauern, Wände
BUILDING (B)	edifice	
B: CHURCH BUILDING	temple	Kathedrale
B: CASTLE/PALACE		Disneyschloß
B: HIGH-RISE BUILDING		Wolkenkratzer, Turm
B: TOWER OF BABEL		Turm von Babel
B: BRIDGE	bridge, bridgebuilding	Brückenschlag
(COMMON EUROPEAN) HOUSE	(Common European) house	(Gemeinsames Europäisches) Haus
DOOR, BACKDOOR, GATE (D/G)	door, exit	Tür, Hintertür, Tor
D/G: GATEKEEPER		Torwächter
WINDOW (TO EUROPE)	window	Fenster (nach Europa)
ROOF	roof	Dach
GABLE		Giebel
HOME	home, shelter	
ROOM(S) (R)		Räume, Zimmer
R: ANTE-ROOM		Vorzimmer
R: KITCHEN		Küche
R: STUDY		Arbeitszimmer
R: LIVING ROOM		Wohnzimmer
R: DRAWING-ROOM		Salon
R: JUNK ROOM		Rumpelkammer
BALCONY		Balkon
CELLAR		Kellerräume
REFUSE DUMP		Müllgrube
YARD	backyard	Hof, Hinterhof, Vorhof
GARDEN/ALLOTMENT		Hintergarten, Schrebergarten
CARETAKER		Hausmeister
FURNITURE		Möbel
(RIGHT OF) TENANCY (T)		Dauerwohnrecht
T: TENANT	people, tenants	Mieter, Untermieter, Bewohner der Beletage
T: LANDLORD	landlord	
T: RENT	rent	Miete

Table 20 Tokens for ARCHITECTURE-HOUSE-BUILDING source concepts in EUROMETA II in order of overall frequency

Source concepts	Tokens in British sample	Sub-total	Tokens in German sample	Sub-total	Tokens overall
(COMMON EUROPEAN) HOUSE	34		283		317
DOOR/GATE	26		161		187
D/G: GATEKEEPER				1	
FOUNDATION	4		56		60
ARCHITECT/ARCHITECTURE	18		27		45
WINDOW	1		22		23
WINDOW TOWARDS EUROPE				11	
ROOF	1		18		19
BUILDING SITE	3		12		15
ABANDONED BUILDING SITE				2	
BUILDING	5		9		14
B: BRIDGE		4		1	
B: HIGH-RISE BUILDING/				2	
B: TOWER OF BABEL				3	
B: CHURCH BUILDING				2	
B: CASTLE/PALACE				1	
ROOMS			13		13
R: JUNK ROOM				1	
R: ANTE-ROOM				1	
R: KITCHEN				1	
R: STUDY				1	
R: LIVING ROOM				1	
R: DRAWING-ROOM				2	
YARD	1		12		13
WALLS	1		10		11
(RIGHT OF) TENANCY	4		7		11
T: TENANT/LODGER		2		5	
T: LANDLORD		1			
T: RENT		1		1	
BLUEPRINT	7		3		10
BUILDING MATERIAL	1		8		9
APARTMENT			6		6
FURNITURE			3		3
HOME	2				2
REFUSE DUMP			2		2
GARDEN/ALLOTMENT			2		2
GABLE			1		1
CELLAR			1		1
BALCONY			1		1
CARETAKER			1		1
TOTALS	108		658		766
Number of passages	89		583		672

may have led to the omission of data from the BoE sample (e.g. morphological variants or instantiations of specialized concepts), it is evident that the ARCHITECTURE-HOUSE-BUILDING domain is represented to a much higher degree in German than in British public debates on European politics. This confirms Schäffner's (1996: 40–1) hypothesis that "references to architects and construction workers, lexicalized as 'Union architects'" as well as the "house" metaphor itself are "more popular in Germany than in Britain".

When we compare the list of concepts in Table 19 with Kövecses's summary of mappings for the conceptual metaphor AN ABSTRACT COMPLEX SYSTEM IS A BUILDING, there are some clear matches. The sources for mappings in Kövecses' list are amply manifested in the corpus data. But some additional aspects are also represented, in particular the PREPARATION aspect, which comprises the notions of ARCHITECTURAL PLANNING, BLUEPRINT, BUILDING SITE etc., as well as the concept of a HOUSE as a PLACE WHERE PEOPLE LIVE TOGETHER (as it is manifested in the various sub-aspects of the TENANCY concept). The reverse of the latter notion is also represented, i.e. the concept of the (EU'S) HOUSE as a PLACE FROM WHICH PEOPLE ARE EXCLUDED, e.g. STANDING/WAITING IN FRONT OF THE DOOR/GATE. This last-mentioned aspect accounts for the substantial number of tokens of the DOOR/GATE concept (cf. Table 20) relating to descriptions of non-EU nations or non-EU citizens (migrant workers or refugees) who *wait outside* or are *being kept outside the EU/EU borders* or also *outside EMU*.[10] Using Kövecses's list of mappings and their elements (cf. above examples 2 and 3) as a starting point and including the aforementioned further aspects, we can draw up a list of scenarios as far as they are represented in the corpus:

6.i ARCHITECTURE-HOUSE-BUILDING scenarios in EU-debates

(a) A POLITICAL/ECONOMIC STRUCTURE FOR THE EU (as a special case of an ABSTRACT COMPLEX SYSTEM) IS A BUILDING (i.e. usually: A HOUSE)
(b) THE STRUCTURE OF THE EU IS THE PHYSICAL STRUCTURE OF THE BUILDING
(c) CREATING A LASTING POLITICAL/ECONOMIC STRUCTURE FOR THE EU IS USING GOOD MATERIALS AND WORKING TO A WELL THOUGHT-OUT ARCHITECTURAL PLAN/BLUEPRINT
(d) AS LONG AS THE POLITICAL/ECONOMIC STRUCTURE IS NOT YET COMPLETE, THE EU IS A BUILDING SITE
(e) THE EXISTING EU NATIONS ARE *IN* THE BUILDING (e.g. as TENANTS/OWNERS)
(f) NON-EU NATIONS (AND THEIR CITIZENS) ARE *OUTSIDE* THE BUILDING (e.g. OUTSIDE THE DOOR/GATE, IN THE YARD)

The HOUSE concept is implicitly represented in all scenarios and, as Table 20 shows, is indeed the overall most frequent explicitly mentioned domain element. It is particularly typical of the German debates in the 1990s: it makes up 43 per cent of all tokens in the German sample (compared with 31 per cent in the British sample). However, its prominence is derived not only from German usage – what made the HOUSE metaphor an international 'star-metaphor' for a while was in fact its adoption by Mikhail Gorbachev, then the general secretary of the Soviet Communist Party and leader of the Soviet Union. From the mid-1980s, he had employed the formulation *Common European House* to promote the political vision of a collaborative way of living together for the European nations, by analogy with an *apartment* or *tenement block* whose *inhabitants* respected each other's *independence* and were ready *to help each other in times of need* (Gorbachev 1987: 61; 1989: 252–4).

The significance of Gorbachev's metaphor for international politics has been noted and analysed in a number of studies.[11] The debates about it provided the background for the discussions about the EU as a *common house* in the 1990s. We thus have a unique opportunity to investigate the emergence and establishment of a specific metaphor tradition in sufficient detail to develop explanatory hypotheses about the main phases and turning points in its conceptual transformations.

The slogan of the *Common European House* is attested in COSMAS since 1985. For the (West) German public, its general appeal had a specific meaning and poignancy, as it could easily be applied to the relationship between the then still separated two German states. The president of the Federal Republic, Richard von Weizsäcker, used the metaphor as a central reference point in his talks with Gorbachev, when he visited Moscow in 1987. In their conversation (as it has been represented by Gorbachev in retrospect), the European states figured as *neighbouring apartments*, with the peoples as the respective *tenants*. The *apartments*, Gorbachev explained, should become more *accessible for reciprocal visits* but should not be the targets of *surprise calls*. Weizsäcker treated the two German states as a *single flat* with a divided *living room:*

(4) *R.v.Weizsäcker:* Es ist ein Bezugspunkt, der uns hilft vorzustellen, *wie die Dinge in diesem gemeinsamen europäischen Haus geregelt werden sollten.* Speziell, was den Umfang betrifft, *in dem die Wohnungen darin für gegenseitige Besuche zugänglich sein werden.* – *M.Gorbachev:* Sie haben ganz recht. Doch möglicherweise *möchte nicht jeder in der Nacht Besucher empfangen.* – *R.v.W.:* Wir sind auch nicht besonders

glücklich darüber, *daß sich ein tiefer Graben durch ein gemeinsames Wohnzimmer zieht.* (Gorbachev 1989: 259)

[*R.v.W.:* It is an important point of reference that helps us to see how things should be organized in the *common European house,* especially as regards the rights of *reciprocal visits from one apartment to another.* – *M.G.:* You are quite right, but not everyone might like *to receive visitors at night.* – *R.v.W.:* We are not particularly happy either *that a big ditch runs right through one communal living-room*].

By the early 1990s, however, with the dissolution of the East German state and the disintegration of the Warsaw Pact and the Soviet Union, which also led to the loss of power for Gorbachev personally, his COMMON EUROPEAN HOUSE concept had started to lose its political appeal. From the cognitive perspective, the ups and downs in the international career of Gorbachev's vision provide fascinating material to formulate hypotheses about conceptual contests across diverse political cultures. Paul Chilton, George Lakoff and others[12] have analysed the Western reception of the *Common European House* slogan as a clash of two distinct, culturally bound ways of conceptualizing states as *houses*: on the one hand, the Soviet/Russian concept of *dom* ['house'], which is "typically associated with a communal tenement block containing separate individual apartments" vs the concept of "a one-family owner-occupied house: a free-standing box-like structure on its own fenced land", assumed to be prevalent in "the United States, Britain and perhaps other parts of Western Europe" (Chilton and Lakoff 1995: 54). According to this analysis, the Russian associations of *dom* – i.e. "collective responsibility, a plurality of separate independent units but common structure (roof, entrance, etc.)" – were replaced in the Western reception by "entailments" that were typical for "American, German, French" settings, namely, "a single unit, a family structure, no internal separations, no common structure, boundary walls or fences" (1995: 54).

This hypothesis about conceptual differences between Russian and Western political cultures can be formulated in two versions. In the 'strong' version, the two contrasting discourses would be seen as each 'allowing' only for one set of "entailments" of the HOUSE metaphor, which would be incompatible with each other. This version is implausible, given the high degree of internationalization of modern political discourse, which ensures the rapid dissemination and translation of prominent slogans, terms and metaphors across various languages. Furthermore, the strong hypothesis can be falsified empirically on the basis of EUROMETA II data: the corpus contains a small but significant number of British and German tokens that *do* include the COMMON HOUSE-AS-TENEMENT BUILDING mapping, as in the following examples:

(5) [...] [Germany] is clearly interested in bringing Eastern Europe and the Soviet Union into the European Community, *to become new tenants of the common European house. There, the united Germany probably won't be the landlord, but it's highly likely to be the one collecting the rent.* (T, 22 September 1990)
(6) Nationale Identität ist so notwendig wie *die eigene Wohnung und die sollte im vielzitierten Haus Europa bezogen werden ohne Untermieter.* (taz, 1 December 1989) [National identity is as essential as *one's own apartment in the much-cited European House, and one should move/live in this apartment without having a lodger.*]

As the figures in Table 20 show, these are by no means the only examples of TENANCY-related concepts in the German or British samples. Thus, any strong version of the hypothesis about exclusive "entailments" in national discourses is refuted.[13] On the other hand, the figures for TENANCY tokens are not particularly high and they can hardly be deemed to be 'dominant' in British and German discourses. A 'weak' version of the hypothesis about Russian–Western differences in understanding Gorbachev's metaphor is therefore still possible, i.e. the proposition that the contrasting meaning aspects are more typical of one discourse than of the other. To strengthen it, the contrasting meaning aspects should be understood as (stereo-)typical presuppositions rather than as logically binding "entailments". Expectations regarding 'normal' housing conditions in a given culture are most likely to function as background assumptions that are associated with the concept of HOUSE on an experiential basis. It could then be argued that in Russian public discourse a phrase like *Common (European) house* typically evokes concepts of a TENEMENT BLOCK with many TENANTS, whereas in Western countries (particularly in the Anglo-American context), this association is not equally strong/immediate. One could expect the Russian HOUSE version to appear briefly in Western discourses at the time of its greatest international prominence and then to become marginal and to be replaced by Western versions. In this context, it is of interest to look at the distribution of tokens for the respective concepts over time; the figures of tokens available from BoE and COSMAS are given in Tables 21 and 22.

The distribution of occurrences of tokens instantiating the notion of COMMUNAL EUROPEAN HOUSE TENANCY in the British and German

Table 21 COMMON-EUROPEAN-HOUSE and TENANCY source concepts in the British sample of EUROMETA II

Source concepts/Years	1989	1990	1991	1992	1993	1994	1995	1996	1997	1998	1999	2000	2001
COMMON EUROPEAN HOUSE	11	4	1			1							1
EUROPEAN HOUSE (not COMMON EUROP. HOUSE)	2	2				3		1	1	1	3	3	
APARTMENT													
(RIGHT OF) TENANCY		1	1										
TENANT/LODGER		1											
LANDLORD		1											
RENT		1											

Discourse History in a Metaphor Corpus 131

Table 22 COMMON-EUROPEAN-HOUSE and TENANCY source concepts in the German sample of EUROMETA II[14]

Source concepts/ Years	1989	1990	1991	1992	1993	1994	1995	1996	1997	1998	1999	2000	2001
COMMON EUROPEAN HOUSE	34	16	2		1	2	5	1	5	1	9	3	
EUROPEAN	20	29	5	4	8	4	11	16	38	31	15	14	9
HOUSE (= *not* COMMON EUROP. HOUSE)				1			1					1	
APARTMENT	2						1		1			1	
(RIGHT OF) TENANCY										1		1	
TENANT/ LODGER	1	1							1	2		1	
LANDLORD													
RENT		1										1	

samples as shown in Tables 21 and 22 shows that the 'weak' hypothesis about an East–West clash of EUROPEAN HOUSE concepts has to be specified and differentiated further. As regards the particular conceptual element of TENANCY, it is effectively disproved: this conceptual aspect can be found in both national samples, and in the German discourse it continues to appear long after the demise of Gorbachev's policies, e.g. in a commentary on the preparations for the EU enlargement process:

(7) Die *Nachbarn* in der geographischen Mitte des Kontinents möchten so bald wie möglich ihren *Mietvertrag* unterschrieben haben. Ihr Problem ist, dass [. . .] die Öffentlichkeit zwar den *Hochglanzprospekt des Westflügels kennt, den Zustand des sie betreffenden Teils der Baustelle aber nicht so genau und das Kleingedruckte (Kosten, Umlagen, Hausordnung) nur in groben Zügen.* (FR, 2 March 2000).[15] [The EU's *neighbours* in the geographical centre of Europe want to have their *tenancy contract* signed as soon as possible. It is, however, a problem for them that their public know *the glossy brochures about the Western wing [of the European House] better than their own part of the building site and are only vaguely aware of the small-print details (rent, communal costs for services and house rules).*]

Apart from the TENANCY-aspect, the overall figures for tokens of the COMMON EUROPEAN HOUSE and the EUROPEAN HOUSE concepts in Tables 21 and 22 seem to bear out the weak hypothesis. After 1991–92, Gorbachev's vision continued to be mentioned occasionally in historical reminiscences, but as a topical policy issue it was soon supplanted by a new initiative, i.e. the reconstitution of the EC as the *European House*. As early as April 1990, the EC Council of Ministers claimed the TITLE to the EUROPEAN HOUSE for themselves, stating that German unification 'was achieved under a *European roof*' ("Wir freuen uns, daß die Vereinigung Deutschlands unter einem europäischen Dach stattfindet", *Presse- und Informationsamt der Bundesregierung*, Bonn, 28 April 1990). This would have been a trivial statement in a mere geographic sense, but it was of high relevance with regard to the fact that the former GDR, by being subsumed in the Federal Republic, was also integrated into the Community. This *European roof* was the ROOF of the EC's HOUSE, not of Gorbachev's pan-European vision. A commentator in the *Frankfurter Allgemeine Zeitung* even drew the conclusion that the newly envisaged EUROPEAN HOUSE did not need to cover all of the available geographical *floor space: a tower building* on less *ground space* would suffice:

(8) Wenn von einem *europäischen Haus* gesprochen wird, *so denkt man, daß das Dach vielleicht so groß sein müsse wie die Grundfläche. Insofern ist das Bild schief. Ein schlanker Turm mag für das, was wirklich gemeinsam – also politisch – geschehen muß, völlig ausreichen.* (FAZ, 29 September 1990) [When people speak of the *European House,* they assume that perhaps *the roof must equal the floor space. In this regard, the metaphor is misleading.* A *slender tower* may well be sufficient to achieve those objectives that really need co-operation, i.e. the political aims.]

The Maastricht Treaty, negotiated in the following year, introduced further *building* terminology by distinguishing three *pillars* of decision making in the EU: "greater powers to the Council of Ministers and the European Parliament, a common foreign and security policy [...], and a parallel process covering police and judicial co-operation" (G, 7 February 1992).[16] A German government advert, published in newspapers, hailed the Treaty as a *reinforcement* of the *foundations* of an already *well-built European house construction*:

(9) Die Europäer haben sich [...] mit der Europäischen Gemeinschaft *ein stabiles Haus gebaut.* Der Vertrag von Maastricht bringt eine weitere *Festigung seines Fundaments*, nämlich die Fortentwicklung der EG. [...] *Das Dach über allem* ist die neu geschaffene 'Europäische Union'. (Z, 18 December 1992) [The Europeans have *built* the European Community as *a solid house.* The Treaty of Maastricht provides a further consolidation of its *foundations,* i.e. the development of its institutions. *The roof over the whole construction* is the newly created European Union.]

There were, of course, also critical voices. One commentator denounced the hubris of Eurocrats who, like the *builders* of the *Tower of Babel,* suffered from a delusion that they were *master architects* (Z, 10 January 1992: "*Handlanger, die sich heute gern als Architekten Europas bezeichnen*"). Another critic saw an *abandoned building site* in the place of an existing – or at least planned – *Common European house* (taz, 6 November 1991: "das [...] '*Gemeinsame Haus*' [ist] keine Lösung [...], denn heute schon zeigt sich wieder einmal, daß dieses Europa *nur noch einer Bauruine gleichkommt*").

However, such critical uses of the EU-AS-A-HOUSE metaphor were rare up to 1997. The majority of examples from that period are references to the EU as a *well-built* or *well-planned house,* and the German government in particular saw it as an appealing vision to persuade other European states to join in the *construction* process:

(10) [. . .] Dr Kohl said he intended using his country's presidency and the subsequent ones of France and Spain to draft plans for a full-scale political union [. . .]. "We want a Europe that's not just an elevated free trade area, but *the construction of a house of Europe as laid down in the Maastricht treaty.*" (G, 6 July 1994)

(11) Kohl erklärte, [. . .] [vor] allem Christdemokraten [. . .] seien die *Architekten des heutigen Hauses Europa* gewesen. Nun gehe es darum, *dieses Haus für künftige Generationen zu stabilisieren*. (MM, 24 July 1995) [Kohl stated that it had been mainly Christian Democrats who had been the *architects of the present European House. Now it was important to stabilize this house for the benefit of future generations.*]

At the same time as the EU-AS-A-HOUSE metaphor was being vigorously promoted, the notion of the COMMON EUROPEAN HOUSE received nostalgic acknowledgement in Germany, e.g. as 'a myth' that had become obsolete (W, 22 May 1993: "Das Ende eines Mythos: *Abschied von der Idee des einen Gemeinsamen Europäischen Hauses*"). In Britain, Gorbachev's metaphor was even openly ridiculed:

(12) Mikhail Gorbachev's *Common European House* always raised heckles *(as anyone who has ever shared a flat with a large, aggressive, rather untidy person with little money will understand)*. (I, 11 September 1994)

Towards the end of the decade the corpus shows only historical references to the once-prominent Gorbachev-slogan in the German sample (examples 13, 14); the one token for 2001 in the British sample is in fact an application of the *Common European House* formula to the EU (example 15):

(13) Doch *sowie das "gemeinsame Haus Europa" beschworen wurde*, geriet die Position der DDR ins Wanken. (BZ, 23 March 1999) [As soon as *the 'Common European House'* was invoked [by Gorbachev], the political status of the GDR began to crumble.]

(14) Das *gemeinsame Haus Europa* war in diesen Monaten 1989/90 bereits Realität. (FR, 1 November 1999) [The *Common European House* became a reality during these months of 1989/1990.]

(15) The present generation of European leaders [...] have been trying *to build a 'common European house' by starting with the monetary roof and working their way down.* (T, 5 July 2001)

The persiflage of Gorbachev's concept in example (12), its historical use in (13) and (14) as well as the uncommented reapplication to the EU as the target topic in (15) show that British and German qualms about the COMMON EUROPEAN HOUSE were in fact not caused by misunderstandings or ignorance of the Russian version of the source concept HOUSE. Rather, they were evidence of a conscious rejection of the former Soviet leader's pan-continental plans. This Western rejection was motivated by political reasons (lingering mistrust of Soviet ideology and Gorbachev's loss of power, which made him a less attractive partner for negotiation), and conceptually it could be expressed as cogently in terms of a TENANCY-related scenario as the Russian proposals (cf. examples 5 and 6).

What mattered for its change in usage was not so much a 'global' clash of concepts but the fact that the role of TENANT in the TENANCY scenario, which had been available to the Soviet Union/Russia in the original proposal, did not fit the perspective of Western European governments in the years following 1990. By the middle of the decade, Helmut Kohl, whose government had arguably derived the greatest profit from Gorbachev's pan-European plans (i.e. national unification for Germany), made a special point of not excluding no European nation from the new EU HOUSE – with the singular exception of Russia:

(16) Zur künftigen Rolle Deutschlands in Europa meinte Kohl: "Ich sage in einem einfachen Bild, daß *wir in einem festen Haus Europa leben."* Darin hätten alle Völker nach ihren Bedürfnissen ihre Wohnungen. [...] *In diesem Haus Europa könne Rußland keinen Mitgliedsplatz haben.* Denn Rußland gehe von Wladiwostok bis an die polnisch–russische Grenze. (W, 11 May 1995). [Kohl described the future role of Germany in Europe: 'To say it in a simple metaphor, we live in a *solid European house.*' There were apartments for all nations in it, according to their needs. However, there was no room for Russia in this house, for Russia extended from Vladivostok to the Polish–Russian border.]

The political motivation of the conceptual change in the HOUSE metaphor is thus made explicit: Russia has become a TENANT *non grata,* officially because of its geographical outsider position but probably also because of its changed political status. In terms of the HOUSE concept, it has joined the ranks of other Eastern European 'problem nations' whose TENANCY rights in the EUROPEAN HOUSE have been questioned from time to time, despite their undisputed geographical status as parts of the European continent. This notion of the Eastern 'outsider' nations that are excluded from *entry* into – let alone *right of abode* or *tenancy* in – the EUROPEAN HOUSE is the opposite perspective to the HEART OF EUROPE solidarity appeals discussed in chapter 4:

(17) [. . .] Europa, das *sein 'gemeinsames Haus' anscheinend ohne die balkanischen* (albanischen, bulgarischen, rumänischen, slowenischen, kroatischen, serbischen usw.) *Bewohner geplant hat.* (taz, 5 March 1994) [Europe, which apparently plans *to build its 'common house' excluding the Balkan inhabitants* (Albanians, Bulgarians, Rumanians, Slovenians, Croatians, Serbians etc.)].

(18) [Vaclav Havel, then President of the Czech Republic in a joint interview with the former EU Commission president Jacques Delors:] "*Ich fürchte schon lange, dass die osteuropäischen Völker, die seit Jahren an den Türen Europas anklopfen, müde werden* und sich am Ende sogar auflehnen gegen dieses reiche und arrogante Europa." (Z, 1 February 2001) ["I have been afraid for a long time that the *Eastern European nations may tire of knocking at Europe's doors* and might eventually rebel against this rich, arrogant Europe."]

(19) The Yugoslav Deputy Prime Minister, Miroljub Labus, warned that *Europe would close its door to Yugoslavia*, [. . .]. (T, 26 June 2001)

On the basis of the EUROPMETA II data, we can draw some conclusions about changes in the EUROPEAN HOUSE concept in British and German public discourse over the 1990s. As Tables 21 and 22 show, the years 1989–1990 mark the climax and at the same time the effective ending of the 'discourse career' of Gorbachev's pan-European vision. With the disintegration of Soviet power, its popularity goes into steep decline, whilst rival versions of the HOUSE COMMUNITY scenario, which have the EC/EU as target input, increase rapidly. Non-EU nations that belong geographically to Europe are perceived as OUTSIDERS, who (with the exception of Russia, cf. example 16) may have a future chance of being allowed into the EUROPEAN HOUSE, by way of an EXTENSION OF THE ALREADY EXISTING HOUSE. This marks a clear change from the scenario of a PAN-EUROPEAN HOUSE that *already* comprised all nations as TENANTS who needed more mutual contact (cf. example 4). The change is not so much the result of a culturally motivated clash of source scenarios (COMMUNAL TENEMENT BLOCK VS SINGLE-FAMILY DWELLING) but rather the outcome of a conceptual contest in which the Western version 'won out' due to political context-conditions. The newly dominant target-mapping THE EC/EU IS ONE BUILDING/HOUSE allows for both single and communal TENEMENT scenarios as well as for further special versions such as those of a TOWER or an (ABANDONED) BUILDING-SITE.

Whilst the tokens for the *Common European House* formula in EUROMETA II dwindle away over the second half of the 1990s, the EU-AS-A-HOUSE metaphor peaks in the German sample in 1997–1998 (cf. Table 22). This increase in popularity is probably due to a factor that we have already encountered in cases such as the PREMATURE BIRTH and HEART OF EUROPE scenarios – that is, prominence of the situation of use and/or of the user. In this case, it was the incumbent German Federal Chancellor until 1998, Helmut Kohl, who 'promoted' the HOUSE concept almost singlehandedly to the status of a central category in German Europolitical debates. The German EUROMETA II sample has a total of 40 passages in which Kohl is quoted advocating the (speedy) *construction/completion* of the *house of Europe* ("Haus Europa"). His tireless promotion of the EU-AS-A-HOUSE concept doubtless helped Kohl's reputation for being both the *architect* (as well as the *father* – cf. chapter 2) of the EU and EMU,[17] but it also earned him some ridicule as a man who was obsessed with being in control of 'his' EUROPEAN HOUSE.[18]

In terms of its 'discourse career', any mentioning of the HOUSE scenario – whether positive or ironical – was advantageous, but even more so was the explicit argumentative adoption of Kohl's already prominent version by commentators and political rivals who wanted to challenge the scenario in detail. In the last two years of his term of office, when he was confronted with the daunting prospect of EU enlargement and problems in meeting the Maastricht Treaty criteria for joining the euro, Kohl had to endure similar challenges to his favourite metaphor as Gorbachev, Major, Blair and Schröder had to suffer in the case of theirs. The SOLID HOUSE scenario version was effectively taken apart:

(20) [Kohl] glaubt an seine Bilder: *"Das Haus Europa wird gebaut, jetzt und nicht irgendwann". Daß die Architektur nicht stimmt, daß dieses Haus ohne neues Fundament zu brüchig ist, um demnächst fünf oder gar zehn neue Mitbewohner aus Osteuropa zu tragen* – das weiß auch Kohl [. . .]. (Z, 20 December 1996) [Kohl believes in his metaphors: *"The house of Europe is being built now – not sometime in the future."* But he knows full well that *the blueprint is not right, that this house is unfit to receive five or even ten new tenants from Eastern Europe if it does not get new foundations.*]

(21) Edmund Stoiber [= Bavarian Minister President and leader of the sister/rival-party of Kohl's CDU, the "Christian Social Union" (CSU)] plagt eine bedrückende Vorstellung. *Die Front des europäischen Hauses könnte ein solider Bau in deutscher Wertarbeit sein, Seitenflügel und Rückgebäude aber aus Holzverschlägen und Pappmaché, beigesteuert von den Italienern und Franzosen. Die Deutschen dürfen das Gebäude dann mit ihrem Geld sanieren.* (SZ, 11 September 1997) [Edmund Stoiber is haunted by one vision: *The European house might be built solidly, i.e. 'made in Germany' on its facade, but the wings and rear-buildings would be of wood or papier-mâché, supplied by the Italians and the French. The Germans would then be left to pay for the necessary renovation afterwards.*]

Whereas in example (20) Kohl's EUROPEAN HOUSE concept was at least taken seriously, though seriously challenged, Stoiber in (21) used it mainly as a point of reference to develop his scenario version of a CONSTRUCTION OF POOR QUALITY (IN ITS NON-GERMAN PARTS), in order to insinuate that Germany was in danger of being duped by other nations. Despite criticism of his scenario as xenophobic (Z, 3 October 1997), Stoiber continued to exploit the BAD CONSTRUCTION theme. He told a CSU party congress that the EU's enlargement strategy of "simply adding storeys or extending the European house" was "no solution" (G, 22 November 1997). Apart from alluding to prejudices about other nations, Stoiber's scenario version of a POORLY BUILT EU HOUSE implied the assumption that the STRUCTURAL STABILITY OF THE HOUSE was not guaranteed, thus contradicting essential parts of Chancellor Kohl's set of presuppositions, which included a firm belief in the SOLIDITY OF THE CONSTRUCTION. Stoiber pursued a strategy similar to Margaret Thatcher's ploy (cf. example 1 in chapter 3, p. 30) of questioning the validity of a particular metaphorical scenario version by denying one of its central presuppositions. Where she had railed against interpretations of the EU integration process as a TRAIN JOURNEY on the grounds that THE TRAIN MIGHT GO IN THE WRONG DIRECTION, the Bavarian politician denounced the EU-AS-A-HOUSE metaphor because THE HOUSE MIGHT BE BUILT PARTLY WITH THE WRONG MATERIAL or WITHOUT ANY PROPER PLAN.

In general, the CONSTRUCTION PROCESS scenario seems to have attracted more pessimistic responses than the COMPLETED HOUSE scenario. In the last few years of the decade the concept of the BUILDING SITE was used as a source input to question the whole purpose of the EU CONSTRUCTION. Thus, *Die Welt* (15 November 1997) pictured EMU as 'a *site* that had so far only been *staked out* and was *waiting for the concrete foundations to be laid*' (*"die Baustelle Euro* [. . .] *ist zwar abgesteckt,* aber die *Fun-*

damente sind gerade erst verschalt"). *Die Zeit* (8 April 1998) likened the whole EU integration project to the real 'building site at the Potsdamer Platz in Berlin, with *pits, puddles, cranes and half-finished buildings everywhere'*, but lacking what even the Potsdamer Platz had, namely an 'infobox' that gave a clear picture of what the site would look like in the future ("Europa gleicht im Frühjahr 1998 dem Potsdamer Platz in Berlin: *überall Baugruben, Schlammlöcher, Kräne, halbfertige Gebäude* [...] *es gibt nicht, wie dort in Berlin, eine Infobox*, wo tüchtige Führer das Bild des Kommenden sichtbar machen"). By November 1998, with Kohl's government voted out of office and the newly appointed finance minister, Oskar Lafontaine, demanding interest cuts from the European Central Bank, the *Süddeutsche Zeitung* (12 November 1998) saw 'the *foundations* of the Maastricht Treaty being shaken' ("ein Umschwung [...], der an den *Grundfesten* des Maastrichter Vertrags rüttelt"). The foreign secretary, Joschka Fischer, called for a realistic approach to 'complement the *vision of the European house'* ("Die Vision vom europäischen Haus muß jetzt durch Realismus ergänzt werden", SZ, 6 November 1998). The once-attractive SOLID HOUSE concept had been supplanted by a scenario in which the EU CONSTRUCTION PROJECT was regarded at best as 'work in progress' or as a somewhat utopian vision.

In the British press, the STABILITY of the EU HOUSE CONSTRUCTION was questioned in an even more fundamental way than in Germany, especially at the end of the decade. In the wake of the 1999 nepotism scandal, the *Times* saw the "European house" as "built on the sands of corruption" (T, 27 January 2000) and five months later, a *Guardian* commentator was not even sure that there was *any* plan to its CONSTRUCTION:

(22) *That Europe is "under construction" is an old conceit.* [...] What is less often mentioned is that *this construction continues without overarching blueprints or plans*, on the basis only of temporary and very partial agreements *between architects, contractors, and clients* – and that, in other words, *it is wonderful that brick stands upon brick at all*. (G, 30 June 2000)

On the one hand, this comment makes use of the conceptual elements of the HOUSE scenario ("agreements *between architects, contractors, and clients*" etc.). However, by denying the existence of *blueprints or plans*, it cancels, so to speak, one of the central presuppositions of a 'constructive' BUILDING scenario. As a consequence, it seems *wonderful that brick stands upon brick at all* – i.e., *the building might fall down at any moment*, and it is not even clear whether the commentator would consider that to be a bad thing. What we find here is a maximum detachment from the HOUSE CONSTRUCTION scenario. It is depicted as an illusion used by the Euro-*architects* to justify their activities – the commentator then reveals its supposedly true nature as a series of AD HOC PARTIAL AGREEMENTS. Other uses of the HOUSE metaphor from the end of the 1990s, which targeted the concept of the "euro" currency, were in no way more optimistic or positive. The common currency was condemned as the "the economic equivalent of a 'burning building with no exits' if things went wrong" by the Conservative leader William Hague (T, 20 May 1998) or as a wrong way to go about the CONSTRUCTION OF THE EU HOUSE *"by starting with the monetary roof and working their way down"* (cf. above, example 15). The most positive CONSTRUCTION-related scenario that a British politician could come up with was not that of a HOUSE at all, but of Britain as "the *bridge* between Europe and America", used by Prime Minister Tony Blair (G, 29 September 1999).[19] What had begun as a visionary project of pan-European politics and was later reinvented as a restructuring programme for the EU finally became a scenario used to express pessimistic evaluations of its capability to develop, both in terms of the STABILITY OF THE HOUSE and of the PLANNING/ORGANIZATION OF THE CONSTRUCTION PROCESS.

6.3 Do metaphors 'evolve'?

The evidence of diachronic patterns in the distribution of EUROPEAN HOUSE metaphors in EUROMETA II shows that corpus data can be used to support hypotheses about historical changes in the metaphorical conceptualization of political topics. The growing disillusionment of the public in Britain and Germany with visions of European integration over the course of the 1990s is mirrored in the changes of architectural scenarios used by the politicians and the press. Two main turning points stand out. Initially, Gorbachev's slogan of the *Common European House*, which dated back to the mid-1980s and denoted a pan-continent political vision, still exerted a strong influence on the HOUSE scenario in debates about the structure of the "European Community". With the collapse of Soviet power at the start of the decade, this concept lost its political relevance; its demise enabled the EC/soon-to-become-EU to take over the role of providing the ROOF and FOUNDATIONS of a new EUROPEAN HOUSE. From then on until the mid-1990s, the EU's CONSTRUCTION plans were most often expressed in the form of optimistic scenarios, such as PUTTING ON A NEW ROOF, ADDING PILLARS or STRENGTHENING FOUN-

DATIONS. From 1997 onwards, however, the perception of Germany and other countries' difficulties in meeting the criteria of the Maastricht Treaty, the urgency of internal reforms as well as external pressures to enlarge the EU led to a gradual increase in the use of more pessimistic versions of the BUILDING scenario. These included CHAOS ON THE EU BUILDING SITE and QUALITY DEFICIENCIES IN THE CONSTRUCTION PROCESS. Towards the end of the decade, even gloomier comments alleged that the PLANS AND BLUEPRINTS FOR THE HOUSE were seriously FLAWED or that the vision of a PURPOSEFULLY CONSTRUCTED HOUSE was an illusory concept altogether.

When viewing these changes from what Dennett and Blackmore might call the 'metaphor-meme's eye's view', we can ask the question (phrased in Dawkinsian imagery): How did the EUROPE-AS-A-HOUSE metaphor manage to 'survive' in a changed meme-pool of public discourse, once the novelty appeal of Gorbachev's formulation had worn out? One basic condition for its success seems to have been its flexibility and adaptability in providing sets of presuppositions suiting almost any argumentative purpose, ranging from enthusiastic endorsements of the *solid construction* of the EC/EU (and its political institutions and projects) to its denunciation as a *construction built on sand, without proper plans* or *dependent on temporary agreements*. The metaphor could undergo both target changes (e.g. from pan-European co-operation to EC-/EU-centred integration) and sweeping source changes, i.e. from COMMUNAL TENEMENT to SOLID HOUSE to FUNCTIONALLY PROBLEMATIC CONSTRUCTION (excluding *outsiders*) to STRUCTURALLY PROBLEMATIC CONSTRUCTION (e.g. *no exit doors, badly built walls, unsafe foundations*) to CHAOTIC BUILDING SITE.

This massive 'depreciation' of the source scenario is of special interest from an evolutionist perspective. We have encountered similar developments in other domains, e.g. the rise of DISASTER scenarios for JOURNEY metaphors (*derailing train, Euro Titanic, dodgy aeroplane*), and the HEART DISEASE and HEART FAILURE variations on the theme of Major's and Blair's appeals to Britain to *be at the heart of Europe*. In all of these cases a common pattern is discernible: an initially affirmative metaphor scenario is first widely reported, applauded and disseminated, then it is questioned and finally it is 'turned around' into highly negatively charged scenarios. In the case of HOUSE metaphors, this pattern covers the great majority of tokens: after the final flourish – and subsequent demise – of Gorbachev's slogan we find first a high quotation and support rate for Kohl's SOLID HOUSE invocations, followed by critical interpretations and negative variations on this once positively viewed concept. In terms of competitive conceptual evolution, such a 'deterioration' appears to be a blessing in disguise: whilst more and more pessimistic evaluations are attached to the scenarios, their semantic core elements survive. The scenarios would in this view be the metaphorical representations that ensure their own replication even at the cost of having to change their evaluative and political value.

Such an interpretation provides more than a mere rephrasing of the corpus findings in evolutionist terminology, for it suggests that there are specific conditions of metaphor evolution. In the first place, we can state that the 'survival' of a metaphor is more probable if it is sufficiently conceptually flexible and at the same time experientially grounded, so as to allow for both conceptual variation and constancy of core elements. Furthermore, a 'metaphor's eye's view' of the 'depreciation' of the HOUSE scenarios can shed light on the question of how an evolutionist approach might provide an explanation for seemingly exceptional cases of conceptual development (Dennett 1995). Why should a conceptual content deterioration develop in the first place and become a stable trend? From the *users' perspective*, the motivation to construct scenarios is tied to communicative purposes, i.e. in the case of politicians, the persuasion of the widest possible section of their target public. Politicians can therefore be expected to be interested in launching optimistic metaphor scenarios to promote their specific agendas and projects. This is indeed the case for Gorbachev and Kohl's praises of the EUROPEAN HOUSE and their initially enthusiastic reception. However, once the euphoria of the initial phase has abated, why do they continue using their increasingly depreciating scenarios, and why does the press prefer to stick to them too (albeit critically), instead of launching new ones?

This 'continuity of usage despite depreciation' is not exceptional in the sense that it would be a rare phenomenon – quite the opposite is the case, as the corpus data clearly demonstrate. But it seems a puzzle from the point of view of rhetorical efficiency: why defend a depreciated, 'worn-out' and argumentatively ineffective scenario when many 'fresh' ones are available? In a slightly different but related form, we encountered this problem in the case of British media and politicians with a clearly Euro-sceptical agenda, who continued to employ versions of the TWO-/MULTI-SPEED scenario in which Britain appeared as the SLOW MOVER in comparison with other states.

From the metaphor's 'point of view' (if it existed), the speakers' political and rhetorical purposes are irrelevant. *Any* use of a metaphor scenario continues its presence in public discourse and enhances its chances of spreading further. According to this perspective, the users are nothing but 'vehicles' (in Dawkins's sense) for the scenarios. The users have their own agendas in formulating specific scenarios, but, first of all, they have to make sure their utterances are noticed and seen as relevant contributions to the public debate. In order to make sure that their contributions are perceived as relevant, they have to respond to any conceptual scenarios that are currently under discussion. No politician or media commentator can afford to neglect a prominent scenario, even if it does not 'lend itself' easily to their political interpretation. And once they have successfully launched a scenario, it may be more important for them to stay in the debate by way of identification with a scenario than to win every single argument or debate. Even if a scenario loses some of its initial persuasiveness due to criticism or parody, it can still serve as a 'flag' concept to rally support for the cause associated with it and to demonstrate one's presence in the debate. Thus, all users contribute to the emergence of scenario-based argumentative traditions, irrespective of whether they 'defend' or 'attack' a scenario and its evaluative bias. The distribution patterns for the scenario in a corpus reflect these traditions by displaying structural changes in the scenario versions over a period of time.

As regards Sperber's (1996) interest in discursive "micro-mechanisms" that exhibit a tendency to produce "contents that require lesser mental effort and provide greater cognitive effects", two aspects seem to be of interest. In the first place, any repetition of assertive formulations such as *'the European house needs strong foundations, a good roof, further pillars'* requires increasingly lesser interpretative effort, provided members of the discourse community can at least vaguely remember its initial use (in a once prominent statement such as Gorbachev's, Kohl's or Major's speeches). Secondly, any ironical or satirical uses of metaphorical formulations or innovative interpretations of pre-established scenarios certainly produce more and "greater cognitive effects". This is precisely what makes them attractive for use: a poignant, witty reformulation of a scenario can achieve enough extra inferences and polemical effects to offset the (in any case rather small) extra "processing" effort on the part of the hearers/readers.

The empirical basis of the EUROMETA II corpus presented here is still too small to regard an evolutionist interpretation as strongly motivated, let alone confirmed. Nevertheless, the 'metaphor's point of view' seems to provide a plausible perspective for the explanation of structural patterns in the conceptual development of metaphors in public discourse. The changes documented in EUROMETA II can be reconstructed as the effect of micro-mechanisms operating on units of representation (i.e. scenarios), which are produced with the aim of fast replication and dissemination in public discourse. The virtual conversation in a discourse community could thus be interpreted as the 'pool' of public representations in which conceptual units are competing. Whilst for their users the competition takes place at the level of political evaluations, the conceptual 'competition' takes place at the level of scenarios (to which the evaluations are attached by way of analogical arguments). The scenarios 'compete' not for political popularity, of course, but for chances of replication. The 'depreciation' pattern that we noted above – together with its political and attitudinal consequences – is a double-effect of this conceptual evolution. Seen from the perspective of individual users, every single formulation is the result of a conscious choice of a public representation to achieve specific communicative aims. When seen from the 'metaphor's perspective', the whole series of instances of individual uses – as they are represented in a corpus – appears to be the product of successive adaptive pressures.

Within the evolutionist framework a corpus represents the discourse section in which the conceptual competition and evolution takes place. Because of the aforementioned statistical imbalances between the national samples and the mother corpora, EUROMETA II can only attempt a modest approximation to a fully representative, contrastive corpus of Euro-political metaphors.

Nevertheless, it has proved to be adequate for the preliminary exploration of metaphor concepts in two discourse communities over a period of time. In particular, changes in the statistical distribution of specific scenarios could be related to changing sociocultural attitudes towards the target topic in the discourse communities. The results are empirically significant: for instance, they appear to contradict strong hypotheses about cultural Russian–Western differences underlying the demise of Gorbachev's *Common European House* slogan. On the other hand, the 'weaker' but more specific hypotheses about the 'discourse career' of the EUROPE-AS-A-HOUSE concept seem to be corroborated by the corpus data rather than being merely illustrated by a few fitting examples. This 'empiricity' should not, however, be interpreted as the application of a strictly inductive or empiricist methodology. The central analytical categories – that is, metaphorical source domains, scenarios, conceptual elements, thematic perspectives – are cognitive and semantic abstractions that are not directly observable. The contrastive and historical distribution patterns of our corpus data represent further abstraction levels.

The methodological justification for these abstracted categories depends on how plausible the analytical inferences based on them are as regards the actual data. The corpus consists only of what Kövecses calls "individual" metaphors. Their origins can be assumed to be mental representations, which are not directly accessible. The corpus data are public representations produced in communicative exchanges between the discourse participants. The pragmatic objectives of individual participants are largely irrelevant for the cognitive analysis that aims at revealing collective discourse patterns. It is, however, important to bear in mind the 'inter-individual' origins of the conceptual structures, lest we fall into the trap of reifying them into pseudo-substances that have a 'life' of their own.

This caution is necessary if we are to envisage developing a theoretical model for the emergence of argumentative tendencies in the conceptual development of metaphors. The corpus analysis as such can aim at giving an account of the emergence and the development of discourse traditions; it cannot in itself capture their actual genesis. For this purpose, we need to go back to the phase in which the transformation of metaphor concepts from "mental" to "public representations" takes place. In the following chapter, we shall discuss examples of *dialogical* metaphor use from EUROMETA II, e.g. interviews and disputations, in which the interpretative/argumentative 'steps' from one scenario to another are made explicit in the form of inter-textual public representations.

7
Metaphor Negotiation

In the preceding chapter, we quoted a dialogue (cf. example 4, p. 127) from a conversation that took place in 1987 between the then presidents of the Soviet Union and West Germany, Mikhail Gorbachev and Richard von Weizsäcker. Both speakers employed the HOUSE-TENANCY scenario to express their views of international relations in Europe. It will serve us here again as a starting point to discuss the way in which metaphors function in dialogical argumentation. Despite the efforts of both speakers to show diplomatic agreement, their scenario versions show significant differences. Gorbachev emphasizes the AUTONOMY OF EACH APARTMENT by pointing out *that not everyone might like to receive visitors at night*. Weizsäcker, on the other hand, insists on the principle of reciprocal VISITING RIGHTS and refers to the East–West German border as a *ditch* that runs through *one communal living room*. This *ditch* seems to be the border between East and West Germany, which implies that Weizsäcker sees Germany as *one (still divided) apartment*. This implication does not necessarily match Gorbachev's understanding of the APARTMENT concept. In his view, all the European states as they existed in 1987 – including both the GDR and the FRG – need to *be secure from visits at night*.

The underlying ambiguity about which states constitute APARTMENTS in the EUROPEAN HOUSE perhaps helped the two speakers to find a common ground whilst voicing different opinions about some crucial political target issues. The conversation took place during a phase of détente in global politics, which would have been unimaginable during the Cold War.[1] But old anxieties and precautions can still be discerned in Gorbachev's warning about *nocturnal surprise visits*. However, the fact that he does not challenge or reject Weizsäcker's version of the two German states *sharing a living room*, shows that the permeability and even the abolition of *dividing walls in the European house* were no longer a taboo, provided such changes were not forced upon the *inhabitants*. Weizsäcker, for his part, does not spell out a demand or assertion that the two German states be regarded as one national APARTMENT; he only implies that scenario.

The Gorbachev–Weizsäcker dialogue casts a spotlight on a historical moment when the international political order established after the Second World War began to be reconceptualized in a radical way. The HOUSE metaphor provides the speakers with a conceptual basis for the negotiation of differing but not incompatible interpretations of the current political situation and the prospects for its peaceful change. In this negotiation, the sets of presuppositions used for the various arguments are not determined by one speaker but by both, and they also change slightly in the course of the conversation. We therefore need to adapt the basic model of analogical argumentation to cover this type of use by differentiating the sets of presuppositions used by the speakers. In our example of the conversation between the Soviet and German presidents, we can distinguish three sets:

7.1 Scenario negotiation in dialogue

(a) a set of source presuppositions P_0 within scenario S that are shared between speakers A and B, e.g. (the continent of) EUROPE IS A HOUSE with nations as TENANTS or APARTMENTS;

(b) a set of further presuppositions P_1 within S_1 (= a specific version of scenario S) plus analogical conclusions C_1 by speaker A, so that $P_1[S_1] \rightarrow C_1$, e.g. NOT EVERYBODY LIKES NOCTURNAL VISITS BETWEEN APARTMENTS: therefore, NATIONAL BORDERS MUST BE INVIOLABLE;

(c) a set of further presuppositions P_2 within S_2 (= a further specific version of scenario S) plus analogical conclusions C_2 by speaker B, so that $P_2[S_2] \rightarrow C_2$, e.g. TENANTS WHO SHARE AN APARTMENT HAVE THE RIGHT TO VISIT EACH OTHER: therefore, THE EAST–WEST GERMAN BORDER MUST NOT BE IMPASSABLE.

Conversation partners can thus 'agree to disagree' about a target topic by sharing a basic set of presuppositions within a scenario and at the same time positing further presuppositions in special scenario versions, which lead to the argumentative conclusions that the speakers want to arrive at (and convince their addressee of). In the Gorbachev–Weizsäcker dialogue, the emphasis is clearly on this agreement aspect. Such a (partial) agreement in metaphorical argumentation is by no means a standard or neutral communicative purpose. Depending on one's political viewpoint, an argument by metaphor leading to (partial) agreement can be given very different interpretations. It can be viewed as a rational, sensible compromise but it can also be condemned as a rhetorical trick designed to persuade or even cheat the audience. Gorbachev's concept of the COMMON EUROPEAN HOUSE, for instance, was suspicious to some West German observers, because to them it seemed to set in stone the existence of two different German *apartments*. Thus, the *tageszeitung* (14 June 1989) quoted a German regional newspaper (*Nürnberger Nachrichten*) accusing the Soviet leader of cunning rhetorical deception:

(1) Gorbatschow erfand jenes *schamlos verführerische Bild vom 'gemeinsamen Haus Europa', das nicht nur (zwecks Durchblick) offene Fenster und Türen, sondern sogar mehrere Einfahrten und – man höre – zwei getrennte deutsche Appartements haben kann.* [Gorbachev invented *the shamelessly seductive image of the 'Common European House'* that may not only have *open windows and doors (for better visibility), but also several entrances and – nota bene – two separate German apartments.*]

The political and moral quality of a speaker's intentions 'behind' the use of a metaphor is very much in the eye of the beholder. As regards the mechanisms of analogical reasoning, however, there is no fundamental difference between 'convincing', 'persuading' and 'seducing' arguments. What does make a difference is the transparency (or lack of it) of the argumentative warrant involved in arriving at a conclusion. In metaphorical argumentation, the warrant is often based on an analogy that connects a new or abstract topic with a well-established and often experientially grounded source scenario. In a dialogical argument based on metaphor scenarios, this connection becomes more explicit than in monologues or meta-communicative comments. The discussion partners (or opponents) construe their thematic perspectives on the spot and express them in their respective scenario versions. We can thus witness the very act of concept-formation in the form of scenario-negotiation. The immediacy of conceptual change is what makes dialogical metaphor use a particularly interesting object for the analysis of analogical reasoning. In this chapter, we shall investigate several further dialogical examples from EUROMETA I and II, using the model in (7.i) as a point of departure for the explication of various other negotiated metaphor scenarios. Printed versions of face-to-face conversations in the press give a grammatically, stylistically – and sometimes also politically – 'cleansed' account of what the interlocutors actually said to each other – for this reason, they cannot be treated as if they were transcripts of what was said. The following analyses of the press versions of metaphorical dialogues should therefore not be seen as attempts to give an account of the actual speech situation. Instead, they concentrate on conceptual aspects of metaphorical argumentation in edited dialogues, with the aim of learning more about the fundamental conditions of co-operative and/or competitive reasoning by metaphor.

The source domain that provides the largest number of examples of dialogical metaphor in Euro-political discourse is that of WAY-MOVEMENT-SPEED, especially the scenarios of the TRAIN and CONVOY JOURNEY. These scenarios seem to be particularly well suited to expressing assessments and comparisons of EU member states' PERFORMANCE as regards their participation in and commitment to the Union's JOURNEY towards closer integration. The TRAIN JOURNEY scenario, for instance, has been used by journalists in interviews to suggest that *the train's smooth progress is in question* and that drastic action is needed to *prevent it from stopping*. The common-sense logic of such measures in the source scenario seems to exert a discursive pressure on some interviewees to stay within the scenario whilst trying to refute the target conclusion. They need to come up with an alternative outcome of the scenario 'plot', as in the cases of two German politicians who had to walk a rhetorical tightrope between reassuring the public that the EU's *progress* was not in question and avoiding the impression of trying to criticize other nations:

(2) Interview with the CDU/CSU chief whip W. Schäuble:
Schäuble: [. . .] Sie werden sehen, *der europäische Zug fährt zügig weiter.*
SPIEGEL: Dann müssen Sie aber die *Bremser rauswerfen, die ständig versuchen, ihn aufzuhalten.*
Schäuble: Tja, aber *wenn Sie jemanden vom Zug werfen, bringen Sie ihn möglicherweise um, und das wollen wir ja nicht. Wir wollen sie nicht vom Zug werfen,* sondern wir wollen sie davon überzeugen, *daβ sie nicht bremsen sollen* [. . .].
SPIEGEL: Da müssen Sie in London noch viel Überzeugungsarbeit leisten. (SP, 30 December 1996)
[*Schäuble:* [. . .] You'll see, *the European train will proceed smoothly towards its goal.*

SPIEGEL: But then you must *first throw those people off the train who constantly try to apply the brakes.*
Schäuble: But *if you throw people off the train, it is possible you may kill them and that's not what we want to do. We do not want to throw them off the train* but we want to convince them *that they should not hold it up.*
SPIEGEL: In that case, you have a lot of persuading to do in London.]

(3) Interview with the Bavarian Minister President E. Stoiber (CSU):
Stoiber: [. . .] wir sagen unseren Freunden klipp und klar: Wir müssen uns auch nach 1997 anstrengen. Da gibt es einige, die sagen, dann haben wir wieder ein bißchen Luft für höhere Staatsschulden. Die deutsche Seite kann so etwas nicht akzeptieren.
SZ: Also müssen wir den Zug anhalten?
Stoiber: Nicht anhalten. Wir müssen den Zug auf das richtige Gleis setzen.
(SZ, 9 December 1996)
[*Stoiber:* [. . .] we are telling our friends absolutely clearly: We must continue to work hard even after 1997. There are some who say: by then there'll be a bit of slack in the budget, so we can risk higher deficits again. The German side can't accept that.
SZ: So we must stop the train?
Stoiber: No, not stop it. We must put the train on the right track.]

In both cases, the TRAIN JOURNEY scenario allows the politicians to meet the interviewers' challenge by transferring the metaphor from a dramatic scenario version of THROWING SOMEONE FROM THE TRAIN or STOPPING THE TRAIN ALTOGETHER to the more conciliatory scenes of DISCUSSION AMONG THE PASSENGERS and PUTTING TRAINS ON THE RIGHT TRACKS. Nevertheless, even though the latter scenario versions introduce target concepts that are diplomatically harmless, they cannot relieve the speakers of all argumentative commitments, which they incurred by taking over the basic scenario. By accepting the basic set of general presuppositions (cf. 7.i.a), they have also accepted assumptions about a normal course of action and roles, and possibly even a specific bias. In the case of the TRAIN JOURNEY scenario, for instance, the bias seems to be a preference for SMOOTH PROGRESS (cf. e.g. Thatcher's protest against "misleading analogies such as the European train leaving the station", quoted in chapter 3, example 1, p. 30). The interviewers' suggestion of PROBLEMS AFFECTING THE TRAIN'S PROGRESS leaves the interviewees with a limited choice of possible answers. By attempting to provide a solution for these problems in terms of the scenario, they accept the implied preference for SMOOTH PROGRESS and implicitly take over specific roles of authority, such as CONDUCTING THE DISCUSSION ON THE TRAIN or PLATFORM MANAGER. Depending on the political context, the assumption of the problem-solving role required by the scenario might be seen as a contentious issue in itself. The argumentative risks of assuming the role of the EU JOURNEY'S LEADER became, for instance, evident in a conflict between the British and German governments over the CONVOY JOURNEY scenario during the mid-1990s.[2] The basic scenario equates each nation with A SHIP IN THE CONVOY and also presupposes that THE CONVOY TRAVELS IN THE SAME DIRECTION, preferably MAKING GOOD PROGRESS. (There may be further associations of this scenario that connect it with the history of attacks on British convoys by German "U-boats" in the two World Wars; however, there were no allusions to maritime warfare in any of the relevant EUROMETA I or II texts.)

The CONVOY scenario thus lends itself to SPEED comparisons for individual nations as SHIPS. During the mid-1990s, German politicians issued repeated warnings *that the EU convoy was held back by certain slower ships*. In a letter to the *Financial Times* to celebrate the change from the "European Community" to the "European Union", Chancellor Kohl tried to square such a warning with an apparent rejection of the TWO-SPEED concept:

(4) In an urgent plea for *continuing progress* towards political as well as economic union, [...] *Mr Kohl rejects the idea of a "two-speed or three-speed Europe"*. At the same time, in a thinly veiled warning to countries such as Britain and Denmark, which have yet to ratify the Maastricht treaty, *he says Germany "cannot accept a Europe, the speed of which is dictated by the slowest ship in the convoy"*. (FT, 4 January 1993)

Kohl's use of the CONVOY scenario here is not part of a dialogue but can be understood as a reaction to previous arguments based on the metaphor DEGREE OF PARTICIPATION IN EU INTEGRATION IS SPEED OF THE EU JOURNEY. Kohl rejects the most contentious formulation of this metaphor in the shape of *"two-speed or three-speed Europe"* slogan and at the same time tries to warn against what he perceives as the imminent threat of that TWO-/MULTI-SPEED EU becoming reality – or of an existing one becoming worse! For if there is *a slowest ship in the convoy that needs to be reminded to go faster*, then there must be some SPEED DIFFERENCE IN THE CONVOY. As example (4) shows, the British commentator read Kohl's attempt as a "thinly veiled warning" to the two countries that had not yet ratified the Maastricht Treaty, i.e. Britain and Denmark. As far as Britain is concerned, this interpretation fits exactly the bias of the MARITIME JOURNEY scenario and of most other JOURNEY scenarios, i.e. that Britain is the principal SLOW MOVER in the EU (cf. above; chapter 3).

Kohl himself repeated the warning to the slowest ship(s), and so did other members of his government, such as the foreign minister, Klaus Kinkel, and the CDU politician Schäuble (e.g. T, 8 September 1994, Z, 9 September 1994 and 10 March 1995). The result of these exhortations was growing irritation on the part of the Conservative British Cabinet, which saw itself put under pressure from a 'partner' government for not being sufficiently proactive about EU integration at a time when it was being attacked at home by Euro-sceptics for being too Euro-friendly. This pressure from both sides eventually led to the outspoken rejection of the German CONVOY-scenario by the then British Foreign Secretary, Malcolm Rifkind, in a speech in Bonn in spring 1997. Although the speech was given four years after the publication of Kohl's letter from 1993, it could have passed as a direct response in a public face-to-face disputation:

(5) [. . .] it was plain that Mr Rifkind was in effect urging the Germans to ditch the ideas of their leader. Each of the Chancellor's favourite metaphors was taken up and dismantled [. . .]. *There was no point in talking about a faster integration which left behind the 'slowest boats' in the convoy: 'We are not talking about convoys, we are talking about democracy'.* [. . .] Rather, *it was the very idea of dividing Europe into fast and slow integrators which would create friction.* Thus old tired metaphors were traded for new. *If European policy was a symphony, it had to be remembered that orchestras could function only on the principle of unanimity – there could be no majority voting among strings or brass.* (T, 20 February 1997)

Here we find the (relatively rare) case of a quasi-official rejection of a specific metaphor associated with the policies of one national government by the foreign secretary of a 'partner' government within the EU. It shows how seriously governments can take metaphors if they consider the target topic to be important enough to require their full conceptual/argumentative attention. Not only does Rifkind discard the CONVOY scenario; he also takes care to refute the analogical conclusions drawn from it. By insisting that there was "no point in talking about a faster integration which left behind the 'slowest boats' in the convoy", he contradicts the implication that high integration speed is essential for all EU member states (just as high speed is required for all convoy ships to reach their destination safely). Instead, he presents a counter analogy: the successful functioning of the EU depends on unanimity among EU states (just as the successful performance of a symphony by an orchestra depends on unanimity in the orchestra).

In conceptual terms, an ORCHESTRA PLAYING A SYMPHONY is as good a source scenario as a CONVOY JOURNEY to depict the EU as a confederation of nation states. Like ships in a convoy, players in an orchestra have to keep the same speed ('tempo') and they have to act 'in concert', i.e. in accord with each other. UNANIMITY is as necessary in a convoy as in an orchestra. However, Rifkind foregrounds UNANIMITY as the most important aspect of the ORCHESTRA PLAYING A SYMPHONY scenario, which he has already set up as an alternative to the CONVOY JOURNEY scenario, whose most salient feature (in his view) is the SPEED aspect. Furthermore, he buttresses his own conclusions by stressing the absurdity of "majority voting among strings or brass", thus making his own scenario appear to be a 'self-evident' refutation of the CONVOY scenario used by Kohl.

The technique of driving a political opponent's metaphor argument to the point of absurdity can also be observed in an example from the field of HEART OF EUROPE concepts. In chapter 5, we analysed the history of statements that 'Britain should be/work at the heart of Europe' and noted a depreciation of the HEART concept from a CENTRAL PART of the EUROPEAN BODY POLITIC to an UNHEALTHY or even DYING ORGAN. These conflicting interpretations were not only often juxtaposed or blended in commentaries; they also appeared in direct argumentative/polemical exchanges. At the 1996 Conservative Party Conference, Sir Leon Brittan, then London's EU Commissioner, who endorsed closer institutional integration, defended Major's formula of *Britain working at the heart of Europe* as an expression of what lay in the nation's interest. His opponent was Norman Lamont, the erstwhile Chancellor of the Exchequer, who since his retirement from the Cabinet had become a prominent spokesperson for the Euro-sceptic faction within the Tory Party. He attempted to turn the analogy around and to arrive at the very opposite conclusion to that which Brittan had favoured:

(6) Sir Leon said that leaving the EU would be "an economic, political and strategic disaster for Britain" [. . .]. *Being at the heart of Europe* did not mean "passively accepting everything that our European partners want, or every new proposal from Brussels". Mr Lamont was strongly critical of the power assumed by Brussels [. . .], he said:

"*There is no point in being at the heart of Europe if the heart is diseased.*" (G, 10 October 1996)

With his doubts about the desirability of BEING AT THE HEART OF EUROPE, Lamont undercut the appeal of the pro-European interpretation of Major and Brittan's version of the BRITAIN-AT-THE-HEART-OF-EUROPE metaphor by shifting the scenario focus. Brittan had employed the HEART-AS-CENTRE concept on the assumption that being at the centre of an entity of positive value is preferable to being distant from it. Lamont twisted that concept around by blending it with the scenario of the HEART SUFFERING FROM A DISEASE. This blend provides a basis for the analogical conclusion that 'Euro commitment is pointless, just as it makes no sense to be close to a diseased heart'. The conclusion achieves a sarcastic effect similar to other ironic variations of Major's metaphor (cf. chapter 5, examples 33 to 38, pp. 106–8). As a response in a dialogue, this conclusion serves as a forceful rejection of Brittan's plea for Britain to engage more positively with the EU. By seemingly following the logic of Brittan's own analogy whilst recontextualizing it in the ILLNESS scenario, Lamont scores a polemical point in 'demonstrating' that accepting the analogy would be a folly.

Discursive reference to a previously established scenario is not always as adversarial and polemical as it appears in the cited denunciations of the CONVOY and HEART-OF-EUROPE metaphors. The following examples of metaphors from the CAR JOURNEY scenario show conceptual elaboration rather than refutation/rejection. The first one is taken from an article written by a strong advocate of Britain's participation in EU integration, the Labour politician Roy Hattersley, at a time when the Tory Eurosceptic tendencies were gaining in strength. The second one is a comment on the significance of the "Inter-Governmental conference" (IGC) preparing the EU for the Amsterdam Treaty, published in the often strongly Euro-sceptical *Daily Telegraph*:

(7) Sensible politicians will warn against *missing the bus*. But the image needs to be extended. *Having watched the* ERM [= the revised European Exchange Rate Mechanism as preparation for Monetary Union] *pull out of the Brussels coach station, we will begin to run after it. Eventually, having climbed breathlessly aboard, we will start to beg, bully and cajole the driver into taking a different route.* His reply is already predictable: "*If you had got on at the beginning, you could have helped to decide the direction, the destination and the speed*". (G, 25 November 1996)

(8) [. . .] just over a year ago, the Government was assuring everyone that the IGC was a non-event. Officials dismissed it as *a "5,000-mile service" for the EU, the equivalent of a change of oil and a new air filter. Now it transpires that the vehicle has been booked in for an overhaul of the bodywork and a full respray.* (DT, 18 April 1997)

In example (7), Hattersley does not refute the basic CAR-TRAVEL scenario (cf. 3.ii.d: A GROUP OF STATES CO-OPERATING IN A POLITICAL PROCESS ARE PARTICIPANTS IN A CAR JOURNEY) but uses it as a platform to launch a new argument. He refers to the scenario as the general position of "sensible politicians", which "needs to be extended". (For the purpose of our analysis, the original authorship of the MISSING THE BUS scenario is irrelevant; it is documented in EUROMETA II as being in use at least since 1991.) Hattersley depicts Britain not only as the stereotypical PROBLEM TRAVELLER on the EU JOURNEY but also as an UNREASONABLE COMPLAINANT. After *belatedly having joined the journey*, Britain criticizes the *route*, only to be told that *it could have had a full say in all decisions, had it made up its mind earlier.* By enriching the CAR-TRAVEL scenario thus, Hattersley makes it much more poignant and persuasive. He 'drives home' a point about the urgent need for a change in Britain's commitment to EU integration by exploiting the potential of the scenario's set of presuppositions in one particular perspective. Focusing on the MISSING THE BUS version of the CAR-JOURNEY scenario, he builds a specific scene that is meant to relate to his readers' imagination of the embarrassing row between *passenger* and *bus driver*. It hardly matters whether anyone has witnessed such a scene in reality: the projection of the concept cluster EMBARRASSING ENCOUNTERS onto the MISSING THE BUS scenario version suffices to achieve the effect of denouncing the alleged unreasonable Eurosceptical attitude of the then still ruling Conservative government, which Hattersley opposed.

In (8), the *Daily Telegraph*'s comment on the Tory government's assurance also starts from an already pre-established scenario, i.e. that of the Inter-Governmental Conference (IGC) as a PIT STOP, which represents one of the sub-variants of the CAR-TRAVEL theme. The reported depiction of the IGC as a *"5,000-mile service"* by the government is interpreted as a "dismissal" because that kind of *maintenance service* involves just *"a change of oil and a new air filter"*. The editor, Philip Johnston, then explains what he sees as the true meaning of the IGC in terms of the extended scenario: *"an overhaul of the bodywork and a full respray"*, i.e. a *substantial repair service*. Again, a sub-variant of the basic scenario is further specified and charged with evaluative terminology ("assuring", "dismissed", "now it transpires") so as to serve as an analogical warrant for a conclusion about the topic, which the readers are left to work out for themselves, i.e. that the ruling government either underestimated or misrepresented the significance of the IGC.

A full analysis of arguments that modify a previously established metaphor scenario would have to be based on more examples than those discussed so far, but the passages presented here allow for some preliminary conclusions concerning the appeal of conceptual metaphor in political dialogues and disputes. The "scenario negotiation" model presented in (7.i) is a special case of a range of argumentative strategies that are available to speakers when responding to previously established metaphor scenarios. We can distinguish four types of such responses – further research will have to establish whether the model needs to be amended:

7.ii Options of scenario modification and negotiation

(a) If a previously established scenario (S_1) provides a set of presuppositions (P_1), which yield conclusions that the speaker also wishes to reach, s/he can enrich that scenario by specifying the presuppositions and adding further ones of the same type (P_1^*), so that the intended analogical conclusion becomes even more conclusive.

(b) If a previously established scenario S_1 provides a set of presuppositions (P_1), which only partly yield the conclusions that the speaker wishes to reach, s/he can offer a new scenario version (S_1^{**}) with a modified set of presuppositions (P_1^{**}), so as to arrive at a modified analogical conclusion (C_1^{**}).

(c) If the previously established scenario (S_1) provides a set of presuppositions (P_1), which yield conclusions that the speaker does not wish to reach, s/he can reject (S_1) and offer an alternative scenario (S_2) with a set of presuppositions (P_2) leading to a new conclusion C_2.

(d) If the previously established scenario (S_1) predominantly provides presuppositions (P_1), which yield conclusions that the speaker does not wish to reach but which are attractive to use (for example, because of the scenario's prominence in public discourse), s/he can blend (S_1) with a further set of presuppositions (P_2) that 'cancels' those parts of (P_1) that are deemed disagreeable. The result is a 'counter-conclusion' (C_2) that contradicts (C_1).[3]

The last-mentioned strategy is also exemplified by the ironical allusions to prominent metaphors discussed in previous chapters (such as Kohl's HOUSE OF EUROPE and Schröder's PREMATURE BIRTH scenarios, or Major and Blair's HEART OF EUROPE promises). In these cases, the commentators do not provide alternative scenarios – as Rifkind does with his ORCHESTRA vision of the European Union – but variations on a previously established thematic perspective, adding crucial new presuppositions that radically alter the purport of the conclusion. As we have seen in the case of the EUROPEAN HOUSE concept, the new scenario versions may in time become so notorious and prominent in public use that they supersede the initial version and establish a tradition of their own.

One type of reaction to metaphor use by previous speakers, which we have not considered yet, is its complete avoidance. Such a stance may be implied in denunciations of metaphors as misleading or deceptive language use, as in Mrs Thatcher's denunciation of EU politicians' metaphors as Orwellian "Newspeak" (cf. example 1 in chapter 3, p. 30). But is a complete omission of metaphors in political argumentation, on account of their deceptive and equivocal use, possible? One philosopher who appears to have formulated such a claim is Thomas Hobbes (1588–1679). In the passage from the *Leviathan* (1651) quoted at the beginning of chapter 1 (p. 1), Hobbes warns his readers to avoid "metaphors" and other "senslesse and ambiguous words". This condemnation of metaphor occupies a famous (to some critics, infamous) place in the history of thinking about metaphor. In *Metaphors We Live By*, Lakoff and Johnson cite Hobbes and John Locke (1632–1704) as the chief proponents of a philosophical trend through which "the suspicion of poetry and rhetoric became dominant in Western thought" and "metaphor and other figurative devices [became] objects of scorn" (Lakoff and Johnson 1980: 190). In his overview of "Metaphor in the Philosophical Tradition" (1981), Johnson ascribes to Hobbes an "Aristotelian view of metaphor as the transference of a name from its proper object to some other object", which made it "natural" for him "to fear that such a transfer was likely to deceive those who had taken the word or name in question as signifying only the original object" (1981: 11–12). Johnson interprets Hobbes's theory as the expression of a "literal-truth paradigm", which is built on three assumptions, namely (1) that "the human conceptual system is essentially literal"; (2) that metaphor is "a deviant use of words in other than their proper senses, which accounts for its tendency to confuse and to deceive"; and (3) that "the meaning and truth claims of metaphor (if there are any) are just those of literal paraphrase" (1981: 12). Similar assessments of Hobbes and of Locke as arch-detractors of metaphor can be found in other historical references – for example, by Cohen (1979), Cooper (1986), Bertau (1996), Goatly (1997), Müller-Richter (1998) and Leezenberg (2001).[4] Considering these verdicts, it may seem perverse to treat Hobbes's theory as being on a par with modern cognitive and semantic approaches. However, as one of Hobbes's aforementioned critics justly points out, a blanket denial of the arguments against metaphor may put us "in danger of overlooking some very thorny underbrush as we scramble over the high road to figurative glory" (Cohen 1979: 1).[5] There are good reasons why Hobbes's criticism of metaphor needs to be taken seriously. First, if it indeed turned out to be a coherent defence of the possibility of 'metaphor-less' communication, it would be worth in principle studying the reasoning behind it. As recent advances in the historiography of metaphor theory have shown – e.g. Dirven 1993/2002, Jäkel 1999, Mahon 1999, Nerlich and Clarke 2002, Mouton (in press), Chamizo Dominguez and Nerlich (in press) – a substantial number of supposedly 'traditional' theories of metaphor offer insights that are not only compatible with but also complementary to the cognitive focus on *mapping* and *blending* relationships of conceptual structures. Furthermore, Hobbes's pronouncements on metaphor are embedded in a theory of political communication, which forms a central part of the *Leviathan* as a treatise that focuses, according to its full title, on "*the Matter, Forme and Power of a Commonwealth, ecclesiasticall and civill*". The central importance of communication for Hobbes's philosophy has been the object of intensive research over the past two decades.[6] Most of this work, however, seems to have been overlooked in those standard references that are critical of Hobbes. In the following chapter, we shall use results of this research in an analysis of key passages from *Leviathan* to reassess the main points of Hobbes's metaphor critique in the context of his general outlook on political communication.

8
Metaphor as Deception

8.1 Metaphors as *ignes fatui*: Hobbes's warnings of political metaphor in *Leviathan*

Hobbes's most notorious condemnation of metaphor, which we already quoted at the beginning of chapter 1, is in itself an argument-by-metaphor in three steps (which are here separated as paragraphs for ease of analysis):

> (1a) To conclude, The Light of humane minds is Perspicuous Words, but by exact definitions first snuffed, and purged from ambiguity; *Reason* is the *pace*, Encrease of *Science*, the *way*; and the Benefit of man-kind, the *end*.
>
> (1b) And on the contrary, Metaphors, and senslesse and ambiguous words, are like *ignes fatui*;
>
> (1c) and reasoning upon them, is wandering amongst innumerable absurdities; and their end, contention, and sedition, or contempt. (Hobbes 1996: 36)

The second part of this statement leaves little doubt that Hobbes condemns what he calls "metaphors" as the very opposite of well-defined, *perspicuous* words. What may strike the reader as a provocation or as an indication of a hidden complexity in the argument, however, is the way in which Hobbes formulates this condemnation. It is itself highly metaphorical: not only does it contain stock metaphors of early enlightenment epistemology, such as the '*light* of the mind', 'words *purged* of ambiguity', but the whole passage forms one elaborate extended metaphor interspersed with a simile. The PACE-WAY-END scenario of reason's 'proper' PROGRESS in the first part (1a) is followed by the comparison of "metaphors" with *ignes fatui*, i.e. *will o' the wisps that lead* the mind (seen as a *wanderer in an unknown region*) *astray* (1b). The dire consequences of such an ABERRATION are explained in the last part of the passage (1c). Confronted with such metaphorical and rhetorical flourish, one wonders whether Hobbes did or did not want his words to be what he called "perspicuous". His condemnation of metaphor is convincing precisely because of its 'metaphor-cum-simile' formulation. It not only proposes but also graphically demonstrates the dangers of "contention, and sedition, or contempt", into which the mind can be *led* by the *false lights* of "metaphors, and senslesse and ambiguous words". Should we therefore treat it as a deliberate paradox?

The matter might still be of little consequence if the passage was just an isolated instance of metaphor use in *Leviathan*, but this is not the case. In fact, the language of *Leviathan* is, as David Johnston (1986: 67) rightly observes, "vigorous, vivid, and rhetorical in character throughout the work", and "simile and metaphor are in constant use". Hobbes's treatise opens with an extended metaphor, which is not only one of the most famous analogical arguments in the history of political philosophy, but also marks a decisive stage in the development of the BODY POLITIC theory tradition (Hale 1971: 127–30). To demonstrate the full strength of Hobbes's use of metaphor for the expository presentation of his theory, we shall look at this passage in detail before proceeding to an interpretation of his thematisations of metaphor in *Leviathan*. (Again, the passage has been partitioned in order to highlight steps in the argumentation.)

> (2a) NATURE (the Art whereby God hath made and governes the World) is by the *Art* of man, as in many other things, so in this also imitated, that it can make an Artificial Animal. For seeing life is but a motion of Limbs, the beginning whereof is in some principall part within; why may we not say, that all *Automata* (Engines that move themselves by springs and wheeles as doth a watch) have an artificall life?
>
> (2b) For what is the *Heart*, but a *Spring*; and the *Nerves*, but so many *Strings*; and the *Joynts*, but so many *Wheeles*, giving motion to the whole Body, such as was intended by the Artificer?
>
> (2c) *Art* goes yet further, imitating that Rationall and most excellent worke of Nature, *Man*. For by Art is created that great LEVIATHAN called a COMMON-WEALTH, or STATE, (in latine CIVITAS) which is but an

Artificiall Man; though of greater stature and strength than the Naturall, for whose protection and defence it was intended; and in which the *Soveraignty* is an Artificiall *Soul*, as giving life and motion to the whole body; The *Magistrates*, and other *Officers* of Judicature and Execution, artificall *Joynts*; *Reward* and *Punishment* (by which fastned to the seate of the Soveraignty, every joynt and member is moved to performe his duty) are the *Nerves*, that do the same in the Body Naturall; *The Wealth* and *Riches* of all the particular members, are the *Strength*; *Salus Populi* [. . .] its *Businesse*; *Counsellors*, by whom all things needfull for it to know, are suggested unto it, are the *Memory*; *Equity* and *Lawes*, an artificall *Reason* and *Will*; *Concord*, *Health*; *Sedition*, *Sicknesse*; and *Civill war*, *Death*. Lastly, the *Pacts* and *Covenants*, by which the parts of this Body Politique were at first made, set together, and united, resemble that *Fiat*, or the *Let us make man*, pronounced by God in the Creation. (Hobbes 1996: 9–10)

The multiple analogies in Hobbes's exposition of his political philosophy form another complex argument-by-analogy. In the first instance (cf. 2a), Hobbes interprets (artificial) ENGINES or AUTOMATA (target concept) in terms of (natural) MOVING ORGANISMS (source concept). In the following rhetorical questions (2b), he inverts the source–target relation by highlighting the mechanical 'nature' of body organs (such as the *Heart*, the *Nerves*, and the *Joynts*). The analogy is thus turned into a proposition of a kind of metaphysical identity, grounded in the basic notion of GOD as an ARTIFICER, with the implication that NATURE IS GOD'S ARTIFICE, which is mirrored ("imitated") in MAN'S ART to make "Artificiall Animals". In the following part (2c), ART itself becomes a metonymic agent ("Art goes yet further, imitating . . .") as the creator of a higher-level "Artificiall Animal" i.e. the STATE (*Leviathan*). This analogy inherits the presuppositions of the preceding one, so that we have a conceptual 'chain' of "artifices": STATE-ENGINE-ORGANISM. The ARTIFICER behind all of them is GOD, with MAN being both one of his artifices and a subordinate ARTIFICER himself.

Hobbes goes on to summarize the implications that follow from the STATE-ORGANISM analogy by characterizing political and social institutions (target) in terms of PARTS and LIFE-CYCLE STAGES of a HUMAN BODY (source). The last sentence in the passage links the BODY POLITIC with the notion of GOD as an ARTIFICER.

This multilayered analogy between the STATE and "that Rationall and most excellent worke of Nature, Man", complete with body and soul, functions as a kind of *leitmotiv* for the political theory that informs the rest of Hobbes's treatise. It is invoked, for instance, in further references (Hobbes 1996: 221) to the biblical book of Job (Job 40–1), where the *Leviathan* is described as a creature that God alone can overpower, in descriptions of other PARTS OF THE BODY POLITIC and its DISEASES as well as in further applications of the BODY metaphor to the church (Hobbes 1996: 166–9, 221–30, 268, 321).

In a detailed analysis of the STATE–*Leviathan* allegory that draws on a long tradition of interpretations,[1] Raia Prokhovnik (1991) has argued that without it, the treatise would just "consist of a set of doctrines without a cohering philosophy, and its rhetoric would lack its central feature" (Prokhovnik 1991: 218). It is because the state ("Commonwealth") is conceived of as both an artifice that it is amenable to scientific analysis and as an organic entity, that the function of its individual MEMBERS as means to achieve a common purpose can be understood. In Prokhovnik's reading, Hobbes derives from this multiple analogy the central conclusion that "the sovereign depends on the subjects who compose him and subjects depend on the sovereign they form" (1991: 207).

Conceivably, it might be argued that Hobbes's exploitation of the *Leviathan* allegory throughout the treatise transcends the figurative level and serves as a 'second-order' literal description of the "Commonwealth" in its parts and in its entirety.[2] Still, such an interpretation would impart an even greater importance to the role metaphor plays in Hobbes's political philosophy. It would emphasize that the allegory is developed from the famous opening statement into a full argumentative warrant intended to *lead* the reader to a valid conclusion – hardly an intellectual *wandering light* put up to *mislead* the reader. The BODY-(ENGINE-)STATE analogy is far from being the only source concept used in the *Leviathan*. Quentin Skinner, in his seminal study of *Reason and Rhetoric in the Philosophy of Hobbes*, counts no less than five major metaphorical themes besides the BODY POLITIC notion in *Leviathan*. Their respective source domains are: READING (of Man's character), PHYSICAL MOVEMENT, USE OF ARMS IN COMBAT, BUILDING-ARCHITECTURE, ENSLAVEMENT/PHYSICAL CONSTRAINT (Skinner 1996: 384–90). Furthermore, Parts III and IV of *Leviathan* abound in comments on whether specific biblical passages should or should not be read metaphorically, exhibiting the whole range of rhetorical tropes. Unless we wish to dismiss the bulk of *Leviathan* as an extended exercise in paradox and self-contradiction, we have to examine Hobbes's reasons for condemning metaphor so emphatically whilst simultaneously making such an extensive use of figurative language in his own argumentation.

8.2 Metaphor and rhetoric

Hobbes's treatment of metaphor and rhetoric is part of the transition from late Humanism, which regarded rhetoric as a key element in education and philosophy, to the early Enlightenment, which sought to find and establish "scientific" methods. Leo Strauss saw Hobbes as a thinker whose work reflected "the fertile moment when the classical and theological tradition was already shaken, and a tradition of modern science not yet formed and established" (Strauss 1952: 5). Hobbes's education and early writings were still couched in the humanistic traditions (Skinner 1996: 238–40), and Hobbes contributed to these traditions by translating Thucydides' *History of the Peloponnesian War* and Aristotle's *Art of Rhetoric* into English. In these works, Hobbes paid particular attention to passages that emphasized the power of rhetoric to excite and move an audience in any way a speaker wanted (Harwood 1986: 31; Skinner 1996: 256–7, 282–3).

This interest in the ethically ambivalent effects of rhetoric became even more urgent in the context of Hobbes's efforts to establish moral and political philosophy as a "civill science" that relied as little as possible on rhetorical flourish. Despite some early warnings against the inflated use of tropes, Tudor rhetoric had "gained a reputation for encouraging an absurdly inflated and euphuistic form of writing", which included a preference for metaphor as part of the *grand style* of public oratory (Skinner 1996: 191). Against this exaggerated, hyperbolic use of metaphor and other tropes, Hobbes formulated a strongly anti-rhetorical stance in *The Elements of Law* (Ms 1640) and *De Cive* (published in Latin in 1642, in English in 1651). In these works, Hobbes systematically exposed and criticized the moral ambiguity of rhetoric and metaphor (Hobbes 1983: 154–5 and 1994: 170–1). But by the time that he wrote the *Leviathan*, within the context of an intensified concern for the relationship between the "Naturall" and the "Civill" or "Morall Sciences", Hobbes redefined the appeal of the latter as depending not just on empirical and logical evidence but also on the eloquence of presentation.[3] His aim was no longer to contrast but to combine scientific truth and rhetorical efficiency: "Reason, and Eloquence, (though not perhaps in the Naturall Sciences, yet in the Morall) may stand very well together" (Hobbes 1996: 385). Johnston (1986: 132) concludes that the aim of *Leviathan* "was not merely to demonstrate the truth of Hobbes's political argument", but rather "to establish the authority of science, and through it to promote rational modes of thought and action, with a superstitious people".

In order to achieve this general objective, the (responsible) use of rhetoric – including metaphor – was indispensable. It thus appears less plausible that Hobbes was absolutely hostile to metaphor in *Leviathan*. But how can this conclusion be reconciled with the explicit condemnation of metaphor? In order to show that Hobbes was offering a coherent synthesis of *Science* and *Eloquence* in which both aspects were integrated, we need to look in detail at the communication theory he presents in *Leviathan*.

The First Part of the treatise, entitled "OF MAN", contains two key passages that can help to explain the apparent paradox of his condemnation of metaphor and his own intensive use of it:

(3) The generall use of Speech, is to transferre our Mentall Discourse, into Verbal [...]. So that the first use of names, is to serve for *Markes*, or *Notes* of remembrance. Another is, when many use the same words, to signifie (by their connexion and order,) one to another, what they conceive, or think of each matter; and also what they desire, fear, or have any other passion for. And for this use they are called *Signes*. Speciall uses of Speech are these; First, to Register, what by cogitation, wee find to be the cause of any thing, present or past; and what we find things present and past may produce, or effect [...]. Secondly, to shew to others that knowledge which we have attained; which is, to Counsell, and Teach one another. Thirdly, to make known to others our wills, and purposes, that we may have the mutuall help of one another. Fourthly, to please and delight our selves, and others, by playing with our words, for pleasure or ornament, innocently.

To these Uses, there are also foure correspondent Abuses. First, when men register their thoughts wrong, by the inconstancy of the signification of their words [...]. Secondly, when they use words metaphorically; that is, in other sense than that they are ordained for; and thereby deceive others. Thirdly, when by words they declare that to be their will, which is not. Fourthly, when they use them to grieve one another [...]. (Hobbes 1996: 25–6).

(4) The sixth [cause of absurd assertions I ascribe] to the use of Metaphors, Tropes, and other Rhetoricall figures, in stead of words proper. For though it be lawfull to say, (for example) in common speech, *the way goeth, or leadeth hither, or thither, The Proverb says this or that* (whereas wayes cannot go, nor Proverbs speak;) yet in reckoning, and seeking of truth, such speeches are not to be admitted. (Hobbes 1996: 35)

Hobbes's characterization of the *uses* and *abuses* of "Speech" in example (3) demonstrates that instead of insisting on a 'literal-truth paradigm',[4] he in fact endorses the expression of anything that people "desire, fear, or have any other passion for" as well as "playing with [...] words, for pleasure or ornament, innocently". The "abuses of speech" are deemed to be dangerous not on account of their figurative status as such, but because "names" here are *not used innocently*. As metaphors serve to deceive others and subvert one of the proper "speciall uses", namely to "counsell" and "teach", they come under the category of abuses.

Passage (4) illustrates the difference between innocent and deceptive use of figurative language. Hobbes here condones the use of so-called 'dead' metaphors like *the way goeth, or leadeth hither, or thither* as "lawfull (...) in common speech", but he excludes them from "reckoning, and seeking of truth". This *seeking of truth* is not just any truthful enquiry or discourse; otherwise, Hobbes's statement would imply that *common speech* consists only of lies. Rather, *reckoning, and seeking of truth* belong in the realms of *science* and *counsel*; and here metaphors are inappropriate, because they obscure the respective topic. Similar points are made in two further remarks:

(5) And therefore in reasoning, a man must take heed of words; which besides the signification of what we imagine of their nature, have a signification also of the nature, disposition, and interest of the speaker; such as are the names of Vertues and Vices; For one man calleth *Wisdome*, what another calleth *feare*, and one *cruelty*, what another *justice*, one *prodigality* what another *magnanimity*, and one *gravity* what another *stupidity*, &c. And therefore such names can never be true grounds of any ratiocination. No more can Metaphors, and Tropes of speech: but these are less dangerous, because they professe their inconstancy; which the other do not (Hobbes 1996: 31).

(6) In Demonstration, in Councell, and all rigourous search of Truth, Judgement does all; except sometimes the understanding have need to be opened by some apt similitude; and then there is so much use of Fancy. But for Metaphors, they are in this case utterly excluded. For seeing they professe deceit; to admit them into Councell, or Reasoning, were manifest folly. (Hobbes 1996: 52)

Again, metaphors are excluded from *counsel, reasoning* and *search of truth*, but the criticism of metaphor is qualified by a comparison with "names of Vertues and Vices". Whereas the latter are maximally deceptive in that the speakers present their own biased uses as correct meanings, the "Tropes of speech", including metaphors, *profess* their semantic inconstancy, i.e. they are transparent *as* "abuses". Due to this transparency, they are less dangerous, and their use in reasoning would be more of a "folly" than a serious case of deception. This relatively 'lenient' assessment might at first appear to be at odds with the more severe verdicts against metaphors as "ignes fatui" and as means of "deceiving others" (cf. examples 1 and 3). However, this apparent conflict can be reconciled by interpreting it as a differentiation of functional types of metaphors: some are 'harmless', such as the inconspicuous phrases in everyday speech (cf. example 4), some are dysfunctional but transparent, *professing their deceit* (cf. examples 5 and 6), and lastly there are metaphors that are employed deliberately to deceive and mislead others.

Before we concentrate on the last type of metaphor as regards its use in political discourse, one further theoretical and terminological differentiation made by Hobbes has to be considered. This is the distinction between "metaphors" and "similitudes". As example (6) shows, the latter are allowed in "Councell" and even in "rigorous search of Truth", even though they do not properly belong in the realm of (logical) *Judgement*, but in that of *Fancy*. What justifies employing *similitudes* in the *search of truth* is their usefulness in "opening the understanding of a scientific topic". *Similitudes* come close to what in present-day terminology would be *similes*, which are based on similar conceptual *mapping* or semantic *interaction* mechanisms as metaphors. This modern understanding of *simile* cannot, however, be directly mapped onto Hobbes's terminology. Hobbes built on humanistic traditions, going back to the famous classic definitions of *simile* as a type of *metaphor* by Aristotle in the third Book of his *Art of Rhetoric* (III, 4 and III, 10),[5] and of metaphor as a shortened simile by Quintilian in his *Institutio Oratoria*.[6] In his own translation-cum-précis of Aristotle's *Rhetoric*, Hobbes combines both perspectives in the definition of *similitude*:

(7) A *Similitude* differs from a *Metaphor* onely by such Particles of Comparison, as these, *As; Even as; So; Even so;* &c.
A *Similitude* therefore is a *Metaphor dilated*; and a *Metaphor*, is a *Similitude contracted* into one Word.
A *Similitude* does well in an Oration, so it be not too frequent; for 'tis *Poeticall*.

An example of a *Similitude* is this of *Pericles*; that said in his Oration, that the Bæotians *were like so many Oakes in a Wood, that did nothing but beate another.* (Hobbes 1986: 110–11)

Given Hobbes's general scepticism towards Aristotle,[7] this definition cannot immediately be assumed to reflect his own views. His critique of "metaphor" in *Leviathan*, for instance, drastically contrasts with Aristotle's praise of metaphor for having – in Hobbes's translation – *"perspicuity, Novity and Sweetnesse"* (Hobbes 1986: 109) and for being among the *"things that* grace *an* Oration, *and make it delightful"* (1986: 115). There is no equivalent contrast between the uses of the term "similitude" in the *Briefe of the Art of Rhetorique* and the *Leviathan*. Instead, as example (6) shows, the latter work distinguishes sharply between "apt similitudes" and "metaphors" – a differentiation that plays no role in the *Art of Rhetorique*. Whilst *metaphor* and *similitude* are only minimally different in Hobbes's translation of Aristotle, they are clearly contrasted in *Leviathan: similitudes* can be "apt", *metaphors* cannot.

Hobbes's principal defence against a conceivable accusation that his treatise was full of *metaphors* in the modern sense is evident: in his terminology (as used and defined in *Leviathan*), they would qualify as "apt similitudes" that are designed to make his treatise more, not less, *perspicuous*. His category of *similitude* covers not just similes as we would understand them, but also the analogies and allegories of the state as a BODY POLITIC, of perspicuous reasoning as PROGRESS ALONG A PATH and of false reasoning as LEADING INTO AN ABYSS. The supposed 'inconsistency' between Hobbes's use of metaphor and his condemnation of it as well as his alleged general dislike of figurative language use thus reveal themselves to be largely products of an unhistorical equation of the present-day meanings of "metaphor" with Hobbes's historical usage and of the oversight of specific terminological distinctions within *Leviathan*. In *Leviathan*, the term "metaphor" denotes in the first place a *functional* concept, i.e. a type of communicative "abuse".

8.3 Metaphor as *sedition*

Hobbes's interest in distinguishing between *uses* and *abuses of speech* was motivated by his appreciation of the fact that rhetoric, in all its forms, is of central importance for the 'well-being' of the BODY POLITIC. *Rhetoric* and *eloquence* were for him not just stylistic flourish or flamboyance; instead they played a crucial role in the constitution of any "Commonwealth", as well as in the "civill science" that analysed it. As far as political decision taking is concerned, this means that rhetoric cannot simply be discounted. Rather, it has to be exposed and disarmed when it puts the Commonwealth in danger. It is in this context of discussing the types of "Councell", in particular encouragement for and deterrence from action ("Exhortation" and "Dehortartion"), that we find a further massive criticism of *metaphor* in the form of a warning against the *deceptive* use of rhetoric:

> (8) Because the office of a Counsellour, when an action comes into a deliberation, is to make manifest the consequences of it, in such manner, as he that is Counselled may be truly and evidently informed, he ought to propound his advise, in such forme of speech, as may make the truth most evidently appear; [. . .]. And therefore, *rash, and unevident Inferences* [. . .], *obscure, confused, and ambiguous Expressions, also all metaphoricall Speeches, tending to the stirring up of Passion*, (because such reasoning, and such expressions, are usefull onely to deceive, or to lead him we Counsell towards other ends than his own), *are repugnant to the office of a Counsellour.* (Hobbes 1996: 179–80)

Metaphor and rhetoric in general can acquire a dangerous power if they are used to entice the hearers to develop attitudinal preferences that translate into rash and violent actions, which are not in their own best interest. If deceptive metaphor use remains unchecked, it can lead to "contention, and sedition or contempt" directed against lawful authority, as expounded in the *ignes fatui*-condemnation (cf. example 1).

Within the framework of the STATE-BODY-analogy in *Leviathan*, "seditious doctrines" are the chief "poyson" or "venime" that ruin the *body politic*, second only to a constitutional lack of sovereign power (1996: 223, 226). Through sedition, even a previously *healthy* commonwealth can be brought to the brink of "Civill warre" (1996: 226, 228) – that is, suffer a relapse into the "warre where every man is Enemy to every man" (1996: 89). This war was what Hobbes dreaded as "the greatest evill that can happen in this life" (1996: 231). He had seen his country divided by it and friends persecuted and killed on account of hatred incited by deceptive rhetoric (witness his homage to Sidney Godolphin in *Leviathan*, as someone who "hating no man, nor hated of any, was unfortunately slain" in the civil war; 1996: 484). During the war, Hobbes himself fled to France where he moved in royalist circles, only to publish the *Leviathan* and return to England when it was still Oliver Cromwell's

"Common-wealth". He subsequently experienced the restoration of the Stuart monarchy, and for the remainder of his life he had to defend himself against accusations of libertinism as well as atheism.[8]

In the rhetorical battles surrounding the political and military conflicts that tore the nation apart, *metaphor* was one of the most powerful weapons. According to Condren (1994: 71), "control of metaphor in the seventeenth century (...) was what we would see as a political concern". The "endeavour to restrict the role of the figurative" helped "to stabilise the political, render it more 'solid' and certain" (1994: 71). Hobbes's impassioned warnings against *deceptive metaphor* can be read as examples of such an attempt at stabilizing the political discourse and political *science* in order to immunize them against *seditious rhetoric*.

The fourth and last part of *Leviathan*, entitled *The Kingdome of Darknesse*, provides a host of examples with which Hobbes tries to expose the deceits, absurdities and insinuations of metaphors in public political and religious discourse. Here is one example of such a false analogy:

> (9) [...] this is another Errour of Aristotles Politiques, that in a wel ordered Common-wealth, not Men should govern, but the Laws. What man, that has his naturall Senses, though he can neither write nor read, does not find himself governed by them he fears, and beleeves can kill or hurt him when he obeyeth not? or that beleeves the Law can hurt him; that is Words, and Paper, without the Hands, and Swords of men? And this is of the number of pernicious Errors: for they induce men, as oft as they like not their Governors, to adhære to those that call them Tyrants, and to think it lawfull to raise warre against them: And yet they are many times cherished from the Pulpit, by the Clergy. (Hobbes 1996: 471)

The political maxim discussed here – that a general law should provide the rules for government, rather than individuals or groups of them – would probably not strike modern readers as particularly problematic, nor would the metaphorical 'personification' of 'the Law' in the agentive role seem to us particularly significant. Neither would it have been too difficult to identify the figurative character of the statement 'that laws *should govern* society' even for a "man, that has his naturall Senses, though he can neither write nor read", as Hobbes himself points out. After all, in the context of *common speech* (and, one might say, of common sense), no adult speaker is assumed to be naïve enough to take the meaning of idioms or proverbs at face value (cf. above, example 4). As regards political discourse, however, Hobbes is not so optimistic. The propagandists of *sedition* and *rebellion* can use the LAW-AS-GOVERNOR scenario, in conjunction with a biased redescription of the monarch as a *tyrant*,[9] as the basis for the conclusion that it is *lawful* to oppose him, because the monarch as a disobedient subject of the 'true' sovereign, the *Law*, deserves no loyalty.

By rebelling against the HEAD of the BODY POLITIC – and a fortiori, by inciting others to rebel through seditious, "metaphorical" confusion of the laws of that BODY POLITIC (its "artificall *Will*", Hobbes 1996: 9) – men act against their own well-understood self-interests. For in Hobbes's view they have ceded their individual will and their "right of nature" to the HEAD of the BODY POLITIC, in order to ensure peace among themselves (*Leviathan*, chapters XIV and XVIII). As an antidote against *poisonous* doctrines of rebellion, Hobbes sketches an alternative commonwealth, whose subjects "would be moved by their own self-interest pursued rationally and without the distorting effects to which myths, superstitions, and other forms of irrationality must inevitably lead" (Johnston 1986: 213).[10]

The specific political conclusions in Hobbes's argument, such as his verdict against any rebellion, may be questionable, motivated as they were by his particular historical experience, i.e. the English Civil War. However, even if one disagrees with these political attitudes, his example of the deceptive use of political vocabulary – i.e. "metaphor" in his terminology – is convincing as regards the analysis of the mechanisms of deception by metaphor. A seemingly innocuous metaphorical formulation, such as that of the *state being governed by law*, can be used by agitators to confuse dissatisfied subjects about what it means to rebel against the sovereign by basing their conclusion on an apparently self-evident scenario. The persuasive power of metaphor – to lead the political thoughts and actions of people *astray* – lies in the underhanded introduction of dubious analogies from which far-reaching consequences are drawn that are ultimately disastrous for society and the individual.

In exposing the effects of deceptive metaphor, Hobbes pursues a critical interest that is not different in principle from Lakoff and Johnson's concerns about the possibility that a "metaphor [...], by virtue of what it hides, can lead to human degradation" (Lakoff and Johnson 1980: 236). His contention that metaphor has an impact on whether political counsel makes "the truth most evidently appear" is also compatible with Stern and Leezenberg's semantic accounts of metaphorical meaning. What Hobbes's metaphor criticism in *Leviathan* adds to the modern analyses is an acute insight into the mechanism of how even seemingly innocuous conceptual mappings can be used to derive possibly catastrophic political conclusions, based on presuppositions that are deemed to 'go without saying'. We have thus arrived at an assessment – however cursory – of Hobbes's *metaphor* concept that stands in contrast to the conventional view of him as being not much more than a historic 'metaphor-basher'. Instead, we have seen that in his critical thematizations of *metaphor* as an "abuse of speech" as well as in his own argumentative practise, Hobbes consistently advocates a critical attitude towards seemingly unproblematic analogies that lead to dangerous conclusions. This disqualification of *metaphor* is not to be equated with the (vacuous) recommendation to speak or think only in literal terms. In the context of Hobbes's theory of communication and his political philosophy, such a position would make no sense at all. What Hobbes *does* recommend is the explicit signalling of all analogical conclusions (i.e. by way of their formulation as "apt similitudes"), so that the grounds for the analogy can be explicated and if need be, criticized.

This brings us back to the question of metaphor negotiation discussed in the preceding chapter. As we saw, the various types of dialogical argument by metaphor – whether they lead to consensual or adversarial or compromise conclusions – can be modelled as choices between sets of presuppositions in the metaphor scenarios that are explicated in the course of a conversation (cf. 7.i, 7.ii). Explicit dialogical argument-by-metaphor goes some way in fulfilling Hobbes's demands for "apt similitude" by definition, because the take-up of a given metaphor scenario by another participant in the debate highlights the presuppositions contained in the scenario, even if the response is not meant as an opposing statement. The greatest danger of political metaphors therefore lies in monological, pseudo-deductive conclusions from supposedly unproblematic maxims (e.g. in Hobbes's example, the conclusion *that it is lawful to rebel against the sovereign* derived from of the proposition *that the Law should govern*). In these cases, the bias of the metaphor source scenario remains hidden and its evaluative perspective is 'closed' for further debate.

Building on Hobbes's model of deceptive metaphor, we can approach the problem of a bias inherent in metaphors from a new angle. Cognitive theory has been successful in destroying the myth of the merely ornamental role of metaphor and in proving its conceptual significance in categorization. The present study has aimed at extending the conceptual analysis to the aspect of argumentation. But in the course of our discussion, we have seen that metaphor is not only a basic mode of categorization and argumentation – it is also an extremely attractive 'tool' in public political discourse. Whether it is politicians 'launching' a figurative catch-phrase or parodying each other's metaphors to score points in public debates, journalists commenting on a politician's favourite metaphor, or Hobbes himself in his *Leviathan* allegory: they all use metaphors and similes in the hope of making their conclusions persuasive and convincing. Is this 'conclusive' effect always just a matter of pseudo-argumentation, deception, make-believe? We might excuse it by claiming that this make-believe was unavoidable because of its functionality for reasoning, but such a position would commit us to a cognitive and ethical relativism, conceding that 'any metaphor goes'. In the concluding chapter we will ask if such a relativistic position is the only possible consequence of recognizing that metaphorical argumentation is based on analogy.

9
Open and Closed Metaphor Scenarios

Hobbes's insights into the mechanism of deceptive public communication are, as we have seen, by no means incompatible with cognitive analysis; in fact they provide essential reasons to explicate the cognitive effects of conceptual metaphor when it is used in argumentation. The analogical relationship of source and target concepts involves not only the transfer of semantic structures but also of emotive and evaluative aspects as integral parts of seemingly self-evident conclusions. Insofar as these conclusions are underwritten exclusively or mainly by presupposed aspects of folk-theory or everyday experience rather than by independently proven facts, they are open to Hobbes's criticism that their persuasiveness is based on false, deceptive analogy.

The metaphors of public discourse on EU politics are no exception to this verdict. The main scenarios from the four source domains analysed in the preceding chapters – FAMILY, JOURNEY, LIFE-HEALTH-BODY and ARCHITECTURE-HOUSE-BUILDING – allow their users to make complex political conclusions appear obvious and unproblematic on account of the analogical link to folk-theories and attached common-sense judgements. Even the explicit identification and criticism of these scenarios often serves as a tactical move in public discourse, e.g. in posing as speaking the 'plain truth' or parodying the opponent's metaphors in new blends. Our own analyses are not value-neutral either, as they are based on interpretative choices – what distinguishes them from party-political metaphor critique is their focus on explicating the mechanism of 'argument-by-metaphor'. We have reconstructed this analogical mechanism as a metaphorical warrant that is based on conceptual scenarios, which provide categorial slots for participants, roles and story-lines as well as 'standard' perspectives for their evaluation. This evaluation is based on socio-cultural stereotypes (e.g. about roles of

FATHERS in the FAMILY scenario, SLOW/FAST MOVERS within the JOURNEY scenario etc., or about 'normal' vs 'extraordinary' courses of action in the BUILDING OF A HOUSE or COMBATING AN ILLNESS). The scenarios and their attached standard evaluations do not logically entail specific conclusions, but they do offer conceptual default frames for actual inferences. Occasionally, a speaker tries to bend the evaluative perspective of a scenario in order to accommodate an unusual conclusion, as for instance the Conservative politician Michael Howard who pleaded in favour of SLOW MOVEMENT towards EU integration for Britain, because this policy was only "falsely called 'the slow track'" (cf. chapter 3, example 10, p. 48). However, in most cases the default conclusion suggested by the scenario is actually drawn.

Other speakers can of course challenge and recontextualize the scenario so as to contradict the default conclusion (e.g. EU-JOURNEY ENDING IN DISASTER, DISEASED HEART, RUINED EURO-HOUSE etc.). This opportunity for contradiction and communicative challenge is in the first place a matter of the sociopolitical environment, i.e. a question of whether (and to what extent) political dissent and opposition is possible in a given discourse community. But it is also a question of how metaphorical warrants are structured. In the case of deceptive metaphor, the warrant rests on seemingly unproblematic source scenarios and on the assumption of their direct applicability to the target topic. The resulting conclusion is designed to silence any criticism by implicitly denouncing it as absurd or inconceivable.

In the case of non-deceptive metaphor (Hobbes's "apt similitude"), on the other hand, the source scenario is presented as a new thematic perspective that invites – but does not prescribe – specific inferences about the most relevant way of conceptualizing the target topic. To indicate that a scenario is open to further discussion and negotiation, speakers can employ hedging formulations or other contextual signals that make it evident to the hearer that the proposed analogy only claims partial applicability. Whether and in which way such an invitation is taken up, depends of course on the further course of the conversation – as the examples in chapter 7 show, some scenarios seem to be especially attractive for discussion partners to extend and elaborate or to modify and reject by suggesting a competing scenario. Individual speakers cannot be held responsible for any later use or misuse of their metaphor scenarios by other participants in the virtual conversation of public discourse. But all speakers have a responsibility to make clear that any conclusion they may draw from a scenario is based on a specific evaluative perspective (as expressed in the scenario) rather than on a supposedly 'objective' or 'self-evident' truth. This means that the scenario should be constructed and presented in a way that leaves it open to critical scrutiny rather than as 'evidence' that closes the argument.

Building on the distinction between open and closed metaphor scenarios, cognitive analysis can help to formulate criteria for assessing the validity of analogical arguments without adopting an objectivist vantage point in a fictitious realm of purely 'literal' meanings, from which metaphorical thought and discourse could safely be criticised. The alternative to a politically or otherwise problematic metaphor is not: no metaphor at all. In actual political debates, the 'deconstruction' of given scenarios and the presentation of counter-scenarios provide efficient and widely used defence strategies against attempts to deceive. Linguistic analysis does not engage directly in the party-political fight for the 'best' metaphor. Instead, it is concerned with reconstructing the sets of presuppositions that are contained in scenarios, and can thus expose the analogical warrants used to legitimize specific conclusions. It would be naive and unrealistic to assume that the 'unpacking' of scenario presuppositions can automatically disabuse their users of the respective conclusions. It is up to the users to judge whether they accept an analogical warrant or not. Any attempt by linguists to give therapeutic admonitions about which scenarios to use or to avoid would most probably be seen as an arrogant infringement of the right to free political debate. On the other hand, it would be irresponsible if linguists adopted a pseudo-neutral stance that refrained from formulating an assessment of the validity or problematic character of analogical warrants used for political categorization or argumentation. As the historic example of the racist metaphor system used by the National Socialists in Germany shows, metaphor scenarios depicting social groups as *parasites that must be got rid of* can inform and precipitate political decisions that lead to the real-life consequence of genocide.

None of the Euro-discourse metaphors analysed in chapters 1–7 includes scenarios that come anywhere near to legitimizing political conclusions with such catastrophic effects. Nevertheless, they, too, reveal deep-seated attitudes and political preferences in the two discourse communities we have investigated. The analyses of scenario distribution in EUROMETA I and II have shown that it is possible to formulate empirically testable hypotheses concerning the predominance of certain metaphor scenarios that underpin the dominant attitudes and argumentative preferences in the British and German discourse communities. Most of these metaphors proved to be part of long-standing traditions of social conceptualization, such as the GREAT CHAIN OF BEING and BODY POLITIC metaphor systems. From an evolutionist viewpoint we can interpret these traditions and micro-historical transformations as evidence of adaptive conceptual developments at the "supraindividual level" (Kövecses). Abstracting from individual uses and focusing on relative distributions of scenarios, we can formulate hypotheses to explain the durability of certain scenarios and the disappearance of others from the metaphor pool and we can identify emerging argumentative trends in a discourse community. Thus the resurgence of *diagnoses* warning of *Eurosclerosis* and the statistical domination of tokens from the ARCHITECTURE-BUILDING-HOUSE domain by scenarios of STRUCTURALLY UNSAFE BUILDINGS or CHAOTIC BUILDING SITES since the mid-1990s can be interpreted as indications of mounting difficulties for EU integration at a time long before these problems were admitted in official declarations or policy documents.

At the "subindividual" level of metaphor analysis, we noted that some of the long-standing metaphor themes and scenarios connect to experiential and folk-theoretical knowledge systems, especially as regards FAMILY- and BODY-HEALTH-related source concepts. These observations tie in with recent research into the relation between metaphor, metonymy and their experiential grounding, which suggests that metaphors do not form a discrete class of phenomena but rather represent one end of *clines of conceptualization*.[1] The significance of these findings for the study of political metaphor clearly needs to be explored further. The 'rootedness' of central mappings and scenarios in primary scenes and experiences is a factor that must be taken into account for any investigation of the reasons of their persistence in folk-theories, idioms, discourse traditions and long-term patterns of sociopolitical conceptualization and argumentation. It may help us to understand why certain scenarios that are notorious for leading to problematic conclusions and prejudicial stereotyping remain popular despite many attempts to open up their sets of presuppositions to critical analysis. Enlightened critics have, for instance, repeatedly exposed the false conclusions inspired by the NATION-AS-FAMILY and social HEALTH-METAPHOR scenarios.[2] But the emotive appeal of these scenarios (as warrants for justifying unconditional 'patriotic' solidarity or elimination of supposed social ILLNESS-factors) seems not to have been significantly diminished or tamed. This observation suggests that metaphoric mappings and scenarios have inherited from the primary scenes a high degree of experiential and emotional immediacy and social management power. If we are interested in understanding and combating their potentially dangerous consequences for political thought and consciousness, we have to acknowledge the strength they derive from the seeming concreteness and vividness that is a legacy of their experiential grounding. Such an acknowledgement does not entail an uncritical acceptance of 'some kernel of truth' in every metaphor scenario. The use of some metaphor scenarios in political thought and discourse may be inescapable. But this only makes their analysis and assessment more, not less, worthwhile. Source scenarios are not dangerous or problematic as such – what makes them into potential *ignes fatui* is the pretence of their users that the analogies based on them, must not be questioned. Instead, scenarios serve best as starting points for further argumentation.

Notes and References

1 Introduction: Metaphor and Politics

1. Cf. e.g. Chilton and Ilyin 1993; Dirven 1994; Chilton, Ilyin and Mey 1998; Chilton and Lakoff 1995; Dirven, Frank and Ilie 2001; Hellsten 2000, 2002; Lakoff 1992, 2001, 2003; Liebert, Redeker and Waugh 1997; Musolff 1994, 1996a, b; Schäffner 1993, 1994, 1996; Zinken 2003; Zinken and Bolotova (in press).
2. Cf. Lakoff's characterization of the main aspects of the two models: (a) for the STRICT FATHER model: "the exertion of moral authority is moral behaviour on the part of the authority figure, and it is immoral for the authority figure to fail to exert authority, that is, to fail to set standards of behaviour and to enforce them through punishment (1996: 78); (b) for the NURTURANT PARENT model: "The primal experience behind this model is one of being cared for and cared about, having one's desires for loving interactions met, living as happily as possible, and deriving meaning from mutual interaction and care" (1996: 108).
3. For a general critique of a 'therapeutic' approach in linguistics cf. Hutton 2001.
4. The project was conducted jointly by the German Department at the University of Durham and the *Institut für Deutsche Sprache* in Mannheim, Germany, and was funded by the British Council and the German Academic Exchange Service (DAAD) under the Anglo-German Research Collaboration programme. For research reports cf. Kämper 1999; Herberg 1999; and Musolff, Good, Points and Wittlinger 2001.
5. For general information on Euro-political developments in Britain and Germany, cf. Baker and Seawright 1998; George 1994; Grosser 1998; Heisenberg 1991; Jones 1996; Marsh 1994; Preston 1994; Ramge 1993; Schoch 1992; Young 1998.
6. For a discussion of the conditions for the emergence of such a 'unified' European discourse community, cf. Schäffner, Musolff and Townson 1996: 6–11.

2 Conceptual Domains and Scenarios

1. Cf. e.g. Lakoff and Johnson 1980; Lakoff, Espenson and Goldberg 1989; Lakoff, Espenson and Schwartz 1991; Lakoff 1994; Deignan 1995; and Kövecses 2002.
2. Cf. e.g. Gibbs 1990, 1994, 1999; Giora 1997; Glucksberg and Keysar 1990, 1993; Glucksberg 2001; Goatly 1997; Steen 1994.
3. This view of public discourse as being fundamentally heterogeneous and argumentative presupposes the opportunity for public debate, as is usual in 'open' societies that grant free speech at least in principle. In a totalitarian dictatorship, on the other hand, there is little or no opportunity for public debate about political concepts or terminology.

4. For further research into "subindividual" aspects of metaphor cf. Johnson 1987; Lakoff and Johnson 1999; Grady, Taub and Morgan 1996, Grady and Johnson 2002.
5. For the theory of conceptual *domains* cf. Lakoff and Johnson 1980; Langacker 1987; and Croft 2002.
6. For the cognitive concepts of "radial"/"prototypical" categories cf. Lakoff 1987: 58–84; Taylor 1995: 38–65; Lakoff 1996: 7, 283–5.
7. Cf. Kövecses 1986, 1995, 2000; Sweetser 1990; Lakoff and Turner 1989; Deignan 1995, 1999; Moon 1998; Niemeier 2000.
8. An abridged version of the pilot corpus is freely accessible on the internet at www.dur.ac.uk/SMEL/depts/german/Arcindex.htm. For preliminary studies of parts of the pilot corpus cf. Musolff 1997, 2000a–c, 2003.
9. Cf. e.g. G, 7 July 1995: "Rifkind to bat for Britain in EU"; E, 9 May 1998: "Wim Duisenberg, in the rough". For abbreviations of newspaper and magazine titles here and below cf. list of abbreviations.
10. Cf. e.g. W, 23 July 1997: "In Deutschland, wo man die 3,0-Marke restriktiv auszulegen pflegt, wird man noch eine Weile damit hadern, daß Frankreich die Punktlandung nicht schon Ende dieses Jahres schafft" [For some time still, politicians in Germany will continue to moan about France not being able to hit the 3.0 spot by the end of this year].
11. Cf. Polenz 1991–99, vol. 2: 391–4; Kluge 1995: 617; Skeat 1993: 335; Kantorowicz 1997: 245–58.
12. This view informs also the metonymical use of the term *Europe* (or in German: *Europa*) for the European Union. The EU is seen by both British and German media (across all Euro-political divides) to be the representative of the whole of ('geographic') Europe, to which any non-members should look as their rightful *family home*. Distinct from this usage is the further, exclusively British interpretation of *Europe* as denoting continental Europe (or, the continental members of the EU), from which Britain is separated by the Channel.
13. For a detailed discussion of the whole range of pragmatic variation in FAMILY metaphors cf. Musolff 2003.
14. For the application of the PREMATURE BIRTH concept to the euro and for other source concepts of CHILDHOOD as part of the LIFE-CYCLE scenario see below, chapter 5.
15. Cf. G, 18 January 1996: "France, *the mother of EMU*, is locked in a bind of (...) savage proportion."; G, 17 March 1999: "In *Europe-as-family* the Commission played the *role of mama, the great dispenser of favours.*"
16. Cf. W, 19 August 1997: "Wie der Mensch sich als Staatsbürger mit seiner Muttersprache identifiziert, so identifiziert er sich auch mit seiner *Mutterwährung*. Beraubt man ihn der ersteren, macht man ihn sprachlos, beraubt man ihn der letzteren, so nimmt man ihm einen Teil seiner staatlichen Souveränität." [Just as individuals identify their national citizenship with their mother-tongue, they also identify with their respective *mother-currency*. Take away the former, and you deprive them of their language, take away the latter, and you rob them of a part of their national sovereignty].
17. For the tradition of male-oriented conceptualizations of politics and patriarchal mythology and terminology cf. R. Lakoff 1975; Pusch 1984.
18. I, 17 June 1997: "Gerhard Schröder, the opposition politician expected to challenge Helmut Kohl in next year's elections, said: 'The days when the

French President and the German Chancellor could decide everything that went on are over. The Franco-German axis must be transformed into a triangle involving London.' "

19. The Latin quotation refers to the traditional slogan advocating the Austrian emperors' policy of territorial gain through dynastic marriage rather than through war. The full text is: "Bella gerant alii! tu, felix Austria, nube! Nam quae Mars aliis, dat tibi regna Venus!"; cf. Büchmann 1898: 407.

3 Analogical Argument in Political Discourse

1. For an extended version of this accusation cf. also her 1992 speech on "Europe's Political Architecture" (Thatcher 1995: 615–16).
2. For further details of the cognitive *metaphor entailment* concept cf. Lakoff 1993: 216–18 and Kövecses 2002: 93–105; for the connection between *entailment* and *metonymy* cf. Radden 2000: 96–105.
3. The following references to Toulmin's model of argumentation do not aim to give a summary or assessment of his theory. What matters here is that non-formal arguments consist of more than bare data, logical operators and conclusions; i.e. that they require some "bridging" element that legitimizes the step from data to conclusions.
4. I use the terms *presupposed* and *presupposition* in a general sense relating to preconditions for understanding an utterance that are not entailments. Unlike the latter, a presupposition typically is not affected by negation or by modal formulation. Thus, *The king of France is bald*, *The king of France may be bald*, and *The king of France is not bald* all presuppose (counterfactually) that there *is* some *king of France*. For the differentiation of semantic and pragmatic theories of presupposition cf. Horn 1997; Lyons 1977, vol. 1: 181–7 and vol. 2: 592–606; Levinson 1983: 167–225; for the application to metaphor theory Stern 2000: 117–43; Leezenberg 2001: 217–27.
5. Cf. Perelman and Olbrechts-Tyteca 1969, Perelman 1979, 1982; for a critical assessment cf. Göttert 1994: 202–3.
6. For the basic model of hypothetical spaces cf. Fauconnier 1994: 31–2.
7. These and the following quotations are taken from the official English version of Fischer's speech on the Internet website *www.auswaertiges-amt.de*; italics by AM.
8. Tables 5–7 do *not* include references to the currency *movements*, e.g. of the euro currency after 1999; for a comparative analysis of conceptual metaphors applied to the euro in the British and German press cf. Charteris-Black and Musolff 2003).
9. **Examples for scenario version: X IS THE PATH/MILESTONE/TIMETABLE FOR THE EU'S JOURNEY**
   (a) [. . .] Maastricht is just *a staging post*. (G, 3 November 1991)
   (b) Die Staats- und Regierungschefs haben [. . .] *die Marschroute* für die Intensivierung des europäischen Einigungsprozesses festgelegt. (FR, 17 December 1990) [The heads of state and government *have determined the route* for a strengthening of the European unification process.]
10. **Examples for scenario version: THE PATH FOR THE EU'S PROGRESS LIES OPEN/IS EASY TO FOLLOW/THE EU MAKES GOOD PROGRESS**

(a) Blair [...] described the launch of the single currency as [...] *the first step on the road towards* building the long period of growth [...]. (T, 16 June 1998)
(b) Amsterdam *ebnet Weg* für erweiterte EU (W, 19 June 1997). [The Treaty of Amsterdam *paves the way* towards an enlarged EU.]

11. Examples for scenario version: THE PATH FOR THE EU'S PROGRESS IS DIFFICULT TO FOLLOW/IS BLOCKED BY AN OBSTACLE/THE EU MAKES SLOW PROGRESS
(a) The trouble is, *nobody knows what the road will be; no one has a map* of what European leaders will decide when they rewrite the EU's treaty (I, 11 September 1994)
(b) *Stolpersteine auf dem Marsch* zum Euro. (SZ, 6 June 1997) [*Stumbling blocks on the way to the euro.*]

12. Examples for scenario version: THE PATH FOR THE EU'S PROGRESS LEADS INTO DISASTER/A CUL-DE-SAC/ONE-WAY-STREET
(a) [The conservative] shadow chancellor Francis Maude said: "[...] the Government [...] *are following their 'new European way'* to tax, to regulate and to spend" (G, 20 November 1998)
(b) *Denn der Weg* von der Stabilitäts- zur Inflationsgemeinschaft *ist kurz*, wenn faule Kompromisse *den Weg zur Union pflastern*. (W, 12 December 1991) [It is only a *short way* from a community of stability to a community of inflation, if *the way toward the Union is paved* with bad compromises.]

13. Example for scenario version: EU MEMBER STATES HAVE REACHED A CROSSROADS
The European Union after Maastricht finds itself confronting the most severe pressures. [...] *We are at a dangerous crossroads* and the recoil from a failed single currency could be profoundly destabilising (G, 11 December 1995).

14. Example for scenario version: X IS OFF THE EU PATH
Small wonder that EMU is becoming increasingly unpopular [...]. Britain is still well advised to stay *on the sidelines*. (G, 28 February 1998)

15. Examples for scenario version: X IS MAKING (TOO) RAPID PROGRESS
(a) Britain is right to stay out [of the single currency]. We could help our partners if we could persuade some of them that *they are in too great a hurry*. (G, 5 May 1998)
(b) France and Germany have taken a *major step towards a single economic government* for the 11 countries that have adopted the euro, isolating Britain inside the European Union [... and .....] signalling *the splitting of Europe into slow and fast lanes.* (DT, 1 June 2000)

16. Definitions of the EU CORE vary: usually they include France, Germany, Benelux (plus, in a few cases, Italy, Austria, Denmark). For the CORE-PERIPHERY imagery in Euro debates cf. Schäffner 1996: 52–6; Reeves 1996: 163–9; Musolff 2000a: 77–86.

17. Examples for scenario version: X IS NOT MAKING FAST (ENOUGH) PROGRESS
(a) *Life in the slow lane* [headline] (...) remaining in the second tier of an integrating Europe will not give us greater autonomy and it will not enhance our ability to control our economy. In fact, *we would be forced to 'track' the policies of the first-tier countries* without having much influence upon them. (NSt, 16 November 1990)
(b) Sleek new Union would *leave UK behind*. (I, 27 June 2000; = headline of *Independent* article on Fischer speech, quoted above)

182 *Metaphor and Political Discourse*

    (c) Bonn hat sich selbst in die *Rolle eines Bremsers* manövriert. (SZ, 12 June 1997) [Bonn has managed to get itself in the role of someone *who applies the brakes* (in EU politics).]

18. Examples for scenario version: X IS OFF TRAIN/TRACK, OBSTACLE IN PATH OF TRAIN, RELUCTANT PASSENGER
    (a) Mr Major and his colleagues are putting it about that *they do not just mean to miss the European train, they are placing themselves squarely in its path*. (T, 10 June 1991)
    (b) Genau wie die beiden Regierungen es vorhaben, wird am 1. Januar 1999 der Euro eingeführt, so daß nun sogar britische Finanzkreise sich Sorgen machen, *sie könnten den Zug verpassen*. (SZ, 8 October 1996) [Just as the two governments [of France and Germany] had planned it, the euro currency will be introduced on 1 January 1999, and this means that even British financial circles are beginning to be *afraid of missing the train*.]

19. Examples for scenario version: X IS ON TRAIN/TRACK, SETTING THE POINTS, LOCOMOTIVE
    (a) Despite Britain's ad hoc alliances, *it is the Franco-German engine that drives the Euro-train*. (ST, 24 March 1996)
    (b) Unter deutscher Präsidentschaft 1988 *seien die Weichen* für die gemeinsame europäische Währung *gestellt worden*. (W, 12 December 1998; quotation from speech by the then Austrian Chancellor, V. Klima) [It was during the German EC-presidency of 1988 that *the points were set* for the common European currency.]
    (c) Die Europäische Währungsunion ist [. . .] *die Lokomotive, die den europäischen Zug seinem Ziel näher bringt*: der immer engeren Union unseres Kontinents. (Z, 19 February 1998) [The European currency union is *the locomotive that takes the EU train closer to its destination*, i.e. the ever closer union of our continent.]

20. Examples for scenario version: THE EUROPEAN TRAIN MAKES GOOD PROGRESS
    (a) *Euro-Express* back *on track*. (G, 26 September 1992)
    (b) *Der europäische Zug ist ein gutes Stück vorangekommen* (Z, 7 January 1999) [*The European train has made good progress*; quotation of a statement made by the then German trade and commerce minister W. Müller]

21. Example for scenario version: THE EUROPEAN TRAIN'S PROGRESS IS IN QUESTION
    Will future historians look back on Maastricht as the moment *when the locomotive of European monetary unity opened the throttle, not to halt again until it reached the terminus, or will they note with mild amusement how it ground to a halt at the next red light*? (G, 16 December 1995)

22. Examples for scenario version: THE EUROPEAN TRAIN'S PROGRESS IS NOT SECURE/WILL END IN DISASTER
    (a) Lady Thatcher warned [. . .] "There is a *fear that the European train will thunder forward, laden with its customary cargo of gravy, towards a destination neither wished for nor understood by electorates*". (T, 20 September 1992)
    (b) To many Britons, Europe seems *like a high-speed train, hurtling its reluctant passengers* into a new millennium of continental government [. . .] (T, 5 December 1998).

23. Examples for scenario version: X IS OFF SHIP, OBSTACLE IN PATH OF SHIP, RELUCTANT PASSENGER (or IS OFF CONVOY, SLOW(EST) SHIP IN CONVOY)
    (a) Mr Kohl [...] says Germany *"cannot accept a Europe, the speed of which is dictated by the slowest ship in the convoy"*. (FT, 4 January 1993)
    (b) Fears grow that *Germany may miss the EMU boat*. (G, 13 January 1996)
    (c) Die Frage, *ob die Briten ins gemeinsame Boot gebracht werden können*, muß zunächst offen bleiben. (W, 7 October 1996) [The question remains open *whether Britain can be brought into the EU boat* (of sharing national policy competencies).]
24. Example for scenario version STATE X IS ON SHIP or FAST(EST) SHIP IN CONVOY
    Der *Geleitzug der Europäischen Union* [...] ist auseinandergerissen. Die schnellsten *Schiffe*, Deutschland und Frankreich, haben sich das Privileg gesichert, das Ziel einheitlicher Währung von 1998 an allein anzukreuzen [...]. (W, 11 December 1991) [The *European convoy has come apart. The fastest ships*, Germany and France, have reserved for themselves the chance *to steer a course towards a common currency* from 1998 onwards.]
25. Example for scenario version: THE EUROPEAN SHIP/CONVOY MAKES/WILL MAKE GOOD PROGRESS
    Europe's single currency will be *launched on a rising tide* of industrial production [...] EU officials yesterday hailed the figures as *providing "a fair wind" for the euro's launch*. (G, 9 April 1998)
26. Example for scenario version: THE EUROPEAN SHIP/CONVOY'S PROGRESS IS SLOW/IN QUESTION
    Launched as smoothly as a sleek ocean liner on January 1, the euro has quickly *encountered some choppy water*. (G, 18 February 1999)
27. Example for scenario version: THE EUROPEAN SHIP/CONVOY'S PROGRESS WILL END IN DISASTER
    Like the Titanic, the euro – one tries to avoid saying the SS Euro – *was regarded as unsinkable. Hence the shortage of lifeboats*. (T, 2 June 1997)
28. Examples for scenario version: X IS OFF CAR/BUS, RELUCTANT PASSENGER, SLOW CAR/MOTOR
    (a) *Europe's political engine* [...] *is certainly sputtering*. [...] *the Franco-German motor* [...] *needs an overhaul*. (E, 9 May 1998)
    (b) *Der einstige Motor Europas, Deutschland*, wird [...] zunehmend zur Bremse. (SP, 16 June 1997) [Germany, *formerly the engine of Europe*, is becoming its brake.]
29. Examples for scenario version: X IS ON CAR/BUS, (TOO) FAST CAR/MOTOR, (TOO) GOOD OVERHAUL OF CAR/ENGINE
    (a) [...] the overriding purpose of yesterday's meeting in Mainz was to show that [...] France and Germany are back *as the "motor of Europe"*, with a unity of purpose and determination. (I, 10 June 2000)
    (b) If the Maastricht treaty was the *juggernaut* that pushed Europe off towards full union, then the "Maastricht 2" conference, beginning in Turin on Friday, is *merely "a 5,000-mile service"*. Or so British ministers [...] would have us believe. [...] Tory Eurosceptics already sniff a sell-out by Britain. *"It is more like ordering a new model than a 5,000-mile service,"* said John Redwood, the former cabinet minister. (ST, 24 March 1996)
30. Example for scenario version: THE EUROPEAN CAR JOURNEY'S PROGRESS WILL END IN AN ACCIDENT/DISASTER

Fischer sagte [...]: Wenn es nicht gelinge, auch zu einer gemeinschaftlichen Wirtschafts-, Sozial und Finanzpolitik zu kommen, *fahre die Währungsunion "krachend gegen die Wand"*. (SZ, 3 April 1998) [Fischer said that if the EU was unable to develop common economic, social and financial policies, EMU *would crash into a wall at full speed.*]

31. **Example for scenario version:** X IS OFF AEROPLANE, AEROPLANE/AIR TRAVELLER OFF COURSE
    (a) It is *as if, out there on the Tarmac, is a jet destined for an unknown location. The danger of not getting on board is that all the best seats in the club class will be taken* and that, when Britain does decide to take the plunge, there will be *only seats in steerage left.* On the other hand [...] the suspicion is *that one of the engines is a bit dodgy.* (G, 10 February 1997)
    (b) Zweifel an *deutscher Punktlandung* für den Euro (W, 20 June 1997). [Germany's *precise euro landing* (to 'hit' the EMU criteria laid down by EU) [is] doubtful]

32. **Example for scenario version:** X IS AEROPLANE ON COURSE
    A return to mission control [headline]. The exchange rate mechanism's original objective was to offer [...] predictability in a world of violently gyrating exchange rates. [...] Yesterday's events offer the first hint *that it may return to the original mission.* (G, 15 September 1992)

33. **Example for scenario version:** THE EUROPEAN PROGRESS MAY END IN AIR CRASH/DISASTER
    [...] by 2002 it will have become clearer whether the single currency [...] *aborts on takeoff.* (G, 15 October 1997)

34. **Example for scenario version:** X, Y ARE PARTNERS ON TANDEM
    Bonn wird sich neuen Pariser Europa-Forderungen gegenübersehen, *die das bewährte Tandem erheblich ins Schlingern bringen können.* (RP, 3 June 1997) [Bonn will be confronted with new French demands, which might well *destabilize the traditional tandem.*]

35. **Example for scenario version:** X IS (SUCCESSFUL) CYCLIST
    [...] mühelos scheint dem sozialistischen Regierungschef [= L. Jospin] mit seinen Maßnahmen zur Annäherung an die Euro-Kriterien das Kunststück gelungen zu sein, *ein wichtiges Etappenziel auf der "Tour d'Europe"* erreicht [...] zu haben. (Z, 23 July 1997) [By getting closer to the EMU criteria, the socialist head of government seems to have pulled off effortlessly the feat of reaching *an important intermediate goal in the 'Tour d'Europe'.*]

36. **Example for scenario version:** X IS (SLOW) BICYCLE
    Margaret Beckett, Labour's acting leader, accused Mr Major of *keeping Britain in the 'bicycle lane' not the fast lane.* (G, 2 June 1994)

37. **Example for scenario version:** EUROPEAN PROGRESS IS BICYCLE: MOVE (FORWARD) OR FALL
    Europe, in Jacques Delors' famous analogy, *is like a bicycle: allow it to stop moving and it falls.* (G, 11 September 1995)

4 Corpora and the Semantics of Metaphor

1. For an introduction to the "Bank of English" corpus cf. the Internet page www.cobuild.collins.co.uk/boe_info.html.

2. For descriptions of COSMAS (version I) cf. the websites:
   www.ids-mannheim.de/kt/corpora.shtml/ and
   www.ids-mannheim.de/kt/textorg.html.
3. For analyses of corpus searches on idiomatic phrases containing metaphors in the "Bank of English" cf. Deignan 1995; 1999; Moon 1998; and Hunston 2002:52–66.
4. For the database cf. http://www.cs.bham.ac.uk/~jab/ATT-Meta/Databank/.
5. The assumption (and, to some extent, successful demonstration) of the 'machine-detectability' of metaphor and metonymy implies the even more fundamental assumption that reliable criteria exist for the *identification* of figurative language use among any language data. For research into this topic, cf. Steen 1994, 1999 and contributions by Steen et al. in *Language and Literature* 11/1 (Steen 2002; Crisp 2002; Heywood, Semino and Short 2002; Crisp, Heywood and Steen 2002).
6. For further WordNet-based analyses of metaphor as well as of metonymy, cf. Markert and Nissim 2003; Peters and Wilks 2003.
7. For the problem of "balanced corpora" cf. Altenberg and Granger 2002b.
8. Due to the word number limitation for the EUROMETA II searches (i.e. 100–500 words), the average word number per passage is considerably lower than in EUROMETA I, where some passages contained the complete articles, numbering up to a thousand words or more.
9. In addition, Searle assumes the operation of two further "principles" concerning the "association" of semantic values of the terms used in a metaphor so that one specific intended value can be identified (1993: 108).
10. Cf. Davidson 1979; Levinson 1983; Rumelhart 1993; Lakoff 1993; Gibbs 1994; Recanati 1995; Stern 2000; Glucksberg 2001; Leezenberg 2001.
11. These arguments do not pertain in the same degree to and thus do not invalidate all pragmatic theories of metaphor. Neither Max Black's essays on metaphor nor Donald Davidson's account of "What metaphors mean", nor Dan Sperber and Deirdre Wilson's Relevance Theory depend on the assumption that language users must go through a process of first pursuing, then rejecting a literal interpretation before arriving at a metaphorical meaning. This does not mean the authors ignore the problem that their concepts of metaphoricity imply corresponding notions of non-metaphorical meaning. Black, for instance, acknowledges a logical derivation of the notion of metaphor from that of literalness but does not accept "literal utterance as an unproblematic standard", by which metaphor could be judged to be 'defective' or 'secondary' (Black 1993: 22). The literalness problem leads Davidson, on the other hand, to the conclusion that metaphor has no special, non-literal meaning at all, but "belongs exclusively to the domain of [language] use" (Davidson 1979: 30–1). Sperber and Wilson acknowledge the metaphorical-literal distinction but reject any notion of metaphor requiring "special interpretive abilities or procedures" (Sperber and Wilson 1995: 237). They see metaphor and other rhetorical tropes as akin to "loose uses of language" that do not require an absolutely literal interpretation "to confirm the presumption of relevance" (1995: 234). In accordance with the principle of relevance, the aspect of "relative indirectness" involved in figurative use must "be offset by some increase in contextual effects" (1995: 235–7; cf. also Goatly 1997: 140–8).

12. Cf. Kittay 1987: 214–24; for historical overviews of semantic field theory cf. Geckeler 1971; Schmidt 1973; Lyons 1977: 250–69; for recent developments cf. Lutzeier 1993; with specific reference to "metaphor (or "image") fields", cf. Kurz 1989; Peil 1993.
13. The term *vehicle* for the 'image' part of metaphorical statements is taken over from I. A. Richards (1936), via Black (1962); cf. Kittay 1987: 25, note 9.
14. Cf. e.g. Glucksberg 2001: 29, 36, 110, 113.
15. This is not to deny the considerable epistemological and methodological differences between the cognitive and neo-semantic approaches. For 'full and frank' exchanges over these differences cf. Lakoff and Johnson 1999: 98–102, 119–29; Lakoff 1993: 236–7; Stern 2000: 176–87; Leezenberg 2001: 135–47; Glucksberg and McGlone 1999: 1541–7, 1555–7; McGlone 2001: passim.

5 Europe as a BODY POLITIC

1. For a criticism of the sole reliance on the most prominent writings in the history of concepts in favour of approaches that also take into consideration minor works, popular media and political documents in order to assess the whole "ideological context" cf. Skinner 1978, vol. 1: xi–xiv.
2. For evidence from BoE for the use of these expressions in current English cf. Deignan 1995: 2.
3. Cf., with reference to the use of physical and medical metaphors in Nazi propaganda and ideology, Sontag 1991: passim; Volmert 1989: 154–7; Schmitz-Berning 1998: 460–4; Hawkins 2001: 44–7.
4. For analyses of spatial imagery in economy-related discourse cf. Boers and Demecheleer 1997; White 2003; Charteris-Black and Musolff 2003.
5. FEVER has not been sub-categorized under ILLNESS/DISEASE concepts due to specific target contextualization; see text below (section 5.3) for details.
6. The German 'loanwords' from English, *fit* and *fitness*, in the sense of 'physical prowess/health' seem to enjoy particular popularity in the German press, whereas they do not figure in the BoE. The only occurrences of *fit* in the context of *Euro* and *Europe* terms in BoE have the meaning of 'matching', e.g. in "Britain would fit into euroland" (T, 1 March 1999). However, *fit* and *fitness* do occur in corporeal sense in the English sample of EUROMETA I.
7. Figures for the sub-domain CURE/THERAPY/CARE appear to be distorted, amounting as they do to just over 50 per cent of those in the pilot corpus. The lexemes known from EUROMETA I were searched but did not yield any significant results. It is, however, highly likely that there are other lexemes in this field for which tokens could be found. The further searches necessary to establish these lexemes were not carried out due to time pressure during the BoE search.
8. For earlier occurrences of the PREMATURE BIRTH metaphor that seem to have received no particular attention in the public cf. e.g. SZ, 25 October 1996 and G, 24 June 1997.
9. Cf. press reports about opinion polls, e.g. SZ, 18 January 1997: "Die Deutschen – sehr skeptische Europäer" [The Germans – very sceptical Europeans!]; Z, 7 March 1997: "Wenn die Mark geht" [When the Deutschmark

disappears]; W, 23 April 1998: "Deutsche trauen dem Euro nicht" [Germans don't trust the euro].
10. Cf. SZ, 28 March 1998: "[Kinkel sagte, es] sei 'falsch und wenig verantwortungsvoll' gewesen, daß Schröder vom Euro als einer *'kränkelnden Fehlgeburt'* gesprochen habe" [Kinkel remarked that Schröder had been wrong and had shown a lack of responsibility in calling the euro a *sickly miscarried child*]; MM, 3 April 1998: "[...] Helmut Kohl ging seinen Herausforderer [...] frontal an: 'Schröders Bemerkung, der Euro sei eine *'kränkelnde Mißgeburt'*, ist nicht zu verstehen'" [Kohl launched a frontal attack on his challenger: Schröder's statement that the euro was a *sick monstrosity* was incomprehensible].
11. Cf. SZ, 28 March 1998: "Schröder stellte [...] richtig, er habe nicht von einer *'Fehlgeburt'*, sondern von einer *'Frühgeburt'* geredet, was ein beachtlicher Unterschied sei". [Schröder put the record straight: *he had not spoken of a miscarriage but of a premature birth*, which made a huge difference.]
12. Cf. e.g. SZ, 4 May 1998: "*Schwere Geburt*" [*Difficult birth*], taz, 17 June 1998: "*die Geburt des Euro* ist durch seine erste schwere Krise *besudelt worden*" [*the birth of the euro has been spoiled* by a first, severe crisis]; G, 5 May 1998: "*Birth pangs* of the euro".
13. The German text contains a pun, as it alludes contrastively to a well-known advertising slogan for a healthy drink: "Nie war er so wertvoll wie heute" [Never was it so valuable as today].
14. Cf. e.g. BZ, 14 March 1998: "In Großbritannien *herrscht das Eurofieber*. Immer mehr Unternehmer und Bankiers bereiten sich auf die Währungsunion vor." [Great Britain is *gripped by euro fever*. More and more companies and bankers prepare for the currency union.].
15. Cf. T, 5 September 1999: "In the 19th century, the vast Ottoman empire was 'the sick man of Europe' but it was also indispensable: if it collapsed, you would get the problems of Iraq, Kosovo, Palestine, even – although more remotely – Chechnya." For the historical tradition of the *sick man of Europe* formula cf. Büchmann 1898: 513–14 (with relevant quotations from, *inter alia*, Montesquieu, Voltaire, and Lord Russell).
16. Cf. the gloss of *Eurosclerosis* as "chronically slow growth" in example (4) of the preceding chapter. For the 1980s usage of *Eurosklerose* in Germany cf. Jung and Wengeler 1995: 110.
17. I owe this observation to René Dirven. For the tradition of 'national' characterizations of diseases cf. Ayto 2000: 207; Radford and Smith 1989: 42; *Brewer's Dictionary of Phrase and Fable* 1999: 488.
18. References to *heads of government, heads of state*, or to institutional *bodies* of the EU (parliament, commission, council etc.) are not included in the corpus, as they represent tokens of standardized terminology whose metaphorical basis seems to be no longer argumentatively active, at least as far as their occurrences in EUROMETA data are concerned.
19. Cf. e.g. the entries for *heart* in *Brewer's Dictionary of Phrase and Fable* 1999: 557–8 and for *Herz* in Röhrich 2001, vol. 2: 704–8.
20. Cf., for example, statements such as "Euro-sceptics will take heart from an ICM poll" (G, 16 February 1995), or "This question goes to the heart of what Europe's economic future will be" (E, 28 November 1998).

21. Cf. CDU/CSU-Fraktion des Deutschen Bundestages 1994: "[...] Hoffnung [...], daß Großbritannien *seine Rolle 'im Herzen Europas' und damit in seinem Kern übernimmt*".
22. Cf. e.g. Z, 14 June 1996: "Die Briten waren *nie wirklich mit dem Herzen in Europa*"; Z, 13 December 1996: "Der Regierungschef, der einst Großbritannien *'im Herzen Europas'* verankern wollte, hat keine feste überzeugung".
23. Cf. E, 28 November 1992: "Today Britain is right to see that [...] as an old, offshore Euro-doubter *that has improbably proclaimed itself to be at the 'heart of Europe'*, it would be perfidious in the extreme for it to scupper a treaty that the rest of Europe still claims enthusiasm for"; G, 9 February 1995: "What am I now to make of John Major, whose *wish 'to be the heart of Europe'* seems to be less than full-blooded?".
24. Cf. e.g. G, 5 September 1995; E, 9 September 1995; G, 30 September 1995.
25. For the tradition of this mapping cf. e.g. Shakespeare's "Something is rotten in the state of Denmark" *Hamlet* I.iii.19-24), and phraseologisms, such as *Rotten Boroughs* (*Brewer's Dictionary of Phrase and Fable*, 1999: 1016). Roslyn Frank has pointed out an important aspect of the blending between the notions of ROT and HEART: in botany, the hard, inner core of a tree trunk is called *heart wood*, and its 'rotting away' is a certain sign of ageing and disease: the tree is 'rotten to the core'. The latter phrase has become a widely used idiom in English and provides one source input for the *rotten heart* metaphor. The common element is the mapping from HUMAN HEART to TREE CORE and to POLITICAL/INSTITUTIONAL CORE. This element of "same basic topology is assigned to both 'bodies' and projected in the 'blend'" (R. Frank, personal communication).
26. Cf. e.g. G, 16 March 1999: "Report *strikes at heart of Europe*"; T, 17 March 1999: "exposure of the corruption and incompetence *at the heart of the European Union*"; *The SUN*, 21 March 1999: "widespread fraud, corruption and cronyism *at the heart of Europe*".
27. Cf. e.g. Z, 13 December 1996: "Die Deutschen verfechten mehr und mehr *ein Europa der kalten Herzen*." [The Germans are pursuing *a policy of a cold-hearted Europe*]; BZ, 16 May 1998: "*Die Leere im Herzen des Kontinents* [...] – in Europa breitet sich erst einmal politische Leere aus." [*The emptiness at the heart of the continent* – a political vacuum is growing in Europe.]
28. Cf. e.g. taz, 13 September 1995; FAZ, 13 September 1995; Z, 15 September 1995.
29. Cf. e.g. G, 1 December 1997; G, 26 October 1998; I, 3 December 1998; NSt, 5 March 1999; E, 20 March 1999; T, 24 February 2000; T, 17 June 2001; FR, 2 January 1998; FR, 19 December 1998; FR, 8 January 1999.
30. For an analysis of the metaphors used in the public debate about the 2001 "foot and mouth epidemic" in Britain cf. Nerlich, Hamilton and Rowe 2002.
31. Other lexical items for body parts and organs, e.g. *arm(s)/Arm(e)*, *belly/Bauch*, *liver/Leber*, *lung/Lunge*, *stomach/Magen*, *nerves/Nerven*, *veins/Adern* or *Venen*, were checked in COSMAS and BoE, but yielded only non-metaphorical or topic-irrelevant results.
32. For further *European muscles* examples cf. T, 5 February 1997; taz, 3 February 1990; FAZ, 5 March 1993; SZ, 16 September 1998; BZ, 29 September 1999.

6 Discourse History in a Metaphor Corpus

1. Lakoff and Turner distinguish between the near-universal "basic Great Chain" concept, which concerns "the relation of human beings to 'lower' forms of existence", and the more specifically Western tradition of the "extended Great Chain" (1989: 167). For further applications of the cognitive interpretation of the "Great Chain" cf. Kövceses 2002: 124–34.
2. Cf., for example, E, 5 June 1999: "Germans must find it [= the label of *the sick man of Europe*] more galling since it was coined in the last century by the Russian tsar, Nicholas I, to describe Ottoman Turkey – a once dynamic polity that failed."
3. For reviews of these strands of historical conceptual research cf. Skinner 1969, 1978; Koselleck 1979, 1998; Busse 1987; Rauff 1987; Ball 1988, 1998; Wengeler 2003. For the history of metaphorical concepts cf. Keller-Bauer 1983, 1984 and the literature recommended in Jäkel 1999; in particular Weinrich 1963, 1964, 1967 and Blumenberg 1960.
4. For Dennett's defence of metaphors in the theory of cognitive evolution cf. Dennett 1987: 298–300; 1995: 213.
5. Cf. the contributions in Aunger 2000, especially Hull 2000 and Kuper 2000.
6. Dennett (1995: 354–8) supports Sperber as regards the difference in the speed of change between gene and meme mutations but does not seem to interpret this as a fundamental counter-argument to meme theory. Dawkins (1999b: x) equally sees no principal problem in admitting a marked contrast in replication fidelity and still maintaining the basic analogy.
7. For further explorations of the 'epidemiological' perspective in relation to meme theory, cf. Dawkins 1993; Brodie 1996.
8. Cf. e.g. for the Old Testament, Ezekiel 44.7 and for the New Testament: St. Matthew 10.6 and 15.24. The other prominent biblical HOUSE metaphor is that of God's "heavenly kingdom" as a "house with many mansions" (St John 14.2).
9. A high number of adjectival and verbal word-forms in BoE and COSMAS that contained the stems *build-*, *bau-* (1,506 occurrences) turned out to consist of non-metaphorical uses or of fully lexicalized terms that did not invoke any relevant BUILDING-scenarios and were therefore excluded.
10. Cf. e.g. E, 17 October 1992: "new candidates are still *queuing up at the European Community's door*"; I, 11 December 1999: "Turkey has been *knocking on the EU's door* since 1963"; taz, 16 July 1992: "*Europas Türen für Flüchtlinge geschlossen*" [Europe's doors closed to refugees]; taz, 12 February 1999: "*Schlüssel, die Polen in den kommenden Jahren die Tore zu Europa öffnen können*" [keys that may open Europe's gates for Poland in the coming years].
11. Cf. Schäffner and Trommer 1990; Bachem and Battke 1991; Schäffner 1993; Chilton and Ilyin 1993; Chilton and Lakoff 1995; Musolff 2000a: 93–104, 2000b; Zinken 2003; Zinken and Bolotova (in press).
12. Cf. especially Chilton and Lakoff 1995; Chilton and Ilyin 1993; Schäffner 1993.
13. A strong version is also implausible in view of the fact that the mapping A NATION IS A SINGLE HOUSE appears to be known in Russian discourse as well. Eleven tokens in the German corpus sample quote an apparently well-

established Russian metaphor for St Petersburg as the 'window to Europe', planned by Tsar Peter I (e.g. taz, 4 April 1992: "Als *'Fenster nach Europa hin'* hatte Peter der Große um 1700 die neue Haupt- und Hafenstadt konzipiert" [Around 1700, Peter the Great designed the new capital and sea port as the *'window to Europe'*]. If one needs a window to look at an entity (here: 'Europe'), it seems most plausible that the onlooker is positioned in a building that is separate from the entity looked at through the window, i.e. *not* in the same building *with* that entity. The above-quoted statement would thus imply that Russia and Europe are conceived of as different HOUSES.
14. COSMAS also provides data for years before 1989 but these are not available for BoE so they have not been included in the table. As regards the phrase *Gemeinsames Europäisches Haus*, the pre-1989 figures appear to reflect a slow build-up to the high point in 1989, i.e. for 1985: 3 tokens, 1986: 4 tokens, 1987: 2 tokens, 1988: 8 tokens. These figures relate only to West German newspapers before unification; East German media and all non-printed sources that are also included in the COSMAS corpora were discounted. The earliest appearance of the slogan in COSMAS is a critical assessment of Gorbachev's détente policy in Z, 14 June 1985: "[. . .] wenn der Parteichef die Europäer einzig und allein als willkommene Hilfstruppen gegen SDI begrüßt, [. . .] *wird er das 'gemeinsame Haus' (Gorbatschow über Europa) nicht nutzen können"* [if the party leader only welcomes Europeans as allies against SDI, *he won't be able to make much use of the 'Common House' (G.'s vision of Europe)*].
15. This example has been supplied by Jörg Zinken; cf. Zinken and Bolotova (in press).
16. The PILLAR metaphor soon found its way into political science analyses of the EU; cf. Jones 1996: 4, 52–4; Buller and Smith 1998: 182.
17. Cf. e.g. E, 23 January 1995: "[. . .] perhaps *Europe's architect* will learn a familiar lesson: *stable buildings cannot be run up in a hurry";* taz, 20 May 1998: "[. . .] wie Kanzler Kohl sich als *Architekt Europas* feiern lasse" [the way Chancellor Kohl gathers plaudits as the *architect of Europe*].
18. Cf. e.g. Z, 16 May 1997: "Helmuts großer Traum, *das Europäische Haus*. [. . .] Wozu er dieses *Haus braucht*, nach so vielen Jahren als Kanzler? Klar doch: *Hausmeister will er werden."* [Helmut's great vision: *the European House*. What does he need this *house* for, after so many years as Chancellor? – Well, it's obvious: *he wants to be its caretaker* (literally: 'house-master')]. BZ, 24 April 1998: "[. . .] Kohl [will], wenn er sich im *Haus Europa aus dem Arbeitszimmer zurückzieht, um in der Küche noch eine Kleinigkeit zu essen,* die Gewißheit haben, *daß im Arbeitszimmer alles seine Ordnung hat* [. . .]." [Once he withdraws from *his study in the House of Europe* to have a snack in the *kitchen*, Kohl still wants to be certain that *everything is in order in the study*.]
19. The few other BRIDGE tokens in the corpus are mainly formulaic uses of idioms such as diplomatic *"bridge-building measures".*

7 Metaphor Negotiation

1. Its German translation was published in 1989, i.e. in a changed political context, when the 'German question' had gained a new quality, due to the

crisis of the East German state (for details cf. Schäffner and Trommer 1990; Bachem and Battke 1991).
2. For a detailed analysis of the British–German conflicts about EU policy as expressed by CONVOY JOURNEY metaphors cf. Musolff 2000c.
3. Options (c) and (d) correspond to the strategies for 'metaphor challenges' outlined by Perelman (1982: 119).
4. Cf. Cohen 1979: 1–5; Cooper 1986: 17–19, 78, 174, 213; Bertau 1996: 81–7; Goatly 1997: 1 [only on Locke]; Müller-Richter (1998); Leezenberg 2001: 1. For a critical assessment of Locke's condemnation of "all the artificial and figurative application of Words Eloquence hath invented" in the *Essay Concerning Human Understanding* (Locke 1979: 508) from the cognitive viewpoint, cf. Johnson 1981: 13; Lakoff and Johnson 1980: 190–1. In a detailed analysis of Locke's views on metaphor in the context of his own epistemological system and of its status in seventeenth-century philosophy, however, Nicolaas Mouton (in press) has challenged this global interpretation. He concludes: "Locke quite reasonably doubts whether metaphors can provide us with 'clear and certain knowledge', but increasingly starts to think that such knowledge is rather limited anyway, and that we have no choice but to rely on metaphors, guesswork, and the likes if we are to cope in this world, given our limitations."
5. Cohen (1979) indeed takes Hobbes's arguments seriously, acknowledging that Hobbes and Locke did each have a "general theory of meaning" which provided the background for their views on metaphor; he also differentiates clearly between Hobbes's criticism of metaphor and the "far less generous and forgiving" condemnation by Locke.
6. Cf. e.g. Ball 1985; Bertman 1988; Condren 1994; Dascal 1983; Isermann 1991; Johnston 1986; Jong 1990; MacDonald Ross 1987; Prokhovnik 1991; Skinner 1978, 1991, 1996; Wagner and Zenkert 1995.

8 Metaphor as Deception

1. Cf. e.g. Baumgold 1988; Brandt 1987; Mintz 1989, 1996; Martinich 1992: 48–9. For an earlier interpretation that highlights the fundamental function of this allegory for Hobbes's system of political philosophy cf. Cassirer 1998 [first published 1932]: 341.
2. Stillman (1995: 799) seems to argue in this direction, when he claims that through the "reasoned analogies between the Leviathan's body and the body politic" metaphor "gives way to similitude and similitude to the promise of a political reading to proceed 'orderly, and perspicuously'". However, Stillman goes on to argue that Leviathan "is so constructed to [...] induce "a state of profound epistemological fear" in the reader (1995: 805) and that power is ultimately "authorized in *Leviathan* by logic and magic" (1995: 815).
3. Skinner (1996: 334–56, 370–2) has traced in detail the changes from Hobbes's 'blanket rejection' of any input from *ars rhetorica* and *elocutio* to civil science, as formulated in *De Cive* and *The Elements of Law*, to the realization of "the inescapable need for an alliance between reason and eloquence, and hence between the art of rhetoric and the methods of science", as expressed in *Leviathan* (Skinner 1996: 346).

4. For a detailed examination and criticism of the *non-sequitur* between the (alleged) "metaphor-bashing" and a "literal truth paradigm" as the essence of seventeenth-century empiricist philosophy cf. Mouton, in press.
5. Cf. Aristotle 1996b: 224: "The *simile* is also a metaphor, as it is only slightly different. For when the poet says 'and like a lion leapt', it is a simile, but when 'a lion leapt', it is a metaphor; for because they are both bold, he spoke of Achilles by the metaphor of the lion"; and 1996b: 235: "For the simile is, as had been said before, a metaphor differing in one addition only; hence it is less pleasant, as it is more drawn out, and it does not say that this is that, and so the mind does not think out the resemblance either."
6. Quintilianus 1970: vol. 2, 463: "In totum autem metaphora breuior est similitudo, eoque distat, quod illa comparatur rei quam uolumus exprimere, haec pro ipsa re dicitur." For Hobbes's perspective on Quintilian's definitions of metaphor and simile cf. Skinner 1996: 345–6.
7. Harwood (1986: 2), on the basis of John Aubrey's short biography of Hobbes, states that "Hobbes held a decidedly mixed view of Aristotle" but "greatly respected the *Rhetoric*: Aubrey had heard Hobbes say that 'Aristotle was the worst Teacher that ever was, the worst Politician and Ethick [. . .] but his Rhetorique and Discourse of Animals was rare.'"
8. Cf. the (auto-)biographical sketches in Hobbes 1994: 231–64, as well as Mintz 1996: passim; Martinich 1992: 19–39 and 1997: 13–18.
9. For a detailed discussion of the techniques of rhetorical redescription or "paradiastole" cf. Skinner 1996: 153–80; for their application to the term *tyranny* in the historical context of the English Civil War, cf. Condren 1994: 36–7, 55–6, 78, 123–4.
10. Feldman (2001) has analysed in detail the demystification of another "metaphor" in *Leviathan*, i.e. the interpretation of the term "conscience" as denoting "the knowledge of private thoughts and facts" rather than "knowledge that is shared and confirmed by witnesses" (2001: 25–6), which Hobbes takes to be its original meaning, as indicated by the etymology of 'conscience' (Hobbes 1996: 48). By suggesting that everyone can be the "judge of good and evil actions" privately instead of relying on "public conscience", the advocates of the metaphorized meaning of *conscience* insinuate a similar justification for disobedience against the HEAD of the BODY POLITIC as those who allege that only 'the Law rules'.

9 Open and Closed Metaphor Scenarios

1. Cf. the contributions in Panther and Radden 1999; Barcelona 2000; Dirven and Pörings 2002.
2. Cf. e.g. the contemporary criticism of Nazi adaptations of BODY POLITIC scenarios by Lovejoy and Tillyard (Lovejoy 1936: 313; Tillyard 1982: 117).

Bibliography

Altenberg, Bengt and Sylviane Granger (eds) 2002a. *Lexis in Contrast: Corpus-Based Approaches*. Amsterdam/Philadelphia: Benjamins.
Altenberg, Bengt and Sylviane Granger 2002b. Recent Trends in Cross-Linguistic Studies. In: Altenberg and Granger 2002a, 3–48.
Aristotle 1996a. *Poetics*. Ed. Malcolm Heath. London: Penguin.
Aristotle 1996b. *The Art of Rhetoric*. Ed. H.C. Lawson-Tancred. London: Penguin.
Aunger, Robert (ed.) 2000. *Darwinizing Culture: the Status of Memetics as a Science*. Oxford: Oxford University Press.
Ayto, John 2000. *Dictionary of Euphemisms*. Revised edition. London: Bloomsbury.
Bachem, Rolf and Kathleen Battke 1991. Strukturen und Funktionen der Metapher 'Unser Gemeinsames Haus Europa' im aktuellen politischen Diskurs. In: Frank Liedtke, Martin Wengeler and Karin Böke (eds), *Begriffe besetzen: Strategien des Sprachgebrauchs in der Politik*. Opladen: Westdeutscher Verlag, 295–307.
Baker, David and David Seawright (eds) 1998. *Britain For and Against Europe: British Politics and the Question of European Integration*. Oxford: Oxford University Press.
Ball, Terence 1985. Hobbes's Linguistic Turn. *Polity*, 17, 739–60.
Ball, Terence 1988. *Transforming Political Discourse: Political Theory and Critical Conceptual History*. Oxford: Oxford University Press.
Ball, Terence 1998. Conceptual History and the History of Political Thought. In: Hampsher-Monk, Tilmans and Van Vree 1998, 75–86.
Barcelona, Antonio (ed.) 2000. *Metaphor and Metonymy at the Crossroads: a Cognitive Perspective*. Berlin and New York: De Gruyter.
Barnden, John A. and Mark G. Lee 2001a. *Understanding Open-Ended Usages of Familiar Conceptual Metaphors: an Approach and Artificial Intelligence System*. Technical Report CSRP-01-05, School of Computer Science, The University of Birmingham, UK.
Barnden, John A. and Mark G. Lee 2001b. *Application of the ATT-Meta Metaphor-Understanding System to an example of MIND PARTS AS PERSONS*. Technical Report CSRP-01-09, School of Computer Science, The University of Birmingham, UK.
Bartsch, Renate 1987. *Norms of Language: Theoretical and Practical Aspects*. London and New York: Longman.
Bartsch, Renate 2002. Generating Polysemy: Metaphor and Metonymy. In: Dirven and Pörings 2002, 49–73.
Bass, Allen M. 1997. The Metaphor of the Human Body in the Political Theory of John of Salisbury: Context and Innovation. In: Bernhard Debatin, Timothy R. Jackson and Daniel Steuer (eds), *Metaphor and Rational Discourse*. Tübingen: Niemeyer, 201–13.
Baumgold, Deborah 1988. *Hobbes's Political Theory*. Cambridge: Cambridge University Press.
Bertau, Marie-Cécile 1996. *Sprachspiel Metapher: Denkweisen und kommunikative Funktion einer rhetorischen Figur*. Opladen: Westdeutscher Verlag.

Bertman, Martin A. 1988. Semantics and Political Theory in Hobbes. *Hobbes Studies*, 1, 134–43.
Black, Max 1954. Metaphor. *Proceedings of the Aristotelian Society*, 55, 273–94.
Black, Max 1962. *Models and Metaphors*. Ithaca: Cornell University Press.
Black, Max 1993. More about Metaphor. In: Ortony 1993, 19–41.
Blackmore, Susan 1999. *The Meme Machine*. Foreword by Richard Dawkins. Oxford: Oxford University Press.
Blumenberg, Hans 1960. *Paradigmen zu einer Metaphorologie*. Bonn: Bouvier.
Boers, Frank and Murielle Demecheleer 1997. A Few Metaphorical Models in (Western) Economic Discourse. In: Wolf-Andreas Liebert, Gisela Redeker and Linda Waugh (eds), *Discourse and Perspective in Cognitive Linguistics*. Amsterdam and Philadelphia: Benjamins, 115–29.
Brandt, Reinhart 1987. Das Titelblatt des Leviathan. *Zeitschrift für Sozialwissenschaft*, 15, 164–86.
Brewer's Dictionary of Phrase and Fable 1999. Ed. Adrian Room (ed.). London: Cassell.
Brodie, Richard 1996. *Virus of the Mind: the New Science of the Meme*. Seattle, WA: Integral Press.
Büchmann, Georg 1898. *Geflügelte Worte*. Ed. K. Weidling. Berlin: Haude and Spener'sche Buchhandlung.
Buller, Jim and Martin J. Smith 1998. Civil Service Attitudes Towards the European Union. In: Baker and Seawright 1998, 165–84.
Busse, Dietrich 1987. *Historische Semantik: Analyse eines Programms*. Stuttgart: Klett-Cotta.
Cameron, Lynne 1999. Operationalising 'Metaphor' for Applied Linguistic Research. In: Cameron and Low 1999, 3–28.
Cameron, Lynne and Graham Low (eds) 1999. *Researching and Applying Metaphor*. Cambridge: Cambridge University Press.
Cameron, Lynne and Alice Deignan 2003. Combining Large and Small Corpora to Investigate Tuning Devices around Metaphor in Spoken Discourse. *Metaphor and Symbol*, 18/3, 149–60.
Cassirer, Ernst 1998. *Die Philosophie der Aufklärung*. Hamburg: Meiner. (First edn 1932).
CDU/CSU-Fraktion des Deutschen Bundestages 1994. *Überlegungen zur europäischen Politik*. Bonn.
Chamizo Domínguez, Pedro J. and Brigitte Nerlich (in press). Metaphor and Truth in Rationalism and Romanticism. In: Armin Burkhardt and Brigitte Nerlich (eds), *Tropical Truth*. Amsterdam and Philadelphia: Benjamins.
Charteris-Black, Jonathan and Andreas Musolff 2003. Battered Hero or Innocent Victim? Metaphors in British and German Financial Reporting. *Journal of English for Special Purposes*, 22, 153–76.
Chilton, Paul and Mikhail Ilyin 1993. Metaphor in Political Discourse: the Case of the 'Common European House'. *Discourse and Society*, 4/1, 7–31.
Chilton, Paul and George Lakoff 1995. Foreign Policy by Metaphor. In: Christina Schäffner and Anita Wenden (eds), *Language and Peace*. Dartmouth: Aldershot, 37–59.
Chilton, Paul, Mikhail V. Ilyin and Jacob Mey (eds) 1998. *Political Discourse in Transition in Eastern and Western Europe (1989–1991)*. Amsterdam and Philadelphia: Benjamins.

Cohen, Ted 1979. Metaphor and the Cultivation of Intimacy. In: Sacks 1979, 1–10.
Concise Oxford Dictionary 1979. Ed. J. B. Sykes. Oxford: Oxford University Press.
Condren, Conal 1994. *The Language of Politics in Seventeenth-Century England*. New York: St. Martin's Press.
Connolly, Bernard 1995. *The Rotten Heart of Europe*. London: Faber.
Conte, Rosaria C. 2000. Memes through (Social) Minds. In: Aunger 2000, 83–119.
Cooper, David E. 1986. *Metaphor*. Oxford: Blackwell.
Crisp, Peter 2002. Metaphorical Propositions: a Rationale. *Language and Literature*, 11/1, 7–16.
Crisp, Peter, John Heywood and Gerard Steen 2002. Metaphor Identification and Analysis, Classification and Quantification. *Language and Literature*, 11/1, 55–69.
Croft, William 2002. The Role of Domains in the Interpretation of Metaphors and Metonymies. In: Dirven and Pörings 2002, 161–205.
Dascal, Marcelo 1983. Signs and Cognitive Processes: Notes for a Chapter in the History of Semiotics. In: Achim Eschbach and Jürgen Trabant (eds), *History of Semiotics*. Amsterdam and Philadelphia: Benjamins, 169–90.
Davidson, Donald 1979. What Metaphors Mean. In: Sacks 1979, 29–45.
Dawkins, Richard 1989. *The Selfish Gene*. New edition. Oxford and New York: Oxford University Press.
Dawkins, Richard 1993. Viruses of the Mind. In: Bo Dahlbohm (ed.), *Dennett and his Critics: Demystifying Mind*. Oxford: Blackwell, 13–27.
Dawkins, Richard 1999a. *The Extended Phenotype: the Long Reach of the Gene*. Oxford: Oxford University Press.
Dawkins, Richard 1999b. Foreword. In: Blackmore 1999, vii–xvii.
Deignan, Alice 1995. *COBUILD English Guides. Vol. 7: Metaphor Dictionary*. London: HarperCollins.
Deignan, Alice 1999. Corpus-Based Research into Metaphor. In: Cameron and Low 1999, 177–99.
Dennett, Daniel C. 1987. *The Intentional Stance*. Cambridge, MA: MIT Press.
Dennett, Daniel C. 1995. *Darwin's Dangerous Idea: Evolution and the Meanings of Life*. London: Penguin.
Dirven, René 1993/2002. Metonymy and Metaphor: Different Mental Strategies of Conceptualisation. *Leuvense Bijdragen*, 82, 1–28; revised version in: Dirven and Pörings 2002, 75–111.
Dirven, René 1994. *Metaphor and Nation: Metaphors Afrikaners live by*. Frankfurt am Main/Bern: Peter Lang.
Dirven, René, Bruce Hawkins and Esra Sandikcioglu 2001 (eds). *Language and Ideology. Volume I: Theoretical Cognitive Approaches*. Amsterdam and Philadelphia: John Benjamins.
Dirven, René, Roslyn M. Frank and Cornelia Ilie 2001 (eds). *Language and Ideology. Volume II: Descriptive Cognitive Approaches*. Amsterdam and Philadelphia: John Benjamins.
Dirven, René and Ralf Pörings (eds) 2002. *Metaphor and Metonymy in Comparison and Contrast*. Berlin and New York: De Gruyter.
Fauconnier, Gilles 1994. *Mental Spaces: Aspects of Meaning Construction in Natural Language*. Cambridge: Cambridge University Press.

Feldman, Karen S. 2001. Conscience and the Concealments of Metaphor in Hobbes's *Leviathan*. *Philosophy and Rhetoric*, 34/1, 21–37.
Fillmore Charles J. 1975. An alternative to checklist theories of Meaning. *Proceedings of the Berkeley Linguistics Society*, 1, 123–31.
Fischer, Joschka 2000. Vom Staatenbund zur Föderation: Gedanken über die Finalität der europäischen Integration (official English version: From Confederacy to Federation: Thoughts on the finality of European integration). Speech in Berlin, 12 May 2000; http://www.auswaertiges-amt.de (accessed August 2002).
Gabora, Liane 1997. The Origin and Evolution of Culture and Creativity. *Journal of Memetics*, 1, http://www.cpm.mmu.ac.uk/jom-emit/1997/vol 1/gabora_l.html (accessed August 2003).
Geckeler, Horst 1971. *Strukturelle Semantik und Wortfeldtheorie*. Munich: Fink.
Gentner, Dedre 1988. Analogical Inference and Analogical Access. In: Prieditis 1988, 63–88.
Gentner, Dedre 1989. The Mechanisms of Analogical Learning. In: Vosniadou and Ortony 1989, 199–241.
Gentner, Dedre, Keith Holyoak and Boicho N. Kokinov (eds) 2001. *The Analogical Mind: Perspectives from Cognitive Science*. Cambridge, MA: MIT Press.
George, Stephen 1994. *An Awkward Partner: Britain in the European Community*. Oxford: Oxford University Press.
Gibbs, Raymond W. 1990. Psycholinguistic Studies on the Conceptual basis of Idiomaticity. *Cognitive Linguistics*, 1, 417–62.
Gibbs, Raymond W. 1994. *The Poetics of Mind: Figurative Thought, Language and Understanding*. Cambridge: Cambridge University Press.
Gibbs, Raymond W. 1999. Researching Metaphor. In: Cameron and Low 1999, 29–47.
Gibbs, Raymond W. and Gerard Steen (eds) 1999. *Metaphor in Cognitive Linguistics*. Amsterdam: John Benjamins.
Giora, Rachel 1997. Understanding Figurative and Literal Language: the Graded Salience Hypothesis. *Cognitive Linguistics*, 7, 183–206.
Glucksberg, Sam 2001. *Understanding Figurative Language: From Metaphors to Idioms*. With a contribution by Matthew S. McGlone. Oxford: Oxford University Press.
Glucksberg, Sam and Boaz Keysar 1990. Understanding Metaphorical Comparisons: Beyond Similarity. *Psychological Review*, 97, 3–18.
Glucksberg, Sam and Boaz Keysar 1993. How Metaphors Work. In: Ortony 1993, 401–24.
Glucksberg, Sam and Matthew S. McGlone 1999. When Love is Not a Journey: What Metaphors Mean. *Journal of Pragmatics*, 31, 1541–58.
Goatly, Andrew 1997. *The Language of Metaphors*. London and New York: Routledge.
Göttert, Karl-Heinz 1994. *Einführung in die Rhetorik: Grundbegriffe – Geschichte – Rezeption*. 2nd edn. Munich: Fink.
Gorbachev, Mikhail 1987. *Rede zum 70. Jahrestag der Oktoberrevolution*. Munich: Heyne.
Gorbachev, Mikhail 1989. *Perestroika: Die zweite russische Revolution*. Munich: Knaur.

Grady, Joseph and Christopher Johnson 2002. Converging evidence for the notions of subscene and primary scene. In: Dirven and Pörings 2002, 533–54.
Grady, Joseph, Sarah Taub and Pamela Morgan 1996. Primitive and Compound Metaphors. In: Adele E. Goldberg (ed.), *Conceptual Structure, Discourse and Language*. Stanford: CSLI, 177–87.
Grice, H. Paul 1975. Logic and Conversation. In: Peter Cole and Jerry L. Morgan (eds), *Syntax and Semantics 3: Speech Acts*. New York, San Francisco and London: Academic Press, 41–58.
Grice, H. Paul 1989. *Studies in the Way of Words*. Cambridge, MA: Harvard University Press.
Grosser, Alfred 1998. *Deutschland in Europa*. Weinheim: Beltz.
Hale, David 1971. *The Body Politic: a Political Metaphor in Renaissance English Literature*. The Hague: Mouton.
Hampsher-Monk, Iain, Karin Tilmans and Frank van Vree (eds) 1998. *History of Concepts: Comparative Perspectives*. Amsterdam: Amsterdam University Press.
Harwood, John T. 1986. Introduction to *The Rhetorics of Thomas Hobbes*. In: *The Rhetorics of Thomas Hobbes and Bernard Lamy*. Ed. John T. Harwood. Carbondale and Edwardsville: Southern Illinois University Press, 1–32.
Hawkins, Bruce 2001. Ideology, Metaphor and Iconographic Reference. In: Dirven, Frank and Ilie 2001, 27–50.
Heisenberg, Wolfgang (ed.) 1991. *German Unification in European Perspective*. London: Brassey's.
Hellsten, Iina 2000. Dolly: Scientific Breakthrough or Frankenstein's Monster? Journalistic and Scientific metaphors of Cloning. *Metaphor and Symbol*, 15/4, 213–21.
Hellsten, Iina 2002. *The Politics of Metaphor: Biotechnology and Biodiversity in the Media*. Tampere: Tampere University Press.
Herberg, Dieter 1999. Der Euro: sprachlich betrachtet. *Sprachreport*, 4/1999, 2–7.
Heywood, John, Elena Semino and Mick Short 2002. Linguistic Metaphor Identification in Two Extracts from Novels. *Language and Literature*, 11/1, 35–54.
Hobbes, Thomas 1986. *A Briefe of the Art of Rhetorique*. In: *The Rhetorics of Thomas Hobbes and Bernard Lamy*. Ed. John T. Harwood. Carbondale and Edwardsville: Southern Illinois University Press, 33–128.
Hobbes, Thomas 1994. *The Elements of Law Natural and Politic. Part I: Human Nature. Part II: De Corpore Politico*. With *Three Lives*. Ed. J. C. A. Gaskin. Oxford: Oxford University Press.
Hobbes, Thomas 1996. *Leviathan*. Ed. Richard Tuck. Cambridge: Cambridge University Press.
Hoenigswald, Henry M. and Linda F. Wiener (eds) 1987. *Biological Metaphor and Cladistic Classification: an Interdisciplinary Perspective*. London: Francis Pinter.
Holyoak, Keith J. and Paul R. Thagard 1989. A Computational Model of Analogical Problem Solving. In: Vosniadou and Ortony 1989, 242–66.
Horn, Laurence R. 1997. Presupposition and Implicature. In: Shalom Lappin (ed.), *The Handbook of Contemporary Semantic Theory*. Oxford: Blackwell, 299–319.
Hull, David L. 2000. Taking Memetics Seriously: Memetics Will be What we Make It. In: Aunger 2000, 42–67.

Hunston, Susan 2002. *Corpora in Applied Linguistics*. Cambridge: Cambridge University Press.
Hutton, Christopher M. 2001. Cultural and Conceptual Relativism, Universalism and the Politics of Linguistics: Dilemmas of a Would-be Progressive Linguistics. In: Dirven, Hawkins and Sandikcioglu 2001, 277–96.
Indurkhya, Bipin 1988. Constrained Semantic Transference: a Formal Theory of Metaphors. In: Prieditis 1988, 129–57.
Indurkhya, Bipin 1992. *Metaphor and Cognition*. Dordrecht, Boston and London: Kluwer Academic Publishers.
Isermann, Michael 1991. *Die Sprachtheorie im Werk von Thomas Hobbes*. Münster: Nodus.
Jackendoff, Ray and David Aaron 1991. Review of George Lakoff and Mark Turner: *More Than Cool Reason: a Field Guide to Poetic Metaphor* (Chicago and London: Chicago University Press). *Language*, 67, 320–38.
Jäkel, Olaf 1999. Kant, Blumenberg, Weinrich: Some Forgotten Contributions to the Cognitive Theory of Metaphor. In: Gibbs and Steen 1999, 9–27.
Johnson, Mark 1981. Introduction: Metaphor in the Philosophical Tradition. In Mark Johnson (ed.), *Philosophical Perspectives on Metaphor*. Minnesota: University of Minnesota Press, 3–47.
Johnson, Mark 1987. *The Body in the Mind: the Bodily Basis of Meaning, Imagination, and Reason*. Chicago: University of Chicago Press.
Johnson-Laird, Philip 1989. Analogy and the Exercise of Creativity. In: Vosniadou and Ortony 1989, 313–31.
Johnston, David 1986. *The Rhetoric of Leviathan*. Princeton: Princeton University Press.
Jones, Robert A. 1996. *The Politics and Economics of the European Union*. Cheltenham and Brookfield, VT: Elgar.
Jong, Willem R. de 1990. Did Hobbes Have a Semantic Theory of Truth? *Journal of the History of Philosophy*, 28, 63–88.
Jung, Matthias and Martin Wengeler 1995. *Nation Europa* und *Europa der Nationen*. Sprachliche Kontroversen in der Europapolitik. In: Georg Stötzel and Martin Wengeler (eds), *Kontroverse Begriffe. Geschichte des öffentlichen Sprachgebrauchs in der Bundesrepublik Deutschland*. Berlin: W. de Gruyter, 93–128.
Kämper, Heidrun 1999. Haltungen zu Europa (Attitudes towards Europe). *Sprachreport*, 2/1999, 25–6.
Kantorowicz, Ernst H. 1997. *The King's Two Bodies: a Study in Mediaeval Political Theology*. With a new Preface by William Chester Jordan. Princeton, NJ: Princeton University Press.
Kaplan, David 1978. Dthat. In: Peter Cole and Jerry L. Morgan (eds), *Syntax and Semantics 9: Pragmatics*. New York: Academic Press, 221–43.
Kaplan, David 1979. On the Logic of Demonstratives. *Journal of Philosophical Logic*, 8, 81–98.
Keller-Bauer, Friedrich 1983. Metaphorische Präzedenzen. *Sprache und Literatur in Wissenschaft und Unterricht*, 51, 46–60.
Keller-Bauer, Friedrich 1984. *Metaphorisches Verstehen: Eine linguistische Rekonstruktion metaphorischer Kommunikation*. Tübingen: Niemeyer.
Kempson, Ruth 1977. *Semantic Theory*. Cambridge: Cambridge University Press.
Kittay, Eva Feder 1987. *Metaphor: Its Cognitive Force and Linguistic Structure*. Oxford: Oxford University Press.

Kluge, Friedrich 1995. *Etymologisches Wörterbuch der deutschen Sprache.* 23rd edn. Ed. Elmar Seebold. Berlin and New York: W. de Gruyter.
Koselleck, Reinhart 1979. *Vergangene Zukunft: Zur Semantik geschichtlicher Zeiten.* Frankfurt am Main: Suhrkamp.
Koselleck, Reinhart 1998. Social History and Begriffsgeschichte. In: Hampsher-Monk, Tilmans and Van Vree 1998, 23–35.
Kövecses, Zoltán 1986. *Metaphors of Anger, Pride, and Love: a Lexical Approach to the Study of Concepts.* Amsterdam and Philadelphia: Benjamins.
Kövecses, Zoltán 1995. Anger: Its Language, Conceptualization, and Physiology in the Light of Cross-Cultural Evidence. In: John R. Taylor and Robert MacLaury (eds), *Language and the Cognitive Construal of the World.* Berlin: Mouton de Gruyter, 181–96.
Kövecses, Zoltán 2002. *Metaphor: a Practical Introduction.* Oxford: Oxford University Press.
Kuper, Adam 2000. If Memes are the Answer, What is the Question? In: Aunger 2000, 175–88.
Kurz, Gerhard 1989. *Metapher, Allegorie, Symbol,* 3rd edn. Göttingen: Vandenhoeck & Ruprecht.
Lakoff, George 1987. *Women, Fire, and Dangerous Things: What Categories Reveal about the Mind.* Chicago and London: University of Chicago Press.
Lakoff, George 1992. Metaphor and War: the Metaphor System used to Justify War in the Gulf. In: Martin Pütz (ed.), *Thirty Years of Linguistic Evolution: Studies in Honour of René Dirven.* Philadelphia and Amsterdam: Benjamins, 463–81.
Lakoff, George 1993. The Contemporary Theory of Metaphor. In: Ortony 1993, 202–51.
Lakoff, George 1994. *Conceptual Metaphor Home Page.* Internet website: http://cogsci.berkeley.edu/ (accessed: December 2003).
Lakoff, George 1996. *Moral Politics: What Conservatives Know That Liberals Don't.* Chicago and London: University of Chicago Press.
Lakoff, George 2001. September 11, 2001. *Metaphorik.de.* Internet website: http://www.metaphorik.de/aufsaetze/lakoff-september11.htm (accessed: December 2003).
Lakoff, George 2003. Metaphor and War, Again. *AlterNet.org.* Internet website: http://www.alternet.org/story.html?StoryID=15414 (accessed: August 2003).
Lakoff, George and Mark Johnson 1980. *Metaphors We Live By.* Chicago: University of Chicago Press.
Lakoff, George and Mark Johnson 1999. *Philosophy in the Flesh: the Embodied Mind and its Challenge to Western Thought.* New York: Basic Books.
Lakoff, George, Jane Espenson and Adele Goldberg 1989. *Master Metaphor List.* Berkeley: University of California Press, Cognitive Linguistics Group.
Lakoff, George, Jane Espenson and A. Schwartz 1991. *The Master Metaphor List,* Draft 2nd edn. Technical Report. University of California at Berkeley.
Lakoff, George and Mark Turner 1989. *More than Cool Reason: a Field Guide to Poetic Metaphor.* Chicago and London: University of Chicago Press.
Lakoff, Robin 1975. *Language and Women's Place.* New York: Harper and Row.
Langacker, Ronald W. 1987. *Foundations of Cognitive Grammar. Vol. 1: Theoretical Prerequisites.* Stanford: Stanford University Press.
Leezenberg, Michiel 2001. *Contexts of Metaphor.* Amsterdam: Elsevier.
Levinson, Stephen C. 1983. *Pragmatics.* Cambridge: Cambridge University Press.

Liebert, Wolf-Andreas, Gisela Redeker and Linda Waugh (eds) 1997. *Discourse and Perspective in Cognitive Linguistics*. Amsterdam and Philadelphia: Benjamins.
Locke, John 1979. *An Essay Concerning Human Understanding*. Ed. P. H. Nidditch. Oxford: Oxford University Press.
Lovejoy, Arthur O. 1936. *The Great Chain of Being*. Cambridge, MA: Harvard University Press.
Low, Graham 1999. Validating Metaphor Research Projects. In: Cameron and Low 1999, 48–65.
Lyons, John 1977. *Semantics*, 2 vols. Cambridge: Cambridge University Press.
Lutzeier, Peter Rolf (ed.) 1993. *Studien zur Wortfeldtheorie (Studies in Lexical Field Theory)*. Tübingen: Niemeyer.
MacDonald Ross, George 1987. Hobbes's Two Theories of Meaning. In: Andrew E. Benjamin, Geoffrey N. Cantor and John R. R. Christie (eds), *The Figural and the Literal: Problems of Language in the History of Science and Philosophy, 1630–1800*. Manchester: Manchester University Press, 31–57.
Mahon, James Edwin 1999. Getting Your Sources Right: What Aristotle Didn't Say. In: Cameron and Low 1999, 69–80.
Markert, Katja and Malvina Nissim 2003. Corpus-based Metonymy Analysis. *Metaphor and Symbol*, 18/3, 175–88.
Marsh, David 1994. *Germany and Europe: the Crisis of Unity*. London: Heinemann.
Martinich, A. P. 1992. *The Two Gods of Leviathan: Thomas Hobbes on Religion and Politics*. Cambridge: Cambridge: University Press.
Martinich, A. P. 1997. *Thomas Hobbes*. London: Macmillan.
Mason, Zachary 2002. CorMet: a Computational Corpus-Based Conventional Metaphor Extraction System. http://www.cs.brandeis.edu/~zmason_(accessed August 2002).
McGlone, Matthew S. 1996. Conceptual Metaphors and Figurative Language Interpretation: Food for Thought? *Journal of Experimental Psychology: Learning, Memory and Cognition*, 24, 432–60.
McGlone, Matthew S. 2001. Concepts as Metaphors. In: Glucksberg 2001, 90–107.
Mintz, Samuel I. 1989. Leviathan as Metaphor. *Hobbes Studies*, 2, 3–9.
Mintz, Samuel I. 1996. *The Hunting of Leviathan: Seventeenth-Century Reactions to the Materialism and Moral Philosophy of Thomas Hobbes*. Bristol: Thoemmes Press (reprint of first edn 1962).
Moon, Rosamund 1998. *Fixed Expressions and Idioms in English: a Corpus-Based Approach*. Oxford: Oxford University Press.
Mouton, Nicolaas T.O. (in press). On the Various Legacies – Purported and Real – of Classical Empiricism Pertaining to the Epistemology of Metaphor. In: Armin Burkhardt and Brigitte Nerlich (eds) (in press), *Tropical Truth*. Amsterdam and Philadelphia: Benjamins.
Müller-Richter, Klaus 1998. Einleitung. In: Klaus Müller-Richter and Arturo Larcati (eds), *Der Streit um die Metapher. Poetologische Texte von Nietzsche bis Handke*. Unter Mitarbeit von Robert Matthias Erdbeer und Daniela Schmeiser. Darmstadt: Wissenschaftliche Buchgesellschaft, 4–30.
Musolff, Andreas 1994. The Mother of Media Wars: Metaphor and simulation in the media coverage of the Gulf war 1991. *Krieg und Literatur/War and Literature*, VI, 11/12, 137–50.

Musolff, Andreas 1996a. False Friends Borrowing the Right Words? Common Terms and Metaphors in European Communication. In: Musolff, Schäffner and Townson 1996, 15–30.
Musolff, Andreas 1996b. 'Dampfer', 'Boote' und 'Fregatten': Metaphern als Signale im 'Geleitzug' der Europäischen Union. In: Karin Böke, Matthias Jung and Martin Wengeler (eds), *Öffentlicher Sprachgebrauch: Praktische, theoretische und historische Perspektiven. Georg Stötzel zum 60. Geburtstag gewidmet*. Opladen: Westdeutscher Verlag, 180–9.
Musolff, Andreas 1997. International metaphors: bridges or walls in international communication? In: Bernhard Debatin, Timothy R. Jackson and Daniel Steuer (eds), *Metaphor and Rational Discourse*. Tübingen: Niemeyer, 229–37.
Musolff, Andreas 2000a. *Mirror Images of Europe: Metaphors in the Public Debate about Europe in Britain and Germany*. Munich: Iudicium.
Musolff, Andreas 2000b. Political Imagery of Europe: A *House* without *Exit Doors*? *Journal of Multilingual and Multicultural Development*, 21/3, 216–29.
Musolff, Andreas 2000c. Maritime Journey Metaphors in British and German Public Discourse: Transport Vessels of International Communication? *German as a Foreign Language*, 3/2000; http://www.gfl-journal.com.
Musolff, Andreas 2003. Cross-Language Metaphors: Conceptual or Pragmatic Variation? In: Kasia M. Jaszczolt and Ken Turner (eds), *Meaning through Language Contrast*. Amsterdam and Philadelphia: Benjamins, vol. 2, 125–39.
Musolff, Andreas, Christina Schäffner and Michael Townson (eds) 1996. *Conceiving of Europe: Diversity in Unity*. Aldershot: Dartmouth.
Musolff, Andreas, Colin Good, Petra Points and Ruth Wittlinger (eds) 2001. *Attitudes towards Europe: Language in the Unification Process*. Aldershot: Ashgate.
Nerlich, Brigitte 1989. The Evolution of the Concept of 'Linguistic Evolution' in the 19th and 20th century. *Lingua*, 77, 101–12.
Nerlich, Brigitte and David D. Clarke 2002. Blending the Past and the Present: Conceptual and Linguistic Integration. In: Dirven and Pörings 2002, 555–93.
Nerlich, Brigitte, Craig A. Hamilton and Victoria Rowe 2002. Conceptualising Foot and Mouth Disease: the Socio-Cultural Role of Metaphors, Frames and Narratives. *metaphorik.de*, 2, 2002, at http://www.metaphorik.de/02/nerlich.htm (accessed August 2003).
Niemeier, Susanne 2000. Straight from the Heart: Metonymic and Metaphorical Explorations. In: Barcelona 2000, 195–213.
Ortony, Andrew 1979. Beyond Literal Similarity. *Psychological Review*, 86, 161–80.
Ortony, Andrew (ed.) 1993. *Metaphor and Thought*, second (revised) edition. Cambridge: Cambridge University Press.
Orwell, George 1976. *Nineteen Eighty-Four*. Harmondsworth: Penguin.
Panther, Klaus-Uwe and Günter Radden (eds) (1999), *Metonymy in Language and Thought*. Amsterdam and Philadelphia: Benjamins.
Peil, Dietmar 1993. Zum Problem des Bildfeldbegriffs. In: Lutzeier 1993, 185–202.
Perelman, Chaim 1979. Analogy and Metaphor in Science, Poetry and Philosophy. In: Chaim Perelman, *The New Rhetoric and the Humanities: Essays on Rhetoric and its Applications*. Dordrecht: Reidel, 91–100.
Perelman, Chaim 1982. *The Realm of Rhetoric*. Translated by William Kluback, Introduction by Carroll C. Arnold. Notre Dame, IN: University of Notre Dame Press.

Perelman, Chaim and Lucie Olbrechts-Tyteca 1969. *The New Rhetoric: a Treatise on Argumentation*. Translated by John Wilkinson and Purcell Weaver. Notre Dame, IN: University of Notre Dame Press.
Peters, Wim and Yorick Wilks 2003. Data-driven Detection of Figurative Language Use in Electronic Language Resources. *Metaphor and Symbol*, 18/3, 161–73.
Polenz, Peter von 1991–99. *Deutsche Sprachgeschichte vom Spätmittelalter bis zur Gegenwart*, 3 vols. Berlin and New York: W. de Gruyter.
Pope, Alexander 1994. *Essay on Man and Other Poems*. New York: Dover Publications.
Preston, Peter 1994. *Europe, Democracy and the Dissolution of Britain: an Essay on the Issue of Europe in UK Public Discourse*. Aldershot: Dartmouth.
Prieditis, Armand E. (ed.) 1988. *Analogica: Proceedings of the First Workshop on Analogical Reasoning*. London: Pitman.
Prokhovnik, Raia 1991. *Rhetoric and Philosophy in Hobbes' Leviathan*. New York and London: Garland.
Pusch, Luise F. 1984. *Das Deutsche als Männersprache*. Frankfurt am Main: Suhrkamp.
Quintilianus, Marcus Fabius 1970: M. Fabi Quintilianii *Institutionis Oratoriae libri Duodecim*, 2 vols. Ed. and transl. M. Winterbottom. Oxford: Clarendon Press.
Radden Günter 2000. How metonymic are metaphors? In: Barcelona 2000, 93–108.
Radford, Edwin and Alan Smith 1989. *To Coin a Phrase: a Dictionary of Origins*. London: Papermac/Macmillan.
Ramge, Hans 1993. Die Deutschen, der Ecu und die westlichen Nachbarn: Sprachliche Stereotype und Einstellungen in deutschen Kommentaren zum Maastrichter EG-Gipfel. *Sprache und Literatur in Wissenschaft und Unterricht*, 72, 48–61.
Rauff, Ulrich (ed.) 1987. *Mentalitäten-Geschichte: Zur historischen Rekonstruktion geistiger Prozesse*. Berlin: Wagenbach.
Recanati, François 1995. The Alleged Priority of Literal Interpretation. *Cognitive Science*, 19, 207–32.
Reeves, Nigel 1996. 'Den festen Kern festigen': Towards a Functional Taxonomy of Transnational Political Discourse. In Musolff, Schäffner and Townson 1996, 161–9.
Richards, Ivor Armstrong 1936. *The Philosophy of Rhetoric*. Oxford: Oxford University Press.
Röhrich, Lutz 2001. *Das große Lexikon der sprichwörtlichen Redensarten*, new edition. 3 vols. Darmstadt: Wissenschaftliche Buchgesellschaft.
Rumelhart, David. E. 1993. Some Problems with the Notion of Literal Meanings. In: Ortony 1993, 71–82.
Sacks, Sheldon (ed.) 1979. *On Metaphor*. Chicago and London: University of Chicago Press.
Schäffner, Christina 1993. Die europäische Architektur: Metaphern der Einigung Europas in der deutschen, britischen und amerikanischen Presse. In: Adi Grewenig (ed.), *Inszenierte Kommunikation*. Opladen: Westdeutscher Verlag, 13–30.
Schäffner, Christina 1994. The Concept of *Europe* in the British Weekly 'The Economist' over the Years 1975–1988. In: Christiane Villain-Gandossi, Klaus

Bochmann, Michel Metzeltin and Christina Schäffner (eds), *Le Concept de l'Europe dans le Processus de la CSCE/The Concept of Europe in the Process of the CSCE*. Tübingen: Gunter Narr, 199–212.
Schäffner, Christina 1996. Building a European House? Or at Two Speeds into a Dead End? Metaphors in the Debate on the United Europe. In: Musolff, Schäffner and Townson 1996, 31–59.
Schäffner, Christina, Andreas Musolff and Michael Townson 1996. Diversity and Unity in European Debates. In: Musolff, Schäffner and Townson 1996, 1–14.
Schäffner, Christina and Sylvia Trommer 1990. Das Konzept des *gemeinsamen europäischen Hauses* im Russischen und Englischen. In: Christina Schäffner (ed.), *Gibt es eine prototypische Wortschatzbeschreibung? Eine Problemdiskussion.* Berlin: Zentralinstitut für Sprachwissenschaft, 80–91.
Schank, Roger C. and Robert P. Abelson 1977. *Scripts, Plans, Goals and Understanding: an Inquiry into Human Knowledge Structures.* Hillsdale, NJ: Lawrence Erlbaum.
Schmidt, Lothar (ed.) 1973. *Wortfeldforschung: Zur Geschichte und Theorie des sprachlichen Feldes.* Darmstadt: Wissenschaftliche Buchgesellschaft.
Schmitz-Berning, Cornelia 1998. *Vokabular des Nationalsozialismus.* Berlin and New York: W. de Gruyter.
Schoch, Bruno (ed.) 1992. *Deutschlands Einheit und Europas Zukunft.* Frankfurt am Main: Suhrkamp.
Searle, John R. 1993. Metaphor. In: Ortony 1993, 83–111.
Sinclair, John 1991. *Corpus, Concordance, Collocation.* Oxford: Oxford University Press.
Skeat, Walter W. 1993. *The Concise Dictionary of English Etymology.* Ware: Wordsworth Editions.
Skinner, Quentin 1969. Meaning and the Understanding of Speech Acts. *History and Theory*, 8, 3–53.
Skinner, Quentin 1978. *The Foundations of Modern Political Thought*, 2 vols. Cambridge: Cambridge University Press.
Skinner, Quentin 1991. Thomas Hobbes: Rhetoric and the Construction of Reality. *Proceedings of the British Academy*, 76, 1–61.
Skinner, Quentin 1996. *Reason and Rhetoric in the Philosophy of Hobbes.* Cambridge: Cambridge University Press.
Sontag, Susan 1991. *Illness as Metaphor: Aids and its Metaphors.* London: Penguin.
Sperber, Dan 1996. *Explaining Culture: a Naturalistic Approach.* Oxford: Blackwell.
Sperber, Dan 2000. An Objection to the Memetic Approach to Culture. In: Aunger 2000, 163–73.
Sperber, Dan and Deirdre Wilson 1995. *Relevance: Communication and Cognition*, 2nd edn. Oxford: Blackwell.
Stalnaker, Robert 1974. Pragmatic Presuppositions. In: Milton K. Munitz and Peter Unger (eds), *Semantics and Philosophy.* New York: New York University Press, 197–213.
Steen, Gerard 1994. *Understanding Metaphor in Literature.* London: Longman.
Steen, Gerard 1999. Metaphor and Discourse: Towards a linguistic checklist for metaphor analysis. In: Cameron and Low 1999, 81–104.
Steen, Gerard 2002. Towards a Procedure for Metaphor Identification. *Language and Literature*, 11/1, 17–33.
Stern, Josef 1985. Metaphor as Demonstrative. *Journal of Philosophy*, 82, 677–710.

Stern, Josef 2000. *Metaphor in Context.* Cambridge, MA: MIT Press.
Stillman, Robert E. 1995. Hobbes's *Leviathan:* Monsters, Metaphors, and Magic. *English Literary History,* 62/4, 791–819.
Strauss, Leo 1952. *The Political Philosophy of Hobbes: Its Basis and its Genesis.* Translated by Elsa M. Sinclair. Chicago: University of Chicago Press (reprint of first edn 1936).
Struve, Tilman 1978. *Die Entwicklung der organologischen Staatsauffassung im Mittelalter.* Stuttgart: Anton Hiersemann.
Struve, Tilman 1984. The Importance of the Organism in the Political Theory of John of Salisbury. In: Michael Wilks (ed.), *The World of John of Salisbury.* Oxford: Basil Blackwell, 303–17.
Sweetser, Eve E. 1990. *From Etymology to Pragmatics: Metaphorical and Cultural Aspects of Semantic Structure.* Cambridge: Cambridge University Press.
Taylor, John R. 1995. *Linguistic Categorization.* 2nd edn. Oxford: Oxford University Press.
Teubert, Wolfgang 2002. The Role of Parallel Corpora in Translation and Multilingual Lexicography. In: Altenberg and Granger 2002a, 189–214.
Thatcher, Margaret 1993. *The Downing Street Years.* London: HarperCollins.
Thatcher, Margaret 1995. *The Path to Power.* London: HarperCollins.
Tillyard, E.M.W. 1982. *The Elizabethan World Picture.* Harmondsworth: Penguin (first edn 1943).
Toulmin, Stephen E. 1958. *The Uses of Argument.* Cambridge: Cambridge University Press.
Turner, Mark and Gilles Fauconnier 2000. Metaphor, metonymy, and binding. In: Barcelona 2000, 133–45.
Volmert, Johannes 1989. Politische Rhetorik des Nationalsozialismus. In: Konrad Ehlich (ed.), *Sprache im Faschismus.* Frankfurt am Main: Suhrkamp, 137–61.
Vosniadou, Stella and Andrew Ortony (eds) 1989. *Similarity and Analogical Reasoning.* Cambridge: Cambridge University Press.
Wagner, Jochen and Georg Zenkert 1995. Rhetorik als Gefährdung der politischen Ordnung: z.B. Thomas Hobbes. In: Josef Kopperschmidt (ed.), *Politik und Rhetorik: Funktionsmodelle politischer Rede.* Opladen: Westdeutscher Verlag, 126–45.
Weinrich, Harald 1963. Die Semantik der kühnen Metapher. *Deutsche Vierteljahreszeitschrift,* 37, 325–44.
Weinrich, Harald 1964. Typen der Gedächtnismetaphorik. *Archiv für Begriffsgeschichte,* 9, 96–104.
Weinrich, Harald 1967. Semantik der Metapher. *Folia Linguistica,* 1, 3–17.
Wengeler, Martin 2003. *Topos und Diskurs: Begründung einer diskursanalytischen Methode und ihr Anwendung auf den Migrationsdiskurs (1960–1985).* Tübingen: Niemeyer.
White, Michael 2003. Metaphor and Economics: the Case of *Growth. Journal of English for Special Purposes,* 22, 131–51.
Worden, Robert P. 2000. Words, Memes and Language Evolution. In: Chris Knight, Michael Studdert-Kennedy and James R. Hurford (eds), *The Evolutionary Emergence of Language: Social Function and the Origins of Linguistic Form.* Cambridge: Cambridge University Press, 353–71.

Young, Hugo 1998. *This Blessed Plot: Britain and Europe from Churchill to Blair.* London: Macmillan.

Zinken, Jörg 2003. Ideological Imagination: Intertextual and Correlational Metaphors in Political Discourse. *Discourse & Society,* 14/4, 507–23.

Zinken, Jörg and Elena Bolotova (in press). Der europäische Raum: Metaphorische Modelle im Diskurs der Europäischen Integration. In: Anatolij Baranov, Dmitrij Dobrovolskij and Lew Zybatov (eds). *Kulturelle Vorstellungswelten: Eine kontrastive Untersuchung metaphorischer Modelle im russischen und deutschen öffentlichen Diskurs.* Frankfurt am Main, Berne and New York: Lang.

Index 1: General

Aaron, David, 113
Abelson, Robert P., 17
Allegory, 162, 167, 172, 191
Altenberg, Bengt, 64, 185
Analogy
  see Argumentation
Argumentation, 6, 32–9, 59–60, 156, 180
  analogical, 30–9, 60, 83–4, 119, 147, 153, 160–2, 167, 170–2, 173–5
  conclusion, 29, 33, 36, 147, 156, 170, 174, 180
  dialogical, 154, 147–51, 153–6, 171
  warrant, 32, 36, 53, 148, 173–4, 176
  see also Presupposition
Aristotle, 34, 37, 163, 166–7, 169, 192
  The Art of Rhetoric, 163, 166–7, 192
  Poetics, 34
ATT-Meta project, 65, 185
Aunger, Robert, 189
Ayto, John, 187

Bachem, Rolf, 189
Baker, David, 178
Ball, Terence, 189, 191
Barcelona, Antonio, 71, 192
Barnden, John A., 65
Bartsch, Renate, 113
Bass, Allen M., 84
Battke, Kathleen, 189
Baumgold, Deborah, 191
Bertau, Marie-Cécile, 158, 191
Bertman, Martin A., 191
Bible
  Job (Book of), 162
  New Testament, 189
  Old Testament, 189
Black, Max, 69–71, 75–6, 79, 185, 186
Blair, Tony, 23, 109–10, 116, 140, 141, 157

Blackmore, Susan, 118, 141
Blending, 36–7, 100–1, 109–12, 113, 119
Blumenberg, Hans, 189
BODY POLITIC theories, 83–4, 115–16, 160–1, 167, 168, 192
  see also GREAT CHAIN OF BEING and Index 2
Boers, Frank, 186
Bolotova, Elena, 178, 189, 190
Brandt, Reinhart, 191
Brittan, Leon, 153–4
Brewer's Dictionary, 187, 188
Brodie, Richard, 189
Büchmann, Georg, 180, 187
Buller, Jim, 190
Busse, Dietrich, 189

Cameron, Lynne, 62, 64
Cassirer, Ernst, 191
Categorization, 1–3, 16–18, 75–7, 83–5, 171–2, 175
Chamizo Domínguez, Pedro J., 158
Charteris-Black, Jonathan, 180, 186
Chilton, Paul, 128, 178, 189
Chirac, Jacques, 22, 40
Churchill, Winston, 122
Clarke, David D., 158
Cognitive theory
  see under Metaphor
Cohen, Ted, 158, 191
Condren, Conal, 169, 191, 192
Connolly, Bernard, 107–8
Conte, Rosaria C., 118
Cooper, David E., 158, 191
Corpus analysis
  Bank of English/COBUILD, 63–9, 82, 87, 88, 112, 122, 123, 129, 184, 186, 188, 189, 190
  COSMAS, 63–9, 82, 87, 88, 112, 122, 123, 127, 129, 185, 188, 189, 190
  concordance, 8, 65–8

206

Corpus analysis – *continued*
  contrastive corpora, 64
  corpus-based analysis of m., 1, 4,
    6–7, 8, 10–12, 61–2, 63–8, 69,
    72, 81–2, 85–9, 93–5, 112–14,
    116, 120–2, 140–5
    EUROMETA I, 11–12, 14–16, 37–8,
      61–2, 66–7, 82, 84–7, 90, 95,
      122, 148, 175, 179
    EUROMETA II, 63–9, 82, 88–90, 95,
      102, 108, 112, 116, 122, 123–6,
      136–7, 140, 143–5, 148, 175
  general vs special corpora, 61–5
Crisp, Peter, 185
Croft, William, 179

Darwin, Charles, 117
Dascal, Marcelo, 191
Davidson, Donald, 73, 185
Dawkins, Richard, 117–19, 141, 142,
  189
Deignan, Alice, 64, 66, 178, 179, 185,
  186
Delors, Jacques, 19, 100, 184
Demecheleer, Murielle, 186
Dennett, Daniel C., 119, 141, 142,
  189
de Silguy, Yves-Thibault, 95
Diepgen, Eberhard, 104
Dirven, René, 71, 158, 178, 187,
  192
Discourse, public
  general features, 4–5, 28–9, 30–3,
    45, 69, 143, 164, 171–2, 173–7,
    178
  d. community, 4–5, 59, 69, 112–13,
    115–16, 120–2, 127–9, 143–4,
    175–6
  d. history, 115, 120–2, 122–40
  virtual conversation, 4–5, 174–5
  see also Rhetoric
Domain
  see under Metaphor

Eloquence
  see under Rhetoric
Embodiment, 9
Empiricism, 10, 114, 144
Entailment, 31–3, 128, 180

Espenson, Jane, 178
Europe/European Union
  see under Politics

Fauconnier, Gilles, 36, 100–1, 180
Feldman, Karen S., 192
Field, semantic/lexical, 73–5, 186
Figurative language, 162, 164, 169
  see also Metaphor, Rhetoric
Fillmore, Charles J., 17
Fischer, Joschka, 39–40, 44–5, 48–9,
  54, 139, 180, 184
Folk-theory, 79, 102, 115, 176
Frank, Roslyn M., 178, 188

Gabora, Liane, 118
Geckeler, Horst, 186
Gentner, Dedre, 36
George, Stephen, 178
Gibbs, Raymond W., 178, 185
Giora, Rachel, 178
Glucksberg, Sam, 73, 75–6, 79, 81,
  178, 185, 186
Goatly, Andrew, 158, 178, 185, 191
Göttert, Karl-Heinz, 180
Goldberg, Adele, 178
Good, Colin, 178
Gorbachev, Mikhail, 127–9, 131,
  134–5, 140, 141, 142, 143, 144,
  146–8
Grady, Joseph, 116, 179
Granger, Sylviane, 64, 185
GREAT CHAIN OF BEING, 84, 115–16,
  123, 189
  see also BODY POLITIC
Grice, H. Paul, 71–2
Grosser, Alfred, 178

Hague, William, 140
Hale, David, 83–4, 160
Hamilton, Craig A., 188
Harwood, John T., 163, 192
Hattersley, Roy, 154–5
Havel, Vaclav, 136
Hawkins, Bruce, 186
Heath, Edward, 107, 109
Hedges, 76, 174
Heisenberg, Wolfgang, 178
Hellsten, Iina, 178

Herberg, Dieter, 178
Heywood, John, 185
History of ideas/conceptual history, 115, 117
Hobbes, Thomas, 1, 7, 31, 157–8, 159–72, 173, 191, 192
  A Briefe of the Art of Rhetorique, 163, 166–7
  The Elements of Law, 163, 191
  De Cive, 163, 191
  Leviathan, 1, 7, 157–8, 159–62, 163–7, 168–72, 191, 192
Hoenigswald, Henry M., 117
Holyoak, Keith, 36
Horn, Laurence R., 180
Howard, Michael, 48, 51, 121, 174
Hull, David L., 189
Hunston, Susan, 64, 66, 185
Hutton, Christopher, 178
Hutton, William, 49–50

Ideology
  see under Politics
Ilie, Cornelia, 178
Ilyin, Mikhail V., 178, 189
Indurkhya, Bipin, 36
Irony, 71
Isermann, Michael, 191

Jackendoff, Ray, 113
Jäkel, Olaf, 158, 189
Johnson, Christopher, 116, 179
Johnson, Mark, 1–2, 8, 31–2, 43, 71, 157, 172, 178, 179, 186
Johnson-Laird, Philip, 36
Johnston, David, 160, 163, 191
Jones, Robert A., 178, 190
Jong, Willem R. de, 191
Jung, Matthias, 187

Kämper, Heidrun, 178
Kantorowicz, Ernst H., 83–4, 179
Kaplan, David, 76–7
Keller-Bauer, Friedrich, 189
Kempson, Ruth, 33
Keysar, Boaz, 73, 75, 178
Kinkel, Klaus, 91, 152, 187
Kittay, Eva Feder, 71, 73–5, 79, 113, 186

Kluge, Friedrich, 179
Kohl, Helmut, 19, 20, 51, 91, 134–5, 137–8, 141, 142, 143, 151–2, 157, 179, 183, 187, 190
Kokinov, Boicho N., 36
Koselleck, Reinhart, 189
Kövecses, Zoltán, 9–11, 18, 43, 84, 108, 114, 122, 176, 178, 179, 180, 189
Kuper, Adam, 189
Kurz, Gerhard, 186

Lakoff, George, 1–5, 8–9, 13, 17, 28–9, 31–3, 37–8, 43, 65, 71, 84, 115–16, 128, 157, 172, 178, 179, 180, 185, 186, 189
Lakoff, Robin, 179
Lamont, Norman, 153–4
Langacker, Ronald W., 179
Lee, Mark G., 65
Leezenberg, Michiel, 71, 73, 76, 78–9, 81, 113, 158, 180, 185, 186, 191
Leviathan
  see under Hobbes
Levinson, Stephen C., 180, 185
Liebert, Wolf-Andreas, 178
Literal-truth paradigm, 157, 164
Locke, John, 157–8, 191
Lockwood, Christopher, 52
Lovejoy, Arthur O., 84, 115, 192
Low, Graham, 10, 62
Lutzeier, Peter Rolf, 186
Lyons, John, 180, 186

MacDonald Ross, George, 191
McGlone, Matthew S., 73, 76, 186
Major, John, 51–3, 105–7, 109, 116, 141, 143, 153, 154, 157, 182
Markert, Katja, 185
Martinich, A.P., 191, 192
Mason, Zachary, 65–6
Memetics
  Meme, 117–22, 141
  Epidemiology of the Mind, 119–22
Metaphor
  conceptual vs linguistic m., 3, 8, 10, 72–82, 112–14
  deceptive m., 1, 7, 30–1, 148, 157, 159, 164–6, 167–72

Metaphor – *continued*
experiential grounding of m., 9,
  101, 102, 114, 176–7
individual m., 9–11, 145
m. idioms, 8
m. mappings, 2, 10, 18–19, 112–14,
  166, 176
m. evolution, 115–22, 141–5
m. negotiation, 146–57, 171–2
primary m., 9, 116–17, 176
subindividual m., 9, 11, 114
supraindividual m., 9–11, 28, 114
see also Blending, Figurative
  Language, Simile
Metaphor domains, 1–2, 17–19, 33,
  41, 61, 73–5, 112–13, 179
Metaphor scenarios, 17–19, 28–9,
  37–9, 44, 48–9, 60, 61, 80–2, 87,
  112–14, 126, 137–8, 141, 145
  147–56, 170, 173–5, 176–7
open and closed scenarios, 173–7
source scenario depreciation,
  141–3, 175
see also Index 2
Metaphor theory
class inclusion theory of m., 75–6
cognitive theory of m., 1–6, 28–9,
  171–2
interaction theory, 69–71, 76, 166
pragmatic theories of m., 71–2
semantic theories of m., 69–82, 113
Metonymy, 71, 72, 102, 104, 111, 179
Mey, Jacob, 178
Mintz, Samuel I., 191, 192
Moon, Rosamund, 179, 185
Morgan, Pamela, 116, 179
Mouton, Nicolaas T.O., 158, 191, 192
Müller-Richter, Klaus, 158

Nerlich, Brigitte, 117, 158, 188
Niemeier, Susanne, 102, 108, 179
Nissim, Malvina, 185

Olbrechts-Tyteca, Lucie, 35, 180
Ortony, Andrew, 76
Orwell, George, 3, 30–1, 157

Panther, Klaus-Uwe, 192
Peil, Dietmar, 186

Perelman, Chaim, 35–6, 180, 191
Peters, Wim, 185
Phraseologism, 64–5
Points, Petra, 178
Pörings, Ralf, 71, 192
Polenz, Peter von, 179
Politics
Political thought, ideology, 1–6, 9,
  10, 13, 20–1, 30–2, 54, 60–1,
  83–4, 101, 104–5, 115, 127–9,
  135, 157–8, 160–2, 167–71,
  176–7
Racism, 84, 175, 186
Stereotypes, 58–9, 60, 129, 155,
  173, 176
European Politics
EU enlargement, 104
European integration, 4
European Monetary Union, 30, 50,
  91–5
British views of EU politics, 4,
  28–9, 30–1, 45, 48, 50, 53–4,
  58–9, 108
German views of EU politics, 4–5,
  28–9, 45, 48, 50, 53–4, 58–9,
  91–5, 103, 108
Treaty of Maastricht, 4, 30, 41, 54,
  59, 90, 96, 111, 133, 139
Treaty of Amsterdam, 4, 41, 90,
  181
Pope, Alexander, 115
Preston, Peter, 178
Presupposition, 33, 36–8, 44–5, 48,
  60, 77–8, 80–1, 129, 138, 147,
  155, 156, 161, 171, 180
Prokhovnik, Raia, 162, 191
Prototype, 11, 17, 73, 179
Pusch, Luise F., 179

Quintilian(us), Marcus Fabius, 166,
  192

Radden, Günter, 180, 192
Radford, Edwin, 187
Ramge, Hans, 178
Rauff, Ulrich, 189
Recanati, François, 185
Redeker, Gisela, 178
Reeves, Nigel, 181

Relevance principle/theory, 120, 143, 185
Representation, 119–20, 144–5
Rhetoric, 3, 31, 35, 64, 75, 81, 100–1, 110, 142, 160, 163–72, 191–2
  Classical Rhetoric, 75, 163, 166–7
  Eloquence, 163–4, 167, 191
  New Rhetoric, 35
  Perspicuity, 1, 159–60
  Paradiastole, 170, 192
  Tropes, 164–6
Richards, Ivor Armstrong, 35, 60, 70, 75–6, 186
Rifkind, Malcolm, 152
Röhrich, Lutz, 187
Rowe, Victoria, 188
Rumelhart, David. E., 185

Santer, Jacques, 107
Schäffner, Christina, 126, 178, 181, 189, 191
Schank, Roger C., 17
Schäuble, Wolfgang, 149–50, 152
Schmidt, Lothar, 186
Schmitz-Berning, Cornelia, 186
Schoch, Bruno, 178
Schröder, Gerhard, 19, 23–5, 91–5, 105, 116, 157, 179, 187
Schwartz. A., 178
Searle, John R., 71–2, 185
Seawright, David, 178
Semino, Elena, 185
Shakespeare, William
  Hamlet, 188
  Romeo and Juliet, 77
Short, Mick, 185
Simile, 75–6, 159–60, 166–7
Similitude, 165–7, 171
Sinclair, John, 64, 66
Skeat, Walter W., 179
Skinner, Quentin, 162, 163, 186, 189, 191, 192
Smith, Alan, 187
Smith, Martin J., 190
Sontag, Susan, 84, 186

Sperber, Dan, 119–21, 143, 185
Stalnaker, Robert, 77
Steen, Gerard, 178, 185
Stereotypes
  see under Politics
Stern, Josef, 73, 74, 76–9, 81, 113, 180, 185, 186
Stillman, Robert E., 191
Stoiber, Edmund, 138, 150
Strauss, Leo, 163
Struve, Tilman, 84
Sweetser, Eve E., 179

Taub, Sarah, 116, 179
Taylor, John R., 17, 179
Teubert, Wolfgang, 64
Thagard, Paul R., 36
Thatcher, Margaret, 30–2, 33, 37–9, 96, 107, 138, 150, 157, 180, 182
Thucydides, 163
Tillyard, E.M.W., 84, 192
Toulmin, Stephen E., 33, 53, 60, 180
Townson, Michael, 178
Trommer, Sylvia, 189, 191
Turner, Mark, 36, 84, 100–1, 115–16, 179, 189

Volmert, Johannes, 186

Wagner, Jochen, 191
Waugh, Linda, 178
Weinrich, Harald, 189
Weizsäcker, Richard von, 127–8, 146–7
Wengeler, Martin, 187, 189
White, Michael, 84
Wiener, Linda F., 117
Wilks, Yorick, 185
Wilson, Deirdre, 120, 185
Wittlinger, Ruth, 178
Worden, Robert P., 118

Young, Hugo, 122, 178

Zenkert, Georg, 191
Zinken, Jörg, 178, 189, 190

Index 2: Metaphor Scenarios and Their Conceptual Elements

THE NATION STATE IS A PERSON, 44
THE NATION STATE IS A FAMILY, 2–6,
  20–1, 34–5, 37, 176, 178
  THE GOVERNMENT IS A NURTURANT
    PARENT, 2–6, 37, 178
  THE GOVERNMENT IS A STRICT FATHER,
    2–6, 35, 37, 178

THE EU IS A BUILDING, 11, 12, 69,
  122–44, 146–7, 173
  THE EU IS A BUILDING SITE, 138–9, 141
  EUROPE/THE EU IS A (COMMON) HOUSE,
    122–38, 140, 146–8, 189–90
  EU-ARCHITECTS, 133–4, 137, 190
  EU-DOOR/GATE, 126, 136, 189
  EU-FOUNDATIONS, 133, 138–9, 143
  EU-PILLARS, 133, 143, 190
  EU-ROOF, 132–3, 135, 140, 143
  EU-TENANCY, 128–31, 135–6

THE EU IS A FAMILY/LOVE-RELATIONSHIP,
  2–7, 11, 13–29, 34–5, 37–9, 44,
  173
  EU-CHILD(REN), 2, 14–18, 27, 29, 34
  EU-COUPLE, 16, 21–6
  EU-FATHER, 2–6, 13–16, 19–21, 34–5,
    95, 137
  EU-LOVE, 16–18
  EU-MARRIAGE/WEDDING, 14–18, 21–9,
    37
  MENAGE A TROIS IN THE EU, 15, 18,
    22–5
  EU-MOTHER, 20, 179
  EU-PARENT(S), 2, 14–18, 20–1

THE EU IS A (HUMAN) BODY, 69,
  83–115, 173, 176

EU/EURO BIRTH/BABY, 16, 90–5, 105,
  115, 121, 186
EU/EURO BODY PARTS/ORGANS, 90,
  101–12
  see also BODY POLITIC
EU/EURO DEATH, 90, 95–6
EUROSCLEROSIS, 63–4, 80, 99–101,
  114, 115
HEALTH/ILLNESS OF THE EU/EURO, 63–4,
  80, 89, 90, 97–101, 106–8, 141,
  154
HEART OF EUROPE, 63, 80, 101–10,
  115, 121, 141, 153–4, 187–8
LIFE CYCLE OF EU/EURO, 85, 90–6
SICK MAN OF EUROPE, 63–4, 80, 97–9,
  109, 114, 115, 189

THE EU IS MOVING ALONG A PATH, 11,
  12, 40–61, 180–4
  TWO-/MULTI-SPEED EUROPE, 40, 45–54,
    121, 151–3
  JOURNEY, 43–60, 141, 151, 173,
    180–4
    AIR/SPACE TRAVEL, 43–4, 57,
      184
    BICYCLE JOURNEY, 43–4, 57, 184
    CAR JOURNEY, 43–4, 56, 154–6,
      183–4
    MARITIME JOURNEY, 43–4, 55–6,
      151–3, 183
    TRAIN JOURNEY, 30–2, 35, 37–8, 55,
      149–50, 182
    WALKING, 45–54, 180–2

THE EU IS AN ORCHESTRA, 152–3
THE EU HAS A CORE AND OUTER CIRCLE(S),
  52, 181